ISBN 13: 978-1-59670-179-3

All interior photos appear courtesy of Collegiate Images

Publishers: Peter L. Bannon and Joseph J. Bannon Sr.
Senior managing editor: Susan M. Moyer
Editors: Doug Hoepker, Steve Contorno
Art director: Dustin J. Hubbart
Interior design: Rachel E. Hubbart
Photo editor: Jessica Martinich

Sports Publishing L.L.C.
804 North Neil Street
Champaign, IL 61820
Phone: 1-877-424-2665
Fax: 217-363-2073
SportsPublishingLLC.com

Printed in the United States of America

CIP data available upon request.

To Dick Herbert, Add Penfield, Jack Horner, Smith Barrier, Ray Reeves, Ron Green, Bill Jackson, and all the other writers and broadcasters who first fueled my love for ACC basketball—I only hope that I can inspire the same passion in some of my readers that each of you imparted to me.

CONTENTS

ACKNOWLEDGMENTS

This book wouldn't have been possible without the cooperation of the players who kindly consented to sit down and talk to me about their most memorable games. To each of them—thank you.

In addition, I have to thank the people at Duke who assisted me in catching up with some hard-to-find players. Mary Dinkins, the director of the Duke Varsity Club, was most gracious with her time and energy. So were Jon Jackson, Duke's director of sports information, and Mike Cragg, the director of the Legacy Fund.

INTRODUCTION

It's easy to pinpoint the exact moment when the Duke basketball program was born. It's well documented that a team coached by "Cap" Card first took the court on March 2, 1905. The Duke Methodists (the nickname Blue Devils was still two decades in the future) lost to Wake Forest that day in the Angier Duke Gym, an aging structure that still stands on the school's East Campus.

It's much harder to identify the moment when Duke basketball became something special in the world of college athletics. That didn't happen in the first half of the 20th Century. Wallace Wade's superb football program was the face of Duke athletics during that era. Even though the basketball team enjoyed considerable success under Eddie Cameron and his successors, the sport remained as obscure at Duke as it did at most football-crazy Southern universities.

It was football money that paid for Duke's magnificent Indoor Stadium, probably the finest on-campus facility in the nation when it opened on January 6, 1940. Cameron worked as an assistant on Wade's football staff and many of his early stars were recruited as football or baseball players. For instance, Bill Werber, the school's first basketball All-American, was better known as a baseball player. He jumped straight from Duke to the major leagues in 1930, eventually becoming the starting third baseman and leadoff hitter for the Cincinnati Reds' world championship team in 1940. He has the distinction of being the first baseball player to bat in a televised game when he led off for the visiting Reds in a game against the Giants that was televised at the New York World's Fair.

By amazing coincidence, Duke's first national player of the year in basketball was also a baseball player who would find fame as the leadoff hitter for a world championship baseball team. But before Dick Groat played shortstop for the 1960 Pittsburgh Pirates, he thrilled Duke basketball fans with his spectacular combination of scoring and playmaking. Groat, the oldest player interviewed in this book, clearly performed at a time when Duke basketball was straining for national recognition. The Blue Devils had already won five Southern Conference titles under Cameron and Gerry Gerard, but it wasn't until Groat's senior season in 1952 that Duke first cracked the national rankings.

Duke basketball really made its entrance onto the national stage a decade later under coach Vic Bubas. His Blue Devil teams won four ACC titles in seven years and reached the Final Four three times. His first Duke team in 1960 would finish at No. 18 in the final AP poll. His next six teams all finished in the top 10. Bubas' teams were fueled by a spectacular array of stars, starting with flamboyant forward Art Heyman and followed by All-Americans Jeff Mullins, Jack Marin, Bob Verga, and Mike Lewis.

Heyman, Duke's second national player of the year and a pivotal recruit in establishing Bubas' program, recounts in this book Duke's controversial 1961 victory over North Carolina that launched that rivalry into the sports stratosphere. It's fair to suggest that before the "Brawl Game" of 1961, football was at the heart of the Duke-UNC competition. Afterward, Duke-UNC was a basketball rivalry—and now clearly ranks as the most important rivalry in college basketball.

Quite a few players interviewed in this book cited Duke-UNC games as their most memorable, including Fred Lind, a benchwarmer who played a crucial role in one of the most remarkable Duke-UNC games ever played. Also included is the story of Steve Wojciechowski, who had the most amazing one-point performance in Duke history to key a historic comeback against the Tar Heels.

There are also quite a few players who recall the postseason games that have made Duke an NCAA Tournament juggernaut. Bobby Hurley talks about the upset of UNLV in the 1991 national semifinals that led to Duke's first national title. Christian Laettner looks back on Duke's 1992 victory over Kentucky in the East Regional title game—voted the greatest game in college basketball history by ESPN. Shane Battier discusses his role in Duke's victory over Arizona in the 2001 NCAA championship game.

Today, the Blue Devils own the best NCAA Tournament winning percentage of any school. Only UCLA, Kentucky, Indiana, and North Carolina have won more national titles. Only North Carolina and UCLA have made more Final Four appearances. Much of that success has been earned by current coach Mike Krzyzewski, who inherited the program in 1980 and has, after a slow start, turned it into one of the nation's best.

Since the start of the modern 64-team NCAA Tournament in 1985, no team (much less no other single coach) has matched Krzyzewski's accomplishments: three national titles; 10 Final Fours; 17 top-10 AP finishes; and an astounding seven No. 1 finishes in the poll.

The story of Krzyzewski's rise to prominence is recounted in interviews with stars ranging from All-Americans Johnny Dawkins and Mark Alarie, the twin terrors of his first great team in 1986, to Laettner and Hurley, the stars of Duke's back-to-back national title teams in 1991 and 1992. Two current NBA general managers talk about their greatest games under Coach K—Danny Ferry and his record-setting trip to Miami, and Billy King and the greatest single defensive performance by a Duke player. National player of the year Jason Williams recounts the game that made him a legend.

There's much, much more, although the rich tapestry that is Duke basketball is too long and too varied to tell every story. Hopefully, the games recounted in this book will provide readers with a fair sampling of the players—and moments—that made Duke basketball what it is today.

CHAPTER 1

STEVE WOJCIECHOWSKI

Basketball excellence didn't come easy to Steve Wojciechowski.

The blue-collar kid from Baltimore was not blessed with many physical gifts. His 5-feet-11 stature was marginal for the college game, especially when complemented by an almost complete lack of leaping ability. His quickness was decent but hardly exceptional.

But "Wojo" did possess some unusual qualities—qualities that are harder to measure than height or vertical lift. He developed a profound understanding of the game, and that made him an exceptional playmaker. He displayed the kind of tenacity on both ends of the floor that coaches cherish. And the longer he played the game, the more the young guard revealed the leadership qualities that were to earn him a significant role in Mike Krzyzewski's program at Duke.

"It didn't happen until late in my high school career," Wojciechowski said of his emergence as a major college prospect. "It wasn't until the summer before my senior season in high school that I felt I had become a real good high school player."

Wojciechowski first attracted attention at Howard Garfinkel's Five-Star Camp in Pennsylvania, where the unknown guard from Baltimore won MVP honors in a class that included such celebrated talents as Stephon Marbury and Vince Carter. Later that summer, the future Duke guard attended the Converse All-American Camp in Ypsilanti, Michigan, where Wojciechowski established himself as one of the premier point guard prospects in the class.

"I played on a team with nine Russians and none of them spoke English," he said. "I ended up having one of the better weeks in my career and at that point, that's when all the big-time schools came after me."

Wojciechowski quickly winnowed his recruiting list to three ACC schools—Wake Forest, North Carolina, and Duke. But there was never any doubt that the kid with an unpronounceable Polish name would play for the coach with an unpronounceable Polish name.

"I felt like I had the best relationship with Coach K of all the coaches," Wojciechowski said. "I trusted him."

Wojciechowski appeared to be joining one of the most solid and successful programs in the country. He signed his letter of intent in the fall of 1993 and watched as Grant Hill led Duke to its seventh Final Four in nine seasons. The Blue Devils had won national championships during Wojciechowski's freshmen and sophomore seasons at Cardinal Gibbons High School in Severna Park, Maryland, and even though Hill's team suffered a heartbreaking loss in the 1994 NCAA title game to Arkansas, the program appeared to be poised to win consistently into the foreseeable future.

But the future is never foreseeable.

THE SETTING

Just days after Wojciechowski and freshman classmates Trajan Langdon and Ricky Price began preseason practice in the fall of 1994, the foundation of the program began to crumble. Junior guard Chris Collins, expected to be one of the team's veteran leaders, broke his foot on the first day of practice. Far worse was to come. Coach Krzyzewski had to leave the team at the end of October to undergo back surgery. Told by his doctors to take six weeks for rehabilitation, Coach K was back on the practice court after 10 days.

At first, it appeared that his will would triumph over his body. Krzyzewski led the 1994-95 Blue Devils to a fast start. Using his trio of freshman guards extensively, Coach K got Duke off to a 9-2 start and as high as a No. 6 national ranking. Wojciechowski played 22 minutes in his first college game, collecting four assists and one turnover against Brown. He started and played 30 minutes in a close loss to No. 16 UConn, then started and played a key role as Duke

Steve Wojciechowski pushes the ball up the court—as always looking to make the pass.

edged Illinois in the first college game ever played in Chicago's United Center.

The fact is Wojciechowski was playing often and well in the first month of his college career. He wasn't scoring a lot of points, but he was already starting to exhibit his remarkable ability to protect and distribute the ball—he would finish his career with the best assist/turnover ratio in Duke history.

Unfortunately, that December honeymoon came to a stunning end in early January. It was actually a long holiday flight to and from Hawaii that exacerbated Krzyzewski's back problem to the point where he had to leave the team.

"I can clearly remember the meeting when he told us he wasn't going with us to Georgia Tech," Wojo's teammate Chris Collins said. "I can't even begin to describe the color of his face. It was kind of gray-green. This guy was always our rock. Now all of a sudden, he's breaking down."

Krzyzewski was "temporarily" replaced by assistant Pete Gaudet, Duke's very popular and respected big man's coach. And suddenly, the nation's best program over the previous decade seemed to fall apart. Duke began the "post-K" era with tough road losses at Georgia Tech and Wake Forest. But the real turning point came back in Durham, when the Blue Devils blew a 26-point second half lead to Virginia before losing in double overtime.

The downward spiral had begun, and Wojciechowski struggled to understand what was happening.

"I felt hurt because who wants to play on a team losing that many games," he said. "But that wasn't his fault. Players, coaches, support staff . . . everybody could have handled that situation better."

It's interesting in hindsight to note that Wojciechowski's playing time dwindled as the losses mounted. After averaging more than 20 minutes a game during Duke's early season success, the young guard disappeared at the end of the bench as the Devils limped to 16 losses in their final 20 games.

A year later, Krzyzewski was back on the bench and Wojciechowski was back in the starting lineup as Duke beat No. 10 Iowa in the championship game of the preseason Great Alaskan Shootout. The Blue Devils weren't an exceptionally talented team in Wojciechowski's sophomore season—the graduation of NBA lottery pick Cherokee Parks and second-round NBA draft pick Erik Meek left the team devoid of big men, while a preseason knee injury sidelined sharpshooter Trajan Langdon for the year. But for most of the season, Coach K maximized the team's abilities and returned Duke to the NCAA Tournament.

The peak of the season came during a four-day stretch in late February, when Wojciechowski passed out seven assists as Duke upset defending national champion UCLA in Cameron, then traveled to College Park and upset Maryland—with Ricky Price hitting the winning shot on a pass from Wojciechowski. Late-season injuries to Wojciechowski and Collins proved too much for the team to overcome in postseason, but Duke's final 18-13 record was a satisfying reversal of the previous season's 13-18 mark.

Wojciechowski's junior season was to be another step forward in the program's struggle to re-emerge as the nation's premiere basketball institution. The return of Langdon and the addition of gritty freshman Chris Carrawell helped the Blue Devils once again compete with the ACC's upper-echelon teams.

So did the development of Wojciechowski's game. He showed up at preseason practice lighter, trimmer, stronger, and faster than the year before. He demonstrated his newfound skills in the Blue Devils opener, abusing celebrated St. Joseph's guard Rashid Bey, while passing out eight assists of his own without a single turnover.

His play only got stronger when within a one-week period Duke ended a seven-game losing streak to North Carolina in Durham, then snapped a nine-game skid against Tim Duncan and Wake Forest in Winston-Salem. But perhaps his pivotal moment came at Virginia in mid-February, when with Duke down one in the final seconds and University Hall in total confusion over a scorer's error, Wojciechowski kept his head and pushed the ball up the court, all the way to the basket. He drew a foul with less than a second remaining in the game, and with the Cavalier fans showering him with ice, he calmly sank the two free throws that gave Duke the one-point win.

As it turned out, that narrow victory was enough to give the Blue Devils the ACC regular-season championship. And even though the perimeter-oriented team ran out of gas in March, Wojciechowski had established himself as a significant player in the league—a second-team All-ACC pick and the team MVP of the regular-season champs.

It was a long way from the depths of Wojciechowski's freshman season. But the Blue Devils still had room for improvement, and with the addition of celebrated big man recruits Elton Brand, Shane Battier, and Chris Burgess, the prospects for the 1997-98 Blue Devils were bright.

Duke started Wojciechowski's senior season ranked No. 3 in the country, behind defending national champion Arizona and Kansas and just ahead of Tobacco Road rival North Carolina.

The Blue Devils would flex their newfound muscle early, smashing the top-ranked Wildcats—which returned all five starters from their '97 title team—in the championship game of the Maui Invitational. The combination of the three young big men, along with senior forward Roshown McLeod and the versatile Carrawell gave Arizona major problems, but the decisive element in the game turned out to be Wojciechowski. The diminutive guard outplayed Arizona's Mike Bibby, driving the All-America point guard to distraction with his ferocious defense.

"It was one of those games you get to play on center stage," Wojciechowski said. "Fortunately, I was able to play well and probably caught Bibby on a cold shooting night."

His performance not only earned Wojciechowski MVP honors for the Maui Tournament, it also started him on the path that would end with his selection by the National Association of Basketball Coaches as its national defensive player of the year.

"I understand that my strength as a defender was the strength of the guys behind me," Wojciechowski said. "We were a terrific defensive team with a lot of long athletes. I benefited from that. I've always said that award was a reflection of our team defense and not necessarily a reflection of just my defense."

The Maui triumph catapulted Duke to the top of the polls. But just as the team was starting to roll, the gifted Brand broke a bone in his foot and was sidelined. It was originally reported the freshman big man would miss the rest of the season.

"Elton was, in my opinion, was well on his way to becoming the best freshman player that this school had ever seen," Wojciechowski said. "When he went down, that certainly changed the face of our team. We didn't have anybody who could replace his low-post presence."

Yet, Duke had won the ACC regular-season title the year before without much of an inside presence and even with Brand missing, the play of Battier and occasionally Burgess provided more strength in the paint than Duke was used to. McLeod, who struggled early to adjust his game to Brand's presence, blossomed in his absence and emerged as a first-round NBA draft pick.

Still, Wojciechowski was the team's floor leader and defensive kingpin as the Blue Devils shrugged off the loss of Brand and began to win at an astonishing rate. The problem was that eight miles away, North Carolina was matching Duke victory for victory. When the two rivals finally met in Chapel Hill on February 5, it was a nationally televised duel between No. 1 Duke (20-1) and No. 2 North Carolina (22-1).

Unfortunately, the eagerly awaited "Rumble in the Jungle" (as dubbed by UNC's Senegalese center Makhtar Ndiaye) turned out to be a lopsided dud. Tar Heel All-American Antwan Jamison exploited the absence of Brand by pouring in 35 points—all from point-blank range—as the Tar Heels dominated. In a way, Duke was blown out twice in one night. UNC built a 19-point lead midway through the second half, but a blowup by the volatile Ndiaye helped Duke fight back to within four points with six minutes left. But UNC promptly responded, spurting back ahead and coasting to a 97-73 victory.

"They were extremely talented," Wojciechowski said of the Tar Heels. "They could match us tit for tat. Vince Carter, Antwan Jamison, Shammond Williams, Ed Cota, Brendan Haywood, Ademola Okulaga . . . you're talking big-time college players down the line. It was one of those situations where, when they got hot in transition, there wasn't anybody better in the country. They took it to us over there."

Duke recovered from its beating in Chapel Hill, winning four straight ACC games before Krzyzewski stunned the media on Tobacco Road by announcing that Brand, recovering faster than expected, would be back in uniform for Duke's February 22 game against UCLA. The Sunday afternoon showcase game attracted the largest media turnout in Duke history—so many writers poured into Cameron that school officials had to abandon the normal press room and set up a temporary media headquarters in nearby Card Gym. Those writers and broadcasters—as well as a national television audience— got to see an incredible performance. Brand didn't start, but he came off the bench and contributed 14 points and seven rebounds in 16 minutes as Duke handed UCLA one of the worst losses in its proud history.

"We wanted to send a message and have a masterpiece-type game," Wojciechowski said. "But one of the emotional highlights of the game was Elton's return. We knew if we were going to do anything special, we needed him at his best."

The 120-84 victory over the Bruins, followed by an easy 76-53 win at Georgia Tech, set the stage for the rematch with North Carolina. Duke (26-2) was back at No. 1 in the nation, while the Tar

Heels (27-2), upset a week earlier by N.C. State, came to town ranked No. 3.

The media turnout was even larger than for the UCLA game. The press packed Card Gym, wondering if the second "Rumble in the Jungle" would live up to the hype.

THE GAME OF MY LIFE
DUKE VS. NORTH CAROLINA, FEBRUARY 28, 1998
BY STEVE WOJCIECHOWSKI

As we came back from Georgia Tech, we understood that the Carolina game was going to determine the ACC regular season championship. That was one of our goals.

For the seniors, the realization that this would be our last game at Cameron only heightened the emotions. We respected the heck out of Carolina and knew we'd have to play our best to beat them. But that's one of the reasons you come to Duke—to play in games like that.

Basically, our feeling going into the game was, there's no alternative: We're going to win it. Really, it was as simple as that. Obviously, we had a game plan. We knew their personnel, and there were things within the game we wanted to stop. But the overriding emphasis was in creating a mind-set so that by the end we were going to be the ones that came away with the win.

The Senior Night ceremony is as emotional a time as you'll experience. I certainly cried. I couldn't help it. Obviously, I'm an emotional player. The range of emotions you go through in that moment is amazing. It's almost like time stops and you're getting all these snapshots of your career flashing before your eyes. All the emotions—the good times and the bad times—all come together at once and you realize, "I'll never play on this floor again after the buzzer sounds." That's a tough thing to deal with right before you've got to stop Vince Carter, Jamison, and those guys.

We started the game and they jumped on us right from the beginning. We were very emotionally charged, maybe to the point it hindered us. And again, they were very good. When they were playing at their best, I'm not sure there was any team in the country better than them. They just took it to us for 30 minutes. We were trying and playing hard, but we weren't getting much done.

That night, one of the things we wanted to do was play a game for 40 minutes. One of the things about their team that year was that they had six guys who played. And they used to rotate them according to the letters of the alphabet. One of our advantages was our depth. We wanted to wear them down, especially in a gymnasium that was hotter than heck that day.

It was very emotional at halftime. Coach was just soaking, ringing wet. He had to change his shirt. People think he ripped his shirt off. It wasn't like Superman or anything. And as a team, we had to change our uniforms. Coach was very emotional because we had invested so much in the game and yet played nowhere near our capabilities. We were all a little shell-shocked. He came in and let us have it. He asked the seniors, "Is this the way you wanted it to end?" Obviously, the answer to that was no.

It still took us a while to get some traction. They were up 17 points with 11 minutes left when we started to come back. I think they were starting to feel fatigued. There wasn't this run where we had a two-minute spurt and suddenly it was down to five and we had a whole new ballgame. We chipped away and chipped away and chipped away, and finally in the last minute we were able to get over the hump.

We went strictly to Elton and Roshown in the second half. Even to the point where we'd dribble to the wing, throw it in to Elton and play off and let him do his thing. Once we saw he had it rolling, we were going to go to that until they made an adjustment. (Of my 11 assists), a vast majority were to Elton.

I don't have a photographic memory, but I do recall turning up the heat defensively. I remember taking it to a side and throwing it to Elton on the block and seeing him go to work. Defensively, I remember a few plays, like one where Cota tried to drive me and I stripped him. There were a number of effort plays that we made in that stretch. I think a lot of that had to do with the fact that we were fresher and we rode the emotional wave of our fans as well.

(With 3.8 seconds left, UNC's Cota went to the foul line with a chance to tie the game.)

I thought we were going to go to overtime. That game had all the makings of an overtime game. I had been involved in an overtime game with Carolina as a freshman and I thought, "Boy, we're coming full circle with this one."

It was shocking for Cota to miss—he was a clutch player for them. But Haywood got the rebound and we fouled him. I knew he wasn't a very good free throw shooter on the year. But the thing that worried me was not so much the free throws as much as the defensive rebounds because they were very athletic and they had just grabbed another one. We huddled up and said, "Look, the shot's coming off. We can't allow them to get a hand on it."

(Haywood missed both free throws.)

Once the buzzer sounded it was just an amazing feeling. That's the scene where I ran to Coach and gave him a hug. It's funny how the game kind of mirrored my career. You start off and you're down by a lot—tough times. Things don't look promising. You keep plugging away and plugging away and you end up winning the game in a really emotional fashion. I think the hug was just that Coach and I shared those experiences and how much he meant to me and how much I meant to him. To share that was amazing.

THE AFTERMATH

Wojciechowski scored exactly one point in Duke's 77-75 victory. He joked, "I'm not sure anybody else would pick as the 'Game of My Life' a game in which he scored one point."

But Krzyzewski put his one point in perspective in immediate aftermath of Duke's win.

"It's one of the greatest one-point performances in the history of the game," he told reporters. "With all of that on the table—with everything at stake today—for him to get 11 assists and one turnover and play great D—it's one of the great performances here. I'm not lobbying for anything, but I'll take my point guard through any alley, through any dark street. I'm not saying he's the most talented or anything, but he was remarkable today. Not just good . . . Steve Wojciechowski was remarkable. He wouldn't let us lose."

Brand garnered much of the postgame attention. He scored 13 of his 16 points in the final 11:30 minutes.

"Brand was great—we couldn't stop him," UNC coach Bill Guthridge said.

But Brand, like Krzyzewski, credited the victory to Wojciechowski.

"He's our leader," Brand said. "I don't care about assists or points or anything. He led us to this victory with his tenacity and his will to win."

Neither Duke nor Wojciechowski were able to recapture the magic in the ACC Tournament a week later. The Blue Devils reached the title game for the first time since 1992, but after hanging with

UNC for almost 35 minutes, watched the Tar Heels score the game's final 15 points for an 83-68 victory. Moments after the game, Wojciechowski—weakened by the flu and the large doses of antibiotics he was taking, collapsed in the shower.

He was able to return for Duke's NCAA Tournament run. The Blue Devils beat Radford and Oklahoma State (with Wojciechowski outplaying future radio talk show host Doug Gottlieb) in Rupp Arena, then knocked off Syracuse in the South regional semifinals in the St. Petersburg Tropicana Dome. It appeared that Wojciechowski was headed for his first Final Four appearance when Duke took a 15-point, second-half lead on Kentucky, but in a game that mirrored Duke's regular-season ending victory over North Carolina, the Blue Devils collapsed down the stretch and lost to the eventual national champs, 86-84.

REFLECTIONS ON DUKE

Steve Wojciechowski's No. 12 jersey does not hang from the rafters at Cameron.

He doesn't rank among the top dozen or so players to play for Krzyzewski. Yet, he remains one of Coach K's favorites—and not just because of their shared Polish heritage. He proved his admiration for Wojciechowski in 1999, when he hired the young Blue Devil alum to join his staff as an assistant coach.

Perhaps one reason for the obvious link between the two coaches is the experience they shared in the mid-1990s, when Krzyzewski had to rebuild his program after his back injury.

"This program was like a Mom-and-Pop shop, where all the plugs plugged into Coach," Wojciechowski said. "It eventually wore him down to where he broke down physically and had to take a year—my freshman year—off. But after that year, he started running this program much more like a Fortune 500 company, where he was the CEO, but he was able to delegate. He had different arms to help him to stay on top.

"My career is kind of the foundation of where the program was going in a changing environment of college basketball. My career was kind of the bridge to the new era in Duke basketball."

Indeed, the only important numbers when it comes to Wojciechowski have nothing to do with his modest scoring totals or even his excellent assists/turnover stats. The numbers to look at are the won-lost totals of his four Duke teams: 13-18 as a freshman, 18-13 as a sophomore, 24-9 as a junior, and 32-4 as a senior.

Wojciechowski, the player, helped restore Duke to the nation's elite. Wojciechowski, the assistant coach, has helped Krzyzewski sustain the Blue Devils' second run of success.

It's worth noting what Wojciechowski's Duke teams started. His 1997 team began an unmatched string of ACC championships—after that year, Duke won either the league's regular-season or tournament title in 10 straight seasons. His 1998 Elite Eight team started a string of nine straight Sweet 16 finishes—the second-longest streak in NCAA history.

That's a pretty good legacy for a 5-foot-11 guard with limited physical skills.

CHAPTER 2

JACK MARIN

Jack Marin had the good fortune of growing up in one of the few basketball hotbeds in football-crazy Western Pennsylvania. The sports scene in Farrell, a small steel town about 70 miles northwest of Pittsburgh, was transformed by a remarkable man—the legendary Ed McCluskey.

"I played for the greatest coach in Pennsylvania history," Marin said. "His program made basketball THE thing to do in my hometown."

Without McCluskey's influence, Marin might have ended up on the gridiron and not the hardwood. His father was a football player at Duquesne (where he played in the first Orange Bowl) and Marin himself played some quarterback in his younger days, but he soon gave up the fall sport to concentrate on basketball. He would go up against the likes of Joe Namath and Mike Ditka in high school—but it would be on the basketball court.

As a sophomore, Marin was a little-used sub on a 30-1 state championship team. In fact, he alternated dressing out with his older brother, Chuck. But McCluskey had the younger Marin in uniform for the playoffs.

"He wanted me to have that experience as a sophomore," Marin said.

McCluskey could see Marin's talent and knew he'd be a key player for the Steelers as a junior. Marin helped make that happen by spending almost the entire summer after his 10th grade season in the school gym, playing in three separate summer leagues that had been organized by McCluskey.

"I'd play a game in the morning, then stay around and shoot until the afternoon game," Marin said. "I might run home—we lived eight blocks from the school—and grab dinner. Then I'd run back and play in the all-star league games at night. People from the mills would come up and watch. The high school was the center of all activity in Farrell."

Graduation stripped McCluskey of his championship talent heading into Marin's junior year.

"I was really the only player we had and I was just getting my feet wet," Marin said. "We had a decent season. We were 17-5 and lost to Sharon, our archrival, in the sectionals. My senior year, we were not supposed to be very good at all. I was a little over 6-5 at the time. My coach decided, since I was a shooter and a decent ball-handler, that I would be the guard. He put a kid who was 5-10—but tough, a mill worker's son—at the center position. We were 23-3. We averaged 53 points a game and I scored 20 of them. We played tough, hard-nosed defense."

Marin believes that playing for McCluskey, who won seven state titles during his career, prepared him to be a standout college player.

"He was tough and made us tough," Marin said. "He routinely embarrassed us in practice, so that we routinely embarrassed the other team in games. Athletes learn to take derision. Coaches do that. Watch Mike [Krzyzewski]—he'll call you every name in the book. He knows that most guys will respond to that. You're never going to get out of yourself what a great coach will get out of you. You just won't do it."

Marin finished his senior year in high school year as a nationally known prospect.

"I was starting to get a bunch of letters," Marin recalls. "The guy who wrote me most was Lefty Driesell [at Davidson]. This was before word processing and he was knocking out letters right and left."

But Driesell—and Duke assistant Bucky Waters, who showed up in Farrell to pursue Marin—faced a difficult task. There was considerable pressure on the Farrell star to attend nearby Pittsburgh. Marin was doing his best to resist that pressure.

"I didn't want to go to Pitt," Marin said. "It had nothing to do with Pitt or the people there. But my Dad was a tough, hard-nosed guy and

Jack Marin—regarded by Vic Bubas as the best all-around player of his era.

he was heavily involved in my life and [had I gone to college close to home] he would have continued to do that. He would have been down there as an assistant coach. I really needed to get a little space."

However, turning Pitt down wasn't easy. Brian Generalovich, the star of the Farrell state championship team two years earlier, was an All-East player at Pitt. One Saturday night, Marin visited Generalovich's home and met Pitt coach Bob Timmons.

"Coach Timmons made plans for us to come down and visit Pitt the next morning," Marin said. "We had a 10 o'clock meeting. My Dad and I get there and there's nobody at the Pitt Fieldhouse. Then it's 10:15 and there's still nobody there. By 10:30, I could see that my Dad was starting to get a little irritated, so I started to play on that, thinking, 'This might get me out of going to Pitt.' So I probably said something like, 'If he's not there to meet us on time, we're probably not that important to him.' We just picked up and drove off."

It was only when the Marins returned to Farrell that they learned the reason for Timmons' absence.

"It was daylight savings time and Coach Timmons hadn't changed his clocks," Marin said. "He called and apologized, but we were never able to reschedule the visit."

Freed of his father's desire that he would stay close to home, Marin looked at a number of schools, but ultimately trimmed his list to Duke and Michigan.

"I came to visit Duke on a spring day when it was beautiful—about 70 degrees, blue skies. Then I visited Michigan and it was cold and foggy and drizzling," Marin said. "So I would say that a significant part of my decision had to do with weather."

Marin could have been part of the same recruiting class as future All-American Cazzie Russell at Ann Arbor. Instead, he signed with Duke and became the classmate of Steve Vacendak, a hard-nosed guard from Scranton. Although the two Pennsylvania prep stars never met in high school, they would become close friends at Duke—and an integral part of one of the nation's best college teams.

THE SETTING

While Marin and Vacendak clicked right away on the court, they struggled as roommates.

"We had a terrible clash because he liked the room hot and I liked it cold," Marin said. "He slept in socks and gloves. I'd get up and crack a window and he'd catch me and close the window. He'd turn up the heat and I'd catch him and turn it down. We could never agree."

On the court, the two Pennsylvania stars excelled for a 14-2 freshman team, combining for almost 36 points a game. But Marin's real education came in practice and in the preseason pickup games, when he was often matched against senior All-American Art Heyman.

"When you first get to school, you'd end up in 'Rat League,'" Marin said. "Everybody on the varsity, the JVs, and a couple of guys who had graduated played. It was make it, take it. You played to 10 baskets. It was kind of routine that if you got up against Heyman's team, you'd go 1-2-3-4-5-6-7-8-9-10 and then you'd sit down. Heyman was the best player ever at Duke . . . there was no more dominant force than Heyman."

The oddity was that Heyman was not nearly the best shooter on the team at the time.

"I was THE shooter in high school," Marin said. "Then I got here and saw Vacendak, who was a good shooter and [Jeff] Mullins, who was a great shooter. But there was also Brent Kitchings, a guy from Philadelphia, who never played much, but he could fill it up. And there was a guy who was on the team and not on the team. His name was Jay Beal and he made everything. Heyman was an okay shooter. He would just post you and if he missed, he'd go get it and put it in. For him, the play was never over until the ball was in the basket."

The exposure to the talent at Duke at that time opened Marin's eyes.

"Vic and Bucky were just hitting their recruiting stride," he said.

That point was driven home in the spring of Marin's freshman year, when Heyman led Duke to its first Final Four.

"I was driving home, listening to Duke play Loyola [in the national semifinals]," Marin said. "I had just come down with mono."

But he was healthy the next fall when Duke opened the 1963-64 campaign with senior Jeff Mullins installed as the go-to guy. That was a veteran team that also featured senior guard Buzzy Harrison and senior center Jay Buckley. Duke again dominated the ACC, was ranked No. 3 in the nation in the final AP poll, and made it all the way to the NCAA title game before losing to UCLA.

Although Marin claimed that his role on the team was to back up Mullins—"and Mullins never came off the floor"—he did play enough to average 7.7 points and 4.7 rebounds. He came off the bench in the title game against UCLA and contributed 16 points and 10 rebounds in Duke's 96-83 loss.

Marin would play a larger role as a junior, becoming a starter on a team that was supposed to be rebuilding after losing three three-year starters. But Marin and Vacendak proved to be stellar performers, while sophomore guard Bob Verga joined the varsity and displayed a spectacular shooting touch. Duke averaged 92 points a game to lead the nation in scoring and climbed as high as No. 5 in the AP poll.

Marin earned first-team All-ACC honors as he averaged 19.1 points and 10.3 rebounds.

"My junior year at Duke was a lot like my junior year in high school," Marin said. "We weren't supposed to be that good either year, and both times we surprised people."

But both of Marin's junior seasons ended on a sour note. Despite Duke's fine record and high national ranking, the Blue Devils were upset by N.C. State in the ACC Tournament finals. In those days, only the tournament winner represented the league in the NCAA Tournament, so the loss to the Wolfpack—on N.C. State's home floor in Raleigh—ended Marin's junior year on a sour note.

However, Duke's prospects for the 1965-66 season were extremely promising. The core of Marin, Verga (a first-team All-ACC pick as a sophomore in 1965), and Vacendak (a second-team All-ACC pick as a junior) were joined by sophomore Mike Lewis, a burly center from Missoula, Montana, giving Bubas four talented scoring options. The fifth spot in the starting lineup belonged to junior forward Bob Reidy, a strong defender and rebounder.

"Early on, we just looked like we were going to be extremely powerful," Marin said. "Offensively, we were so multifaceted—we had four guys who could make critical baskets—four go-to guys. [Lewis] was tough inside. Steve could score when he had to, and he obviously scored a lot of clutch baskets for us. Then Verga was a pure scorer."

Duke flexed its muscles early, routing two-time defending national champion UCLA on back-to-back nights in Durham and Charlotte. Just before Christmas, the Devils rallied from a huge second-half deficit to knock off No. 3 Michigan in Detroit's Cobo Hall. And just after Christmas, the rampaging Devils routed Notre Dame in Chicago as Marin, Vacendak, and Verga combined for an astonishing 94 points (35 by Marin, 32 by Vacendak, and 27 by Verga).

"I played on a team where nobody was hiding from the ball," Marin said. "You were always measuring your man."

The twin victories over UCLA vaulted Duke to its first-ever No. 1 national ranking. The Blue Devils held the top spot in the AP poll for eight weeks until a late December upset at West Virginia, which just happened to be coached by former Blue Devil assistant Bucky Waters.

"It was just one of those games where they had a great game and we didn't," Marin said. "I was happy for Bucky."

Duke's loss allowed unbeaten Kentucky to claim the top spot in the polls. It ignited a long-range war of the words—who was the best team in college basketball? Was it Bubas' offensive machine or was it Adolph Rupp's "Runts"?

That question was expected to be answered at the Final Four, but Duke almost failed to make its appointment. Once again, the life-or-death aspect of the ACC Tournament threatened to prevent the Devils from playing in the NCAA Tournament. The first hurdle was North Carolina in the semifinals and the debut of Dean Smith's Four Corners delay game. The Tar Heels spread the floor, and when Duke refused to chase, the game turned into the ACC's first great deep freeze.

"That nearly killed my father," Marin said. "My mom said he left the building several times. They wouldn't play, and there was nothing we could do to get them to play. All I remember is we were down 17-12 with seven minutes to go and somehow we pulled it out. Mike Lewis made a free throw to win the game [21-20]. We had guys who would step up and do what it took."

One night later, Duke was on the verge of a second straight title-game loss to N.C. State when Vacendak made a number of plays down the stretch to salvage the victory—Bubas' fourth ACC championship and his third in four years.

Marin didn't play well in the tournament, and that, coupled with Vacendak's clutch performance in the title game, led to a most unusual vote for ACC player of the year. In the All-ACC voting, taken before the tournament, Marin (and Verga) earned first-team honors, while Vacendak was voted to the second team for the second year in a row. But when the ACC player of the year vote was taken after the tournament, Vacendak edged Marin 31-29 in the voting—becoming the only second-team All-ACC player to win the league's player of the year award.

"I remember some disappointment with that," Marin said. "But as I look back, in retrospect, I'm really pleased that Steve was player of the year in the conference. He was a great teammate for four years.

He was truly a great clutch player and he was the catalyst for our team in a lot of ways. You had other people shining, but he played tough every night. He was very instrumental in our success."

Marin got his game back on track in the Eastern Regionals, played on the same Reynolds Coliseum court where Duke had just won the ACC Tournament. He was instrumental in a 76-74 victory over No. 5 St. Joseph's; Marin had 18 points and 15 rebounds and hit six clutch free throws in the final 90 seconds to keep the Hawks at bay. One night later, he outshined Syracuse All-American Dave Bing in the East title game, scoring 22 points and grabbing nine rebounds in Duke's 91-81 victory.

The win propelled No. 2 ranked Duke to a spot in the Final Four and the long-awaited matchup with No. 1 Kentucky. The semifinal game between the two Southern powers was widely perceived to be the real national title game.

"Duke is the best team I've seen all year," UCLA's John Wooden said. "But I haven't seen Kentucky. Let's just say [the champion will be] the winner of Duke-Kentucky."

Wooden was one of many observers to overlook No. 3 Texas Western, which was matched against Utah in the other semifinal. But it was the presence of Don Haskins' predominately black team from El Paso that would transform the 1966 Final Four into a historical turning point and turn the Duke-Kentucky game into the prelude for one of college basketball's pivotal moments.

THE GAME OF MY LIFE
DUKE VS. KENTUCKY, MARCH 18, 1966
BY JACK MARIN

I think the problem with all the buildup going in is that we kind of knew midweek that we wouldn't have Bobby Verga (who was hospitalized with strep throat). Everything else was clouded by that. We didn't have a backup—more than anything because guys other than the starters didn't play. We were always on the floor unless we were in foul trouble . . . and I don't think Verga was ever in foul trouble. We always had his presence and he was a monster.

When we got there, we heard that their Larry Conley was not feeling well either, but there was no comparison between the losses. I think with Verga, we were certainly capable of beating Kentucky.

The game started really well for us and for me particularly. Pat Riley was guarding me and we backdoored him two or three times early in the game. They were applying heavy pressure and we knew that, and we'd worked on this thing. Steve came down and gave me this good fake entry pass into the wing. Pat overplayed it and I got three quick lay-ups out of that.

There probably isn't anything better in a game like that, in an environment like that, than to get a couple of hoops early. It gives you a psychological boost that's dramatic. And if it goes the other way and you miss one or two early, sometimes it's not easy to recover. You birdie a couple of early holes and the round's pretty easy.

There were a lot of lead changes. I know we were fighting and clawing. Bob tried to play, but he was dehydrated and weak and didn't have his game. The guy who played behind him, Ronnie Wendelin, did a pretty decent job for someone who got very little opportunity to play during the season. He wasn't a force, but he carried his weight. We had to deal with (Louie) Dampier in the backcourt and he did a good job.

Lewis had a misstep late that I think he will always remember. He caught the ball in one of those situations where he was wide open and lost the sense of where he was. He turned to put the ball in the basket and missed essentially a lay-up. It's one of those things you understand in the end. It's not like it's a choke. It's just that he wasn't where he thought he was.

(Duke's 83-79 loss to the Wildcats set up the historic Texas Western-Kentucky championship game—a landmark game in college basketball matching the all-black Miners against the all-white Wildcats.)

We didn't pay too much attention to that. It was interesting going in because there were two Southern teams meeting in the semifinals. It wasn't really uncommon. UCLA had come in (with an integrated lineup) . . . Cincinnati had been a fairly black team in the past and Loyola of Chicago (the 1963 NCAA champs started four blacks). It wasn't really uncommon if you had a Southern team with a bunch of white kids playing in the championship game. Kentucky was white, and we were too. Utah was a (racially) mixed team.

The (championship) game wasn't good theater. Texas Western was in control the whole way.

Yeah, I've thought about what would have happened if we had played them in the finals. I don't know why we couldn't have handled them. We handled Michigan and they started Bill Buntin, Oliver

Darden, and Cazzie Russell. We handled UCLA and their pressure. I brought the ball up against UCLA. It wasn't that our guards couldn't handle the pressure, but I had a much easier time bringing it up against somebody my size than the other guys.

I think quickness would have been an issue, but we'd run up against some quick teams. If Verga was healthy, I think we were the best team in the country.

GAME RESULTS

But Duke finished third in the nation that year, not first.

Marin led the Devils with 29 points against the Wildcats, hitting 11 of 18 shots from floor. His shooting kept Duke close throughout the second half. The Wildcats seized the lead in the first minute after the break and led by seven with 12 minutes to play. Duke fought back to tie six times, but could never regain the lead. The Wildcats were up 73-71 when Lewis missed inside, and a fast-break basket by Riley gave Kentucky the margin they would hold the rest of the way for the 83-79 victory.

Lewis added 21 points for Duke and Vacendak 17, despite foul trouble. Verga played just 22 minutes and missed five of seven from the floor. His four points were 14 under his season average. Conley played 28 minutes and scored 10 points—almost exactly his season average.

"I don't want a man to go out of this room and say that I said we could have beaten Kentucky with a well Bob Verga," Bubas told the media after the game. But he couldn't help adding, "We are better— a whole lot better—when he is healthy."

Verga played a little better in the consolation game 24 hours later, scoring 15 points in Duke's 79-77 victory over Utah. Marin was again the Blue Devils' leading scorer with 23 points, although he hit just nine of 26 shots from the floor.

"That was a funny night," Marin said. "Those consolation games were good for getting your average. I took 26 shots that night and I thought 25 of them were dead center. I bet I had 10 balls bounce straight back at me from the back of the rim. I was shooting deep, and every one of them felt perfect."

Late in the game, Utah had a chance to force overtime, but Bubas called two timeouts in a row to ice free-throw shooter Dave Black.

"He did something I've never seen before or since," Marin said. "After the timeout, the ref hands him the ball and he hands it back and wipes his hands on the official's jersey. I turned to [Utah star Jerry] Chambers and said, 'You lose.'"

That was Marin's final moment in a Duke uniform. After the game, he showered, changed, and went to watch the historic Texas Western-Kentucky game—the landmark moment that his Duke team came so close to crashing.

REFLECTIONS ON DUKE

Although Marin was highly coveted by the NBA, he insisted throughout the spring of 1966 that he was going to attend Duke Medical School rather than play pro basketball.

"St. Louis said they would draft me fourth," Marin said. "Marty Blake called me and I said, 'Marty, I'm not going. I'm not going. I'm not going.' So they didn't draft me. So the Bullets, who had never contacted me, drafted me fifth."

Marin was still determined to attend medical school, but in the end, the Baltimore Bullets made him an offer he couldn't refuse.

"They made me the third highest paid rookie in the league," he said. "I got $18,500. I got more than Dave Bing—he started at $16,500."

Marin ended up playing 11 seasons in the NBA, averaging as many as 22 points a game and twice making the All-Star team. When his career was over, he returned to Duke and earned a degree from Duke's Law School.

The former Blue Devil star had success representing pro basketball players—both in the NBA and overseas—and served for almost two decades as special counsel for the NBA Retired Players Association. He also enjoyed success on the Celebrity Golf Tour.

Marin still follows the Blue Devils closely.

"I would have loved to have played for Coach K," Marin said. "He reminds me a lot of Vic, especially the way he coaches defense. We relied on the same overplaying man-to-man defense. And the whole thing about slapping the floor? That was started by Vic."

Marin still cherishes his career at Duke and is very proud of Bubas' declaration that he was the most complete player of that era.

CHAPTER 3

ART HEYMAN

It's possible to argue that Art Heyman was the player that single-handedly changed the focus of the Duke-North Carolina rivalry from football to basketball.

When Heyman first emerged as a schoolboy sensation on Long Island, the ACC's great basketball rivalry was North Carolina versus N.C. State. Duke was still a football power. While the school enjoyed moderate basketball success in the 1950s, the Blue Devils couldn't compete with the basketball juggernaut Everett Case had built at N.C. State. The "Gray Fox" dominated the final years of the Southern Conference and the first years of the new ACC, winning nine conference titles in 10 seasons between 1947-1956.

The first real challenge to Case's dynasty came from Chapel Hill, where former St. John's coach Frank McGuire drew on his New York roots to establish a pipeline—celebrated as his "Underground Railroad"—to bring talented New York players to Tobacco Road. His efforts paid off in 1957 when a team featuring five starters from the Big Apple not only ended Case's reign in the ACC, but also reeled off 32 straight wins to become the first team on Tobacco Road to bring home a national championship.

Of course, Case did not surrender without a fight. He sent his energetic young assistant, Vic Bubas, on the road to find the talent to combat McGuire's New York pipeline. Bubas found big man John Ritcher and point guard Lou Pucillo in Philadelphia, then ventured into Lexington, Kentucky, to steal sharpshooter Jon Speaks from Adolph Rupp's backyard. McGuire countered by replacing his championship squad with more New York talent. Between 1957 and 1961, his Underground Railroad delivered such gifted players as Lee Shaffer, Doug Moe, York Larese, and an electric leaper known as Billy "The Kid" Cunningham.

The prize gem of McGuire's New York recruiting machine was supposed to be Heyman, a bullish playground legend in New York who made his reputation playing against—and abusing—many of the older prospects who had found their way to Chapel Hill. Future coaching legend Larry Brown was a particularly bitter rival for Heyman, but there was also a mutual respect between them and it was long assumed that the two Jewish players from Long Island would room together at Carolina.

Heyman did make a perfunctory recruiting visit to Duke in the spring of 1959, but that was after head coach Harold Bradley had left Duke for Texas and before athletic director Eddie Cameron had named a replacement. Several Duke players escorted Heyman around campus, but they hardly bonded with the brash New Yorker. In fact, Heyman teased his hosts, boasting what he was going to do to them under the boards.

Cameron, who had gone 226-99 as Duke's head basketball coach in the years between 1929-42, was less concerned with landing the obnoxious New Yorker than he was with finding a new coach. He focused in on Case's right-hand man, luring the 31-year-old Bubas from Raleigh to Durham. He introduced Bubas to the media on May 5, 1959, with the words, "Gentlemen, this is our new basketball coach. We hope he is our coach forever."

Privately, he had another message for his new coach: "Don't you think it's time you go recruiting?"

It was awfully late in the recruiting season, but few men were as knowledgeable about the recruiting landscape as the new Duke coach, and Bubas knew something that gave him hope of pulling off a miracle. He had heard that Heyman's stepfather, Bill Heyman, harbored a deep dislike for McGuire. Bubas continued to pursue Heyman, even after his target signed a formal letter-of-intent with the Tar Heels. His persistence paid off when Bill Heyman and McGuire got into a shouting match one night at the Carolina Inn—an argument that nearly came to fisticuffs.

Art Heyman—the wide smile hiding a fierce, competitive nature.

"I had to step in between them," Heyman said. "My stepfather called Carolina a basketball factory and McGuire didn't like that. They were about to start swinging at each other."

Under the rules then in place, Heyman's letter-of-intent did not become binding until July 1, and as that date approached, Bubas continued to recruit the Long Island star. Or more precisely, he recruited his parents.

"He charmed my mother and stepfather," Heyman said. "They made me go to Duke. All my friends from New York were at Carolina. If Duke hadn't picked me up at the airport, I would have gone down the road and started school there."

THE SETTING

Bubas' successful quest for Heyman energized the Duke program and turned the Duke-Carolina rivalry into a raging inferno. McGuire never forgave Heyman for reneging on his commitment and he never forgave Bubas for his role in the event.

"Frank hated Duke and he hated the Duke kids," Heyman said. "He hated the way the kids over there used to mimic him. They'd wear suits and slick back their hair and pull on their ties and their cuffs like he always did . . . it drove him nuts."

It wasn't long before Bubas returned McGuire's hatred of Duke.

"Vic learned that they had hired a private investigator to follow me around and try to catch me doing something wrong," Heyman said. "I remember we played Navy in Greensboro. At the time, there was an unwritten rule that ACC coaches didn't give scouting reports to teams from outside the conference. But Frank and the Navy coach [Ben Carnevale] were friends, and during the game, they knew everything we were going to do. After the game, Vic saw McGuire standing there and they went at it. Frank adjusted his tie, like he always does, and said, 'Vic, I love you and Art.' Vic started shouting, 'Frank, you are full of shit . . . I'm going to clock you!' I had to step in between them."

North Carolina's enmity for Heyman boiled over during his freshman season. At the time, first-year players could not play varsity basketball. Instead, the freshmen would play a schedule of games against other freshman teams. That first winter, Heyman's Blue Imps played UNC's Tar Babies in at a high school gym in Siler City, North Carolina—a small town about 20 miles southwest of Chapel Hill.

Future Duke coach Bucky Waters, who coached the Duke freshmen in 1960, expected the UNC team to try to provoke the hotheaded young Blue Devils star.

"Before the game, I sat down with Art and told him, 'You've got to prepare yourself for anything. If you explode, you'll make them happy,'" Waters said. "Then the game started and they began with this line of rhetoric, right in front of us, 'Jew! Christ-killer!' It was vicious. I called time out and got real close to Art and said, 'This is what we've been expecting. You can fight them, but if you punch back, expect to hear the same thing every night.' I took two time outs back to back so I could keep talking. I told him, 'Play hard and kick their butts, then at the end of the game, you can point to the scoreboard as you walk off.'

"Well, Art was incredible, and we won the game. Or we were about to win it when [UNC freshman Dieter] Krause cold-cocked Art. Just a cheap shot, just a punch from out of nowhere. I lost it. I was so convinced that it was all premeditated that I had [UNC freshman coach Kenny Rosemond] by the lapels and I was bouncing him off the scorer's table. I kept pushing him into the [scoreboard controls] and the scoreboard was going nuts. Here I worked so hard to convince Art to keep his cool, then I lost mine."

The Siler City brawl was only a preview of what would become the most celebrated fight in ACC history.

When Heyman moved up to the Duke varsity in the fall of 1960, he found himself surrounded by a close-knit, older group of players—the same players he had once taunted on his recruiting visit.

Bubas had led that junior-dominated team to a mediocre 12-10 regular-season record in his first season as head coach. But the team caught fire in the 1960 ACC Tournament. After an opening victory over South Carolina, the fourth-seeded Blue Devils upset top-seeded North Carolina in the semifinals. The next night, Bubas' miracle workers upset second-seeded Wake Forest—a burgeoning power with sophomore center Len Chappell and junior guard Billy Packer—in the title game. A week later, Duke beat Princeton and St. Joseph's in the NCAA Tournament before losing to NYU in the East Regional finals.

All five starters from that title team returned for Heyman's sophomore year. But from day one, there was no question as to who was Duke's star—it wasn't center Doug Kistler, the ACC Tournament MVP, and it wasn't forward Carroll Youngkin, who had poured in 30 points in the upset of UNC. It was Heyman, who simply amazed onlookers with his power and his determination. He wasn't the greatest shooter, but he was an unstoppable driver and a dynamo on the boards.

"He's just like a king in a checker game," Bubas told reporters. "I can move him anywhere and he gets the job done."

From that point on, Heyman became known as "King Arthur."

"He was a step above," Waters said. "No player ever took over a game or put a team on his back like Art. And he was such a great, great passer."

Heyman was proud of his playmaking skills.

"That's what everybody forgets," he said. "We didn't keep assists in those days, but I know I led the team by a wide margin. Of course, I also had the ball in my hands 99 percent of the time."

His eagerly awaited debut lived up to the hype as Heyman scored 28 points in the 1959-60 opener against LSU. He continued his torrid pace through an early-season slate that included West Virginia, Florida, Marquette, and Georgia Tech. Heyman was averaging 26 points a game as Duke got off to a 9-0 start before running into North Carolina in the finals of the Dixie Classic in Raleigh.

Heyman opened the game by abusing UNC for 11 points in a little more than five minutes. At that point, McGuire called time out and switched All-American Doug Moe onto the Blue Devil star. Moe, one of the college game's best defenders, limited Heyman to five points in the game's final 25 minutes, and UNC was able to pull out a 76-71 victory. His failure gnawed at the brilliant young player. Heyman reacted by ripping a picture of Moe out of the Durham newspaper and pasting it on his dorm wall.

Heyman continued to think about Moe as Duke resumed its triumphant march after the loss to Carolina. The Blue Devils reeled off six more wins in a row to reach the rematch with Carolina at 15-1—and an all-time best national ranking of No. 4 in the Associated Press poll. The Tar Heels arrived in Durham with a 14-2 record and a No. 5 national ranking. The UPI (the 1961 equivalent to the modern USA Today Coaches' Poll) had UNC at No. 4 and Duke at No. 5.

It was still early in the ACC season and whatever the outcome of the game, the two rivals would still be jockeying with powerful Wake Forest for ACC supremacy. Yet, that situation did nothing to diminish the anticipation of what Bubas called "the biggest game ever played in the South."

Duke's Cameron passed up the chance to get national TV exposure—unheard of in that day and time—when he refused to move the game from its scheduled 8 p.m. start to an early afternoon tip off. A sleet storm paralyzed the state, guaranteeing a huge Saturday night audience in the state for the regional telecast of the game.

The atmosphere in Duke Indoor Stadium (not yet renamed for Cameron) was electric, although there was an undertone of ugliness. It showed up during the preliminary game between the two freshman teams, which got so out of hand that the UNC Tar Babies ended up with just three players on the floor after five players fouled out and three others were ejected for fighting. Freshman Jeff Mullins led the Blue Imps to a lopsided victory then hurriedly dressed and returned to the court to watch the varsity game that followed.

As the two varsity teams took the court, the tension grew. All of the background—the bitter recruiting battle for Heyman, the ugly scene in Siler City, the memories of Duke's ACC Tournament win in 1960 and UNC's Dixie Classic victory earlier that season, the near-fight between Bubas and McGuire in Greensboro—hovered over the court.

"We'll win the game because we're the better team," Moe told reporters before tip off. "I don't know exactly how we're going to do it—whether it will be rebounding or shooting—but we're going to win. We'll do what we have to do to win."

Heyman felt the same way, but for once the normally loquacious New Yorker kept his mouth shut. He was determined to do his talking on the court.

THE GAME OF MY LIFE
DUKE VS. NORTH CAROLINA, FEBRUARY 4, 1961
BY ART HEYMAN

I never played with a grudge. But that game, I had a grudge.

Moe was guarding me and he kept spitting on me. Every time I took a shot, he would spit on me. I told him I was not going to take that. I told him I had a cold, and if he wanted to keep spitting, I'd let him have some real nasty stuff. I wanted to fight him, but Doug was a blowhard and he backed down and all we did was dance a little. McGuire got upset when our trainer, Jim Cunningham, came off the bench to get between Krause and us. He didn't know that Cunningham knew Krause from high school.

Doug was frustrated. I wasn't on that night . . . I was focused. He couldn't stop me. I hit nine of my first 11 shots and got him in foul trouble.

(UNC led 35-34 at the half when an incident occurred that was to haunt Heyman in the coming days.)

At the time, both teams ran off the court at the same end. There was a Carolina cheerleader there, whacking his players on the butt as they ran off. For some reason, he whacked me as I ran by. I turned around and whacked him back. I didn't think anything about it at the time, but Blackwell Brodgen (a Durham lawyer and a UNC fan, who was seated in the end zone) saw it and filed assault charges against me. Nothing came of it— the case was thrown out of court—but the story went all over the country that I had hit a cheerleader. They didn't make it clear that it was a male cheerleader. My mother was playing cards when she heard about it and she called me up and asked me how I could hit a woman!

That was nothing. The other fight—between Larry (Brown) and me—that's the one everyone remembers. Larry is so full of it; he says I sucker punched him. Nothing like that happened. But that's Larry: He's only happy when he's unhappy.

What happened was that I grabbed him to prevent him from making a lay-up. Larry threw the ball at me and started swinging. It was right in front of their bench and before I knew it, everybody was hitting me. But I was strong and I fought my way back to my feet and I fought back. They were beating the hell out of me and I was just fighting back.

THE AFTERMATH

It took 10 Duke policemen 10 minutes to clear the floor of brawling players and students. Afterward there was some confusion as to the departure of Heyman. Referee Charlie Eckman reported that Heyman was ejected for fighting, although Bubas claimed that his star had merely fouled out on the initial play, before the fight.

Amazingly, Brown was allowed to stay in the game and shoot two free throws. It made little difference as Duke wrapped up the 81-77 victory. Heyman had been magnificent—36 points on 11-of-13 shooting from the floor and 14 of 17 free throws. He added eight rebounds and an uncounted number of assists. He got some sweet revenge on Moe, who managed a mere 11 points before fouling out with more than 10 minutes to play.

"It was his finest game," Bubas said of his young star.

But the aftermath of the game presented more problems for the Blue Devils. Eckman's official report to the commissioner blamed Heyman for throwing the first punch and so did most of the postgame news reports. The criticism of the Duke star became so harsh that Bubas took the unusual step of calling a midweek press conference, then rolling the game film for the assembled media. He slowed it down and replayed it several times to demonstrate that Brown, not Heyman, threw the first punch. The film showed that the most despicable blow in the fight was delivered by future NBA executive Donnie Walsh, who came off the UNC bench to hit Heyman from behind, knocking him to the floor.

The film also showed that while the majority of the Carolina team jumped the Duke star, none of his teammates came to his rescue.

"That bothered me," Heyman said. "I told them, 'If somebody swung at you, I'd be right there.' They told me, 'It's not our nature.' I don't think there was an animosity there, but we weren't that close. They were older guys and most of them were married. I was closer to Jeff Mullins and the guys in his class."

Heyman was even more upset a week later when he prepared to board the Duke bus for a trip to Winston-Salem, North Carolina, where the Blue Devils were scheduled to battle Wake Forest for first place in the conference.

"Mr. Cameron called me into his office and told me I was suspended and couldn't play at Wake Forest," Heyman said. "That's when I really got upset. I told Mr. Cameron that if he didn't back me, I was leaving. I had done everything they asked; I went to class, I was never in trouble. I used to make all these trips to the hospital—not for publicity or anything. I hadn't done anything wrong. I felt like if Duke wouldn't back me, I was leaving."

Cameron decided to appeal Heyman's suspension, a tactic that allowed the Duke star to play at Wake Forest. Since the team bus had already left, Heyman jumped in a car with assistant coach Fred Shabel and a reporter from *Sports Illustrated* and made the 90-minute drive to Winston-Salem for the game.

Unfortunately, Duke lost a close game to the powerful Deacons. And within days, ACC commissioner Jim Weaver issued his ruling, which dealt the same penalties to Heyman, Brown, and Walsh. All three were suspended for their teams' remaining regular-season ACC games. Heyman was allowed to play in two non-conference games and in the ACC Tournament, but without his energetic presence, Duke stumbled down the stretch.

"That cost us a national championship," Heyman said. "I really believe that. We lost our focus after that. Even when I came back for the tournament, it wasn't the same."

Wake Forest represented the ACC in the NCAA Tournament and the Deacons reached the East Regional finals before losing to St. Joseph's.

RELECTIONS ON DUKE

Heyman didn't get to play in the 1961 finale at North Carolina, when the Tar Heels pulled out a 69-66 victory in overtime to win the ACC regular-season title. But he did play against UNC four more times in his career and never again lost to the Heels. He wrapped up his career much as Dick Groat did 12 years earlier—by scoring his career high in his final regular-season game at home. Heyman said his goodbye to the Duke crowd by scoring 40 points in a 106-93 rout of the Tar Heels.

But Heyman's career was not done. He won ACC Tournament MVP honors as he led the Blue Devils to the ACC title, then teamed with Mullins to spark the Devils to the East Regional title and the first Final Four trip in school history. The drive to the national championship game ended in the semifinals against eventual champion Chicago Loyola, but Heyman was so impressive in that defeat and in the third-place victory over Oregon State that he was voted the MVP of the Final Four.

Heyman, the ACC's first consensus national player of the year, was the first player taken in the 1963 NBA draft, picked by his hometown New York Knicks. Although his power game didn't translate well into the pro game, he did give the Knicks one solid season, averaging 15.4 points and earning a spot on the all-rookie team. That was his only strong NBA season. Heyman did bounce back in the new ABA. He was a mainstay for the 1968 Pittsburgh Pipers, averaging 18.5 points and 3.8 assists a game for the league champions. But after one more productive season (14.4 points per game in 1969), Heyman quickly faded and retired to open a restaurant and bar in New York City.

"I could have been something special," Heyman later said of his pro career. "Maybe I wasn't mature and I didn't grow up. I just wasn't ready. It's really sad, but I have no one to blame but myself. It was all my fault."

Heyman left Duke with one regret: The school had decided not to retire his No. 25 jersey. Bubas always made it clear that it was an honor his first star player deserved.

"Everybody talks about how great Dick Groat was," Bubas said after Heyman scored 40 in his finale against UNC. "Groat was a great player. I guarded him. But Heyman is bigger and stronger. He's got to be the best player ever to put on a Duke uniform."

Unfortunately, Cameron vetoed any jersey retirements. He believed that only Groat—a two-sport All-American—deserved to be honored. That meant that Heyman, Mullins, Bob Verga, and all the other great players of the Bubas era were out of luck.

Heyman's snub became even more glaring when—with Cameron gone—Duke coach Bill Foster managed to get Mike Gminski's No. 43 jersey retired in 1980. Now, Gminski was a great player, but his accomplishments pale in comparison to Heyman's. And as the first stars of the Mike Krzyzewski era—Johnny Dawkins and Danny Ferry—were honored, Heyman's omission became even more embarrassing.

Luckily, Krzyzewski was a student of the game and understood the important role Heyman played in Duke history. He worked behind the scenes, and on March 4, 1990—just over 27 years after Heyman's last home game—his No. 25 jersey was lifted into the rafters.

"I was the first break for Bubas," Heyman said. "I started all that down there."

CHAPTER 4

JEFF MULLINS

Jeff Mullins is usually referred to as a native of Lexington, Kentucky. There's a wonderful irony in the fact that Duke coach Vic Bubas stole one of the Blue Devils' greatest players from under the nose of Kentucky legend Adolph Rupp.

But it's not quite that simple.

Mullins only lived in Lexington for three years before coming to Duke. He actually grew up in the small New York community of Staatsburg, located about 100 minutes north of New York City.

"It was a real small town," Mullins said. "The last year I was there, our high school graduated just three seniors. We never had enough boys for football, but we did a lot of Huck Finn things along the river."

Mullins' life changed just before his sophomore year in high school when IBM transferred his father, Vincent Mullins, to Lexington—smack dab in the middle of the nation's rabid basketball heartland. The gangling 15-year-old had played more baseball than basketball back in New York, but he soon found himself one of 80 prospects trying out for the basketball team at Lafayette High School.

"That was a little frightening," Mullins said. "The coach, Ralph Carlisle, was a legend in Kentucky high school circles. He was also a real demanding, authoritarian type. You did it his way or else. I found that out my first day. He started out by showing us how to make a lay-up, how to approach the basket from 45 degrees . . . which foot to use . . . which hand to use . . . how to lay it off the glass. He wanted somebody to demonstrate a lay-up from the left side, which meant you had to use your left hand. Well, wouldn't you know, but out of all the boys there, he picked me to demonstrate. I had always shot with my right hand, even from the left side, and I just could not use my left hand. I stood there and bricked about three in a row and just looked awful.

"Well, after that we scrimmaged and during the scrimmage, I had a steal and was all alone for a lay-up. The only problem was that I was coming in from the left side. As I got close to the basket, I was asking myself, 'I know I can make it if I shoot right-handed, but Coach said to shoot left-handed from the left side.' I was still thinking about it when I got to the basket and shot left handed—and missed badly. I thought I had really screwed up and Coach Carlisle blew his whistle, stopped practice and came running down from the bleachers. Then he said, 'This boy is going to make the team because he listens and follows instructions!'"

Mullins did make the team, although he played junior varsity basketball as a sophomore before moving up to the varsity as a junior, where he played second fiddle to a sharp-shooting guard named Jon Speaks.

"Jon was very accomplished—to this day, I still believe he had one of the best jump shots I've ever seen," Mullins said. "We were pretty close. We both lived outside the district and I'd ride to school with Jon, then we'd stay after school and work out one on one."

Speaks was such a good player that he attracted the interest of a bright young assistant coach from Everett Case's powerhouse program at N.C. State. In those days before limits on recruiting contacts, Wolfpack assistant coach Vic Bubas was often on hand at practice to watch Speaks. But he also watched as Mullins slowly developed over the course of his junior year. As Bubas recruited Lafayette's senior star, he began to forge a strong relationship with the team's budding junior.

Of course, it was Lexington, Kentucky, and in that era, Rupp owned the state. He could have had Speaks—and probably Mullins— had he not committed a major recruiting blunder.

"He had not recruited Jon all year, but that spring, Rupp was the speaker at our athletic banquet," Mullins said. "Jon and I were together before the banquet when Coach Rupp came up to us. I started to walk away, but he told me to stay. Then he turned to Jon and

Jeff Mullins—the gifted forward that Vic Bubas stole from Adolph Rupp.

said, 'Son, I want to offer you a scholarship.' Jon was very interested, but he told Coach Rupp he needed to talk to his parents about it. Rupp said, 'No, I want to announce it tonight. If you don't accept tonight, I'll give it to somebody else.' He got pretty mad—his face turned red. It really turned me off."

Speaks signed with Bubas at N.C. State and enjoyed a fine career (winning first-team All-ACC honors as a senior) before dying tragically in an auto accident just weeks before graduation. But Rupp's mishandling of Speaks was to have worse consequences for the Wildcats when Mullins blossomed during his senior year at Lafayette High School into Kentucky's Mr. Basketball and into one of the nation's top prospects.

Rupp recruited Mullins hard, twice bringing in the governor to try to convince the Lexington product to stay in state. But Mullins was still a New York kid at heart and he had the best long-term relationship with Bubas, who had just been named the new head coach at Duke.

He visited the Durham campus over Thanksgiving and was in the stands when North Carolina whipped the Duke football team 50-0. That didn't shake his interest in Bubas' new school. However, after returning to Lexington, he began to hear stories about Bubas' first recruit—a brash Long Island product named Art Heyman.

"Between Thanksgiving and spring, every other coach had stories about Art Heyman," Mullins said. "That's one of the main reasons why I made another visit to Durham in the spring. I didn't meet Art on my first visit and I wanted to see what he was like. From Day One, we hit it off."

And from that moment, Mullins was Duke bound, although he admits that he wasn't quite sure he'd make it to Durham until he and Speaks—who drove down to Tobacco Road together from Lexington in the fall of 1960—crossed the Kentucky state line.

THE SETTING

Despite their early chemistry, Heyman and Mullins didn't really get to know each other in 1960-61. Heyman joined the varsity, while Mullins practiced and played with the freshman team.

The newcomer from Kentucky got closer to his classmates—especially Jay Buckley, a long, lanky 6-foot-10 center with an IQ reported to be around 160, and Buzzy Harrison, a smooth guard with a great outside stroke. All three would start for three consecutive seasons on the varsity and all would play a major role in Duke's 1964 NCAA Tournament run.

But Buckley and Harrison would be overshadowed in that era by the Heyman-Mullins show. The two All-America forwards were a contrast in style and personality. Heyman, one year ahead of his running mate, was an outspoken—and often outrageous—character, who played with an emotional fire that was obvious to any onlooker. He was just a so-so shooter, but he was a powerful driver and an excellent passer. Mullins was a quiet, unassuming player who was much admired (even by Duke's rivals). The curiously archaic term frequently used to describe him was "a gentleman." He was also a deadly shooter, a strong rebounder, and a good defender.

"We were very different," Mullins said of Heyman. "We went our different ways on campus and we played our own brand of basketball. What we shared was that we both wanted to be special players. We both wanted to win."

The important point was that Mullins was Duke's second banana. As good as he was—three times a first-team All-ACC pick who averaged almost 21 points a game in his first two seasons—he was always overshadowed by Heyman, who scored more points, took most of the big shots, and garnered most of the media attention.

Heyman won national player of the year honors in 1963, leading Duke to its first Final Four. After his graduation that spring, there was considerable skepticism about the Blue Devils' future. True, Bubas returned four starters, including an All-America-quality player in Mullins, but could the quiet, seemingly unemotional sidekick become a leader?

"Losing Art was a huge hole to fill," Mullins said. "But we had enjoyed a lot of success in our career. We had learned how to do it. It had become part of us."

It helped that Mullins took his game to Heyman's level. Comparing their senior-year stats is eye opening:

Heyman (1963): 24.9 ppg; 10.8 rpg; 46.9 FG%; 69.1 FT%
Mullins (1964): 24.2 ppg; 8.9 rpg; 48.9 FG%; 82.0 FT%

The team's enjoyed similar success, too. Heyman's '63 Devils won the ACC regular-season title with a 14-0 record, swept the ACC Tournament, and finished 27-3 after losing to eventual champ Chicago Loyola in the national semifinals. Mullins '64 Devils also won the regular-season (13-1 with a one-point loss at Wake Forest), swept the ACC Tournament, and finished 26-5 after losing to UCLA in the national title game—Duke's first appearance in the championship game.

Mullins, who claimed the ACC player of the year award and was selected first-team All-America by the Basketball Writers, doesn't take all the credit for the success of the 1964 team. He points to a lineup change by Bubas after a late December loss to Michigan, in which the Duke coach replaced sophomore Steve Vacendak at point guard with junior Denny Ferguson. While Vacendak was the more talented player (he would earn ACC player of the year honors as a senior), Ferguson provided more experience and better playmaking, while Vacendak continued to contribute as a sixth man.

However, Mullins still believes that the real turning point in Duke's season came in mid-February, when Jay Buckley came out of his shell.

"Jay was my suitemate and he was a brilliant student," Mullins said. "But he wasn't a very assertive player."

That changed when Lefty Driesell brought a Davidson team ranked No. 4 in the nation to Durham to take on No. 5 Duke. The game was a sensation on Tobacco Road, thanks to the theatrics of Driesell, a Duke grad who had burst on the scene the year before when his unknown team stunned unbeaten and No. 2-ranked Duke in Charlotte. Leading up to the rematch, a Charlotte newspaper reporter compared the two teams position by position, concluding that Davidson was the clear cut winner at just one spot—in the middle, where center Fred Hetzel was far better that Buckley, described as "Duke's one weak link."

Mullins recalls sitting behind Buckley at a pregame meeting, where Bubas read the article out loud, challenging his senior center.

"I could see the hairs on the back of his neck stand up," Mullins said. "Then he went out and just played great. He became a man that night. And it didn't stop there. After that game, it was like a whole new light came on. He was a great player for us the rest of the way."

Indeed, Mullins believes that Buckley deserved the ACC Tournament MVP award for his play that March weekend, when he averaged 19.7 points per game and 10.7 rebounds per game as Duke swept Big Four rivals N.C. State, North Carolina, and Wake Forest to earn a second straight ACC championship.

"I was glad we won, but it was a mediocre tourney for me," said Mullins, who averaged 19.3 points in the three games, but shot a sub-par 21-of-50 from the floor. "Today, players have no concept of shooting percentage. I always looked at my shooting percentage. My high school coach always preached that a guy should shoot 50 percent from the floor. He said it wasn't a good game if you didn't score more than you shot."

Mullins was determined to play better in the NCAA Tournament, which opened six days later on the same Reynolds Coliseum court that had just played host to the ACC Tournament. In that era before the NCAA field was seeded and balanced, Friday night's East Regional semifinals matched Duke, ranked No. 3 in the nation, against No. 7 Villanova in the first game. The second game would match Princeton, which featured All-American Bill Bradley, against unknown Connecticut, coached by former Duke assistant Fred Shabel.

It was widely believed that the Duke-Villanova game would produce the East champion. Duke's prowess had been tested in the tough ACC, while Jack Kraft's Wildcats had dominated eastern basketball with a backcourt that boasted future pros Wally Jones and Bill Melchionni, plus future NBA big man Jim Washington. That wasn't all—the team's top scorer was 6-foot-4 sophomore Richie Moore.

Moore had scored 25 points as Villanova routed Providence in the first-round of NCAA Tourney in Philadelphia to set up the matchup with Duke, which enjoyed a first-round bye. The Wildcats were extremely confident, so much so that Melchionni told a Philadelphia newspaper that Mullins "wasn't so much" and that Villanova "would take the starch out of Duke."

The confident senior guard would get a chance to make good his boast when Duke and Villanova clashed in Raleigh.

THE GAME OF MY LIFE
DUKE VS. VILLANOVA, MARCH 13, 1964
BY JEFF MULLINS

I remember reading an article earlier that year that talked about how Wally Jones and UCLA's Walt Hazzard had been high school teammates and how they planned to meet up at the Final Four. I can't say it was something that fired me up, but I do remember thinking about it.

Villanova was a very good team with three really good players in Jones, Melchionni, and Washington, plus a good scorer in Moore. They were a very unorthodox team. They ran that Jack Kraft zone, which had four guys in a zone and let Jones roam—almost like a box-

and-one, except instead of guarding one man, Jones would float all over the floor. We practiced against it and thought there were some holes we could exploit. (Assistant coach Bucky Waters, who did the scouting report) emphasized that we could only take it so far against their defense, then we had to pull up and shoot the jumper.

After the game, there were articles about how I worked on my bank shot after shooting so poorly in the ACC Tournament. I don't remember that. What I do remember vividly is sneaking Steve Ludweder into the game. At the time, the NCAA only allowed you to have 14 guys on the bench. Steve was a small kid who served as a ball boy and as our good luck charm. We used to sneak him in zipped up in a ball bag. We'd take the balls out and carry them under our arms, while one of the big guys—Jay or (Hack Tison) would carry the bag with Steve in it.

The other thing I remember is something Vic said before the game. Right before tip-off, he told me, "You get this one for us, and I'll get the next one."

After that, it's kind of a blur. It seems like I had a lot of shots from the corner. I can remember running the baseline, then popping free and getting a pass. The one shot I do remember is the one right before halftime.

(Mullins beat the halftime buzzer with a shot he banked in from just over midcourt, giving him 28 points at the break.)

I didn't even realize my stats; I thought I had about 18 points at halftime. I just had no idea. In my career, I had a lot of big halves. I'd have 21 in the first half, and then score six in the second. My junior year, we were playing West Virginia in a nationally televised game. Art was all pumped up about proving he was a better player than Rod Thorn. But Art had a nervous half and Rod held him down. I had 22 points in the first half, and Art grabbed me at halftime and said, "You're not going to touch the ball in the second half." Then he went out and scored 20 in the second half, while I just scored a couple.

I never considered myself a pure scorer. I do remember that when they got close (in the second half), we had a play for me and I got a lay-up at a key time.

I thought it was one of those magical games. We felt like they were our obstacle to the Final Four. And afterwards, we felt like we beat a very good team. But we were a driven team. Early in the year, Vic had bought a record player and assigned (reserve guard) Ron Herbster to get some records. One of the records he got was "Going to Kansas City." That was appropriate because the Final Four that year was in Kansas City. We used to play it in the locker room every day. From day one, that was our one ambition.

GAME RESULTS

Mullins finished with 43 points and 12 rebounds as Duke beat Villanova 87-73. He hit 19 of 28 shots from the floor and five of six from the foul line. In addition, he guarded Richie Moore all night and held the Wildcats leading scorer to eight points on four-of-12 shooting.

"If anybody was looking for All-America players here tonight, we certainly showed them one, didn't we?" Bubas told reporters after the game. "Jeff was great, great, great—just like he's been all year."

Villanova's Kraft wasn't quite as generous with his praise.

"Actually, Mullins didn't have a good night," Kraft told disbelieving reporters. "He made some mistakes out there tonight that I know he wouldn't do."

The only person who gave any credence to Kraft's criticism was Mullins himself.

"I saw Kraft's comments," the Duke star said. "I was a little shocked, but I didn't really play as well as I could have in the second half. If he was talking about that, he had a point."

Still, Mullins' 43-point night was his career best—10 points more than his previous high, a 33-point effort in a double-overtime victory over Tennessee. He followed it with a 30-point performance as Duke coasted by Connecticut 101-54 in the East Regional title game.

"It was an easier 30," Mullins said.

Many fans were disappointed that the Duke star didn't get to match up against Bill Bradley in the regional finals. The game would have had a lot of resonance, since Bradley came so close to playing with Mullins at Duke. The Princeton star actually signed with Duke (preventing Bubas from signing future Davidson All-American Fred Hetzel) and only changed his mind in the days before he was due to arrive on campus.

But Shabel employed a slowdown in the regional semifinals and limited Bradley to 22 points in a 52-50 victory.

"It was a surprise matchup," Mullins said. "We didn't have much of a scouting report."

It didn't matter as Duke won easily to fulfill the promise of its 1964 theme song. The victory earned the Blue Devils a trip to the

Final Four in Kansas City. That long-awaited trip almost turned into disaster as Duke's plane slid off the end of the rain-soaked runway in Kansas City and ended up stuck in the mud.

"Then we got to our hotel and our rooms weren't ready," Mullins said. "Then we went to the arena to practice and we couldn't get in our locker room because they were being painted."

Despite all the bad omens, Duke upset No. 2 Michigan in the semifinals. The powerful Wolverines, led by All-American Cazzie Russell and Bill Buntin and Oliver Darden, had drilled Duke 83-76 in Ann Arbor, Michigan, just before Christmas. But this was a different Duke team with Ferguson steady at the point and Buckley playing like a monster in the middle.

"My job was to keep Darden off the boards," Mullins said. "Well, the first shot went up, I got position, and he was so strong, he just shrugged me out of the way. But as he went up, Jay came over and he caught one of Jay's elbows right above the eye. I didn't have any more problems after that."

It was Buckley's 25 points and 14 rebounds—more than Mullins' 21 points and eight boards—that pushed Duke into the title game for the first time in school history. Unfortunately, the Blue Devils had the misfortune of running into John Wooden's first great UCLA team, which blitzed Duke 98-83 to win the title.

"People talked about them being small, but they had three guys who played in the NBA for 30 years between them," Mullins said.

REFLECTIONS ON DUKE

Mullins capped his college career by earning a spot on the 1964 U.S. Olympic Basketball team. Duke's first basketball Olympian earned a gold medal in Tokyo. He was drafted sixth in the first round of the 1964 NBA draft by the St. Louis Hawks.

Mullins had a difficult transition to the pro game. His biggest problem early in his career was his ball handling. After playing forward his entire career at Duke, he struggled to make the transition to wing guard in the NBA. His solution was hard work—he began to work out in a pair of half-glasses. The bottom halves were blacked out, forcing him to dribble without looking at the ball.

As his ball handling improved, so did his playing time and his scoring average. After tallying less than six points a game in his first two seasons with the Hawks, he moved to the San Francisco Warriors and blossomed into a 13-points-a-game scorer in his third year, 18.9 in his fourth, and 22.8 in his fifth year. That was the first of four straight 20-point scoring averages for the former Duke star. He played in three all-star games and earned an NBA championship ring as a key reserve for the 1975 Golden State Warriors.

Mullins retired in 1976 after scoring 16,037 points in 12 seasons.

The former Duke star pursued business ventures for a decade before he was lured back to basketball. He became athletic director and head basketball coach at UNC Charlotte in 1985. The program had fallen on hard times after a 1977 Final Four trip under former coach Lee Rose. Mullins restored some of the 49ers' luster, taking the team to three NCAA appearances and a 182-142 record in his 11-year tenure.

He was still coaching at Charlotte when Duke retired his No. 44 jersey on December 6, 1994. Mullins ended his career at Duke as the school's No. 3 all-time scorer. His total of 1,884 points has since been passed by a number of four-year players, but his career average of 21.9 points a game at Duke is behind only Dick Groat, Art Heyman, and Bob Verga.

Mullins holds one interesting distinction—he's the only player in Duke (or ACC) history to score in double figures in every one of his career games.

That's a measure of his consistency. That's one reason his 43-point performance against Villanova was so memorable—it was a unique night for a player who rarely sought the limelight.

CHAPTER 5

GARY MELCHIONNI

Gary Melchionni was in the stands at Reynolds Coliseum on the night of March 13, 1964, when Jeff Mullins exploded for 43 points in Duke's NCAA Tournament victory over Villanova.

He was pulling against the Blue Devils.

"Duke meant little or nothing to me at that point," the future Duke star said.

Instead, the members of the Melchionni family were all Villanova supporters. Gary's older brothers Bill and Tom played for the Wildcats. Bill, who would later play in the NBA, was one of the three stars on that '64 'Nova team, along with Wally Jones and Jim Washington.

"My mom and dad packed my younger brother and me in the family sedan and we cruised down [from Pennsauken, New Jersey, just across the river from Philadelphia] to Raleigh," Melchionni recalled. "It was March and I remember being struck by how the weather changed as we drove south. The grass turned green and it got a lot warmer. I realized the weather was a lot nicer down there."

But his family was disappointed by the outcome of the game with Duke.

"Villanova was a very strong team that year," he said. "But the game was in Duke's backyard. I know Jeff Mullins had a great game—I vividly remember the shot he banked in from just beyond midcourt just before halftime—but what really made the difference was their size. With [Jay] Buckley and [Hack] Tison, they dominated inside."

Melchionni remained a Villanova fan through his high school years. How could he help it, growing up with three brothers who played for the Wildcats?

"Our backyard games were, in a word, intense," Melchionni said. "There was a bit of an age gap. Bill was so much older. We'd play to 22 and you had to win by two. He'd let us get up 20-0, then he'd come roaring back and beat us 22-20."

That experience honed Gary's game while teaching him humility.

"I'm not sure I ever thought of myself as an exceptional player," he said. "I was just following in my older brother's footsteps."

Melchionni played for an undefeated team at Pennsauken High and drew moderate recruiting interest from a number of schools. His first choice was Princeton—a power in that era with a succession of stars such as Bill Bradley, Geoff Petrie, and John Hummer.

"I loved Pete Carril," Melchionni said. "But if I had gone there, my parents would have had to pay a few bucks. All the other places I could go would pay my way."

So Melchionni opted for his second choice—Villanova.

"The short version of what happened is that I thought I had committed to Villanova, then [coach] Jack Kraft came back and said they didn't have a scholarship for me. I had to go back to some of the schools that had turned me down and see if any of them had a scholarship left."

The first place he turned was Duke, which was undergoing a coaching change. Vic Bubas, who had guided the program to unprecedented heights in the 1960s, had decided midway through the 1968 season to retire. The school brought former Bubas assistant Bucky Waters back from West Virginia to sustain the program.

"I had been mildly recruited by Bubas and his staff, but I was recruited a lot more by Bucky when he took over," Melchionni said. "Luckily, he still had a scholarship for me when I came back to him. A lot of my friends told me I was making a mistake; that they had brought in all these All-Americans and I would never play there.

"Maybe it was stupidity. Maybe it was confidence. I thought I was a player and I wasn't afraid of the challenge."

THE SETUP

Melchionni did find himself surrounded by talent when he arrived at Duke in the fall of 1969. He was part of an outstanding

Gary Melchionni (No. 25) goes up with the left hand to score against Richmond.

recruiting class that would become the most successful freshman team in Duke history.

The Blue Imps featured three promising guards—sharpshooter Jeff Dawson from Illinois, scoring machine Jim Fitzsimmons from Boston, and Melchionni. Freshman coach Jack Schalow molded that backcourt trio with 6-foot-10 Alan Shaw and 6-foot-4 swingman Richie O'Connor into a dominant aggregation.

"Jack Schalow was the best coach I ever played for," Melchionni said. "Maybe pure fear was the reason we played so well. Jack was an ex-paratrooper in the 82nd Airborne and he was tough as nails. He was also a great coach who used his non-scholarship players well. We were a pressing, running team and we had a terrific season."

Indeed, the Duke freshmen finished 16-0—Melchionni's second undefeated season in a row.

But there were early signs of the problems that were to sink Duke's basketball program into mediocrity in the early 1970s. Fitzsimmons, a brilliant offensive player, left Duke after one semester and transferred to Harvard (where he later led the Ivy League in scoring). On the varsity, promising forward Don Blackman also departed.

"That really hurt Duke in that period," Melchionni said. "We lost so many good players in that era. It was a shame."

Over the next two years, Melchionni's class would also lose Dawson and O'Connor. The next recruiting class would lose center Dave Elmer and forwards Ron Righter and Sam May.

"It was crazy the way we were losing guys," Melchionni said. "The first game of my junior season, Coach Waters tried to put Dave Elmer into the game, but Elmer told him he was hurt and couldn't play. Coach went to [trainer] Max [Crowder] and asked what was up. Max didn't know what he was talking about. It turned out Elmer was planning to transfer the next day and he didn't want to waste a year of eligibility."

Elmer was a promising big man who had thoroughly outplayed future N.C. State All-American Tommy Burleson in a freshman game. Later, he would return to the area and lead Miami of Ohio to a victory over North Carolina in Chapel Hill. O'Connor was leading the Duke team in scoring when he quit during his junior season. Dawson would later lead Illinois in scoring.

"We lost some good players—too many good players," Melchionni said. "It was just too much to overcome."

In hindsight, Melchionni is not really sure who is to blame for the exodus. He noted that Waters and assistant Hubie Brown were hard-nosed coaches who didn't handle players gently. But he also acknowl-edged, "We had a lot of prima donnas, who when they met adversi-ty, didn't handle it well."

Duke still had a lot of talent when Melchionni joined the varsity for the 1970-71 season. Center Randy Denton, forward Rick Katherman, and guard Dick DeVenzio were all seniors and three-year starters. The influx of four lettermen from that undefeated freshman team should have made the Devils contenders in the ACC.

"We had a lot of good players, but it was a senior-sophomore team," Melchionni said. "The seniors were all recruited by Bubas and didn't respond all that well to Bucky. We had chemistry problems. We were still pretty good—we finished 20-10, but we should have fin-ished 25-5."

Melchionni's sophomore season was marred by a succession of physical problems. He battled a bad case of mono early in the year. Then, just as he was rounding into form, he suffered a sprained ankle. Later, he battled a thigh injury.

Still, he ended the season in the starting lineup, averaging 4.5 points and finishing third on the team in assists.

"It was an up-and-down year for me and the team," he said.

Melchionni's junior year also started with an injury as he blew out an ankle against Virginia.

"It seemed to take forever to get back," he said.

But once he did return, Melchionni began to demonstrate just how good a player he could be. He upped his scoring average to 11.7 points a game and led the team in assists. He helped engineer a mon-umental upset of No. 3 North Carolina at home on the day that Duke Indoor Stadium was renamed Cameron Indoor Stadium.

"I hit Robbie West with a nice pass and he knocked down the game-winning shot at the buzzer," Melchionni recalled.

Unfortunately, the parade of player defections was starting to pile up. Dawson and Elmer left without playing a game. O'Conner departed with eight games left in the season. Duke struggled to a 14-12 finish, including a 6-6 ACC mark that matched the school's worst ACC record in 20 seasons.

But something worse was yet to come. In the off-season, Duke was cited for recruiting violations in pursuit of the great David Thompson. The charges were minor—a businessman Waters engaged to help him land the future superstar had bought Thompson a sports coat and driven him from his home in Shelby, North Carolina, to the

ACC Tournament in Greensboro. As a result, Duke was placed on one-year probation by the ACC.

"It seemed to be such a trivial thing, especially in that era," Melchionni said. "It seemed bizarre, preposterous. It was not a good way to start the season."

The talent drain—promising forward Ron Righter had joined the stampede in the off-season—had left Duke ill-equipped to compete in an ACC dominated by powerhouse teams at N.C. State, Maryland, and North Carolina. If that wasn't enough, the Duke fan base was starting to turn on embattled coach Bucky Waters.

"The thing about getting rid of Bucky, that really started to intensify," Melchionni said. "To say that was a distraction would be an understatement."

Melchionni's senior season got off to a terrible start when he suffered an injured Achilles tendon.

"The treatment in those days was just to stay off it," he said. "I missed the entire preseason practice period. I did nothing for weeks. Then the season started and I was trying to get in shape and play at the same time."

Duke opened the season with an easy home court victory over William & Mary and then hit the road facing a brutal schedule. Just three of the team's next 16 games were at home. The losses started to pile up. The Blue Devils hit rock bottom at Georgia Tech in late January, losing 88-86 to a bad Yellow Jacket team.

"We threw the game away," Melchionni said. "Georgia Tech had no business being in the game with us. Bucky was so frustrated that he kicked a trashcan across the locker room."

Duke was 8-9 as the Devils returned home for a game against Lefty Driesell's powerful young Terps. Maryland, which entered the game ranked No. 3 in the nation, was led up front by junior All-America big men Tom McMillen and Len Elmore. Forward Jim O'Brien and guard Howard White—Driesell's first two great recruiting gets at Maryland—were seniors with talent and experience.

But Maryland's sparkplug was a player Waters knew all too well. Point guard John Lucas, a product of Durham's Hillside High School, had passed up the local school to play for Driesell at Maryland. Taking advantage of the NCAA rule change that allowed freshmen to compete on the varsity level, Lucas became the first great freshman performer in ACC history.

It was a wonderfully balanced, extremely talented, and sublimely confident team that showed up in Cameron Indoor Stadium to take on the slumping Blue Devils.

GAME OF MY LIFE
DUKE VS. MARYLAND, FEBRUARY 3, 1973
BY GARY MELCHIONNI

We had a week off after the Georgia Tech game. We decided to change our offense—to get away from our pattern offense and go to a looser, motion-type offense.

Maryland was a great team. We knew there was a lot of talent on that team. Give Lefty credit, he never got in the way of his talent.

As good as they were, we felt like anytime we played at home, we could win. It didn't matter what the opponent was like, what the issues were or who had left the team that week. If we were at home, we thought we could win.

Cameron was a great place to play. In those days, there were a heck of a lot more students. They had a large portion of the seats upstairs. When ACC teams and good teams came in, the place filled up. The students seemed to be a lot closer to the action. You didn't have press row to separate the fans from the court. They were right on the court. It was a much more intimidating crowd. We certainly had an edge on them.

Of course, by that time, a lot of the fans were coming just to yell and scream at Bucky. Every game we had to deal with that. But our fans also took special delight at tormenting Lefty when Maryland came to town. The Terps had a forward named Jim O'Brien, who had bright red hair and a receding hairline. The fans called him "Bozo the Clown," and there would always be somebody wearing a Bozo head-piece.

As the game started, we didn't have any trouble scoring against Maryland. We got good shots and we were knocking them down. I don't think that bothered them. They wanted to run up and down the court. If you wanted to run with them, they were fine with that. Their attitude was, "We've got better horses, and if you run with us, at the end, we'll be ahead."

I know I knocked down some jumpers in the first half. I had maybe 12-14 points at the half. I felt pretty good.

I had been a little frustrated (by the team's struggles) and I remember thinking that I had been unselfish for too long. I decided to take things into my own hands a little more. It started that game.

Late in the game, we had a small lead (66-60) when we decided to spread things out and make them chase us. You could do that in those days with no shot clock. In that situation, I felt like I could blow by anybody they put on me. They weren't running anybody else at me, so I had a lot of room to operate. I don't know how many times in a row I either took it to the rim or pulled up for a short jumper. I decided that until they stopped me, I wasn't going to stop taking it to the rim. (Melchionni scored 11 straight points to push Duke's lead to 77-62 with two minutes left.)

We got a little sloppy at the end and they were able to crawl back in it. But there was never any fear that they were going to steal it. We were in control all the way.

Afterward, I remember thinking, "Finally, a good win . . . thank God." There was almost a sense of relief that we had put it together. Personally, there was a lot of satisfaction in how I played. I knew (my point total) was up around 40, but I had lost track. It was surprising—I don't think I ever scored 30 in a high school game. I had always considered myself the ultimate team player, but maybe I had become too unselfish on those Duke teams.

THE AFTERMATH

Melchionni hit 17 of 25 shots from the floor and finished with 39 points in Duke's 85-81 victory. It was not only his career high, but turned out to be the most points scored by a Blue Devil in the decade between Bob Verga's 41-point explosion against Ohio State in 1966 and Tate Armstrong's 40-points against N.C. State in 1976.

"Fabulous," Maryland's Driesell said of Melchionni's performance. "He played very well. We helped him a little at the end."

Driesell was talking about the defense—or rather non-defense—Maryland played against the Duke star. Melchionni started by burning the smaller, but quicker White.

"He's quick, but I'm taller, and once I got him inside, I knew I was too big for him to stop my shot," Melchionni told reporters after the game.

The Blue Devil senior also burned Bob Bodell, a 6-foot-4 defensive specialist, and the gifted Lucas.

"I guess that as I was getting more and more confident, it didn't matter who was playing me," Melchionni said. "Everything seemed to be dropping for me. I never really dreamed I'd dominate a game the way I did."

Postgame attention was focused on Duke's spread offense—which looked suspiciously like Dean Smith's infamous "Four Corners" at North Carolina. But Waters told reporters that his delay game, which he called "The Mongoose" was different—a variation of a strategy developed by Chuck Noe.

"The truth lies somewhere in between," Melchionni said with a laugh when asked about comparisons between the Mongoose and the Four Corners. "There's not that much difference between the two. If you had the ballhandlers, it's a very effective strategy in the era before the shot clock."

And few players ever ran it more effectively than Melchionni did against the Terps. On five straight possessions, he took it to the basket—converting five straight field goals, including one three-point play. That 11-point run gave Duke the 15-point lead that assured the victory and caused Duke's Waters to dub the game, "The Gary Melchionni Show."

Duke was able to build on its upset of the Terps, beating Wake Forest, Virginia, and Notre Dame in succession to improve to 12-9. But a home-court loss to powerful N.C. State killed the team's momentum and sent the Devils into a four-game losing streak to end the season.

Melchionni never quite lost the personal momentum he gained against the Terps. He finished the season averaging 15.8 points a game and again leading the team in assists. Even though Duke finished in the second division with a 4-8 ACC record (the worst ACC finish in school history up to that time), Melchionni joined David Thompson, Tommy Burleson, Tom McMillen, and George Karl on the All-ACC first-team—ahead of such future NBA players as John Lucas, Bobby Jones, Walter Davis, Len Elmore, Barry Parkhill, and Mitch Kupchek

REFLECTIONS ON DUKE

Melchionni, like his older brother Bill, got his chance to play in the NBA. He was drafted in the second round by the Phoenix Suns and played two seasons in the desert with the likes of Connie Hawkins, Charlie Scott, and Dick Van Arsdale.

The Duke grad averaged eight points and two assists as a reserve guard in his two seasons. But he was cut just before the start of the 1975-76 campaign.

"It was a bad time to be cut," he said. "There wasn't time to link up with another team. I went over to Italy and played a year there."

Melchionni decided not to chase a pro career after that season. Instead, he returned to Duke and earned a law degree. He's built a successful practice in the Philadelphia suburb of Lancaster. His name reappeared in Duke basketball lore recently when his son Lee joined the Blue Devils, emerging as a key reserve on the Blue Devil teams from 2003-06.

"I can say this in all honesty," the elder Melchionni said. "You go to Duke to play basketball and it becomes more than playing basketball. That's the same for my experience and for Lee's experience."

In return, the elder Melchionni provided Duke with a rare bright moment during one of the darkest periods in its basketball history.

CHAPTER 6

GENE BANKS

Gene Banks is without question the most celebrated recruit in Duke basketball history.

True, Duke has signed other players who have been regarded the No. 1 players in their class—Danny Ferry, Elton Brand, maybe Art Heyman—but none have arrived on campus with anything like the hysteria that surrounded the Philadelphia schoolboy legend known as "Tinkerbell." And no other player—with the possible exception of Heyman—ever arrived at such a crucial time for the school's basketball fortunes.

But Banks' start on the hardwood began much earlier playing with his father.

"I really didn't like basketball," he said. "It was just a chance for me to hang out with my dad. He played a lot of basketball at the rec center or the YMCA. He was playing against guys like Frank Card, Earl Monroe, Guy Rodgers, and Wayne Hightower—playground greats."

Banks' father was a high school star who never got the chance to play college basketball. He entered the military service instead. But his game would be passed down to his son.

"He was a pretty good player," Banks said. "And a lot of the way I played was like the way he played. After he played, he'd take me out and we'd shoot. He made it fun for me. After a while, he started putting me on his teams. I got my butt whipped a lot. But after playing with the older guys, when I started playing with guys my own age, that was a big advantage."

There was no organized AAU circuit in those days, but Philadelphia was a basketball hotbed with a myriad of youth leagues.

59

Banks bounced from team to team, building a strong reputation. He became more prominent when he was selected to get bussed from his all-black West Philadelphia neighborhood to a junior high school in South Philly.

The majority of students at Furness Junior High were blue-collar whites from the Irish and Polish neighborhoods. Banks, a friendly, loquacious young man, won over an entirely new constituency—not only with his basketball skill but also with his personality. The school offered an accelerated academic program that would help prepare Banks for the scholastic demands of college.

"I didn't understand it then, but it was really a product of my destiny, I guess," he said.

Banks was, in his own words, just "a whisper" in the Philadelphia sports scene when he entered junior high school. That changed when the 13-year-old Gene Banks abused LaSalle star Billy Taylor in a rec-league game in front of a huge crowd in Chester, Pennsylvania. From that point on, Banks was more than a whisper—he was the loudest voice on the Philadelphia basketball scene.

Banks continued to excel at West Philadelphia High, where he teamed with future Kentucky standout Clarence Tillman to anchor the nation's No. 1-ranked high school team. Coaches touted him as the best Philadelphia prospect since Wilt Chamberlain emerged at Overbrook High—which, incidentally, was West Philly's main rival. Philly fans, starved for a winner, made Banks an icon—his high school games were moved to the Palestra and even the Spectrum. Just before his final game, Banks cemented his celebrity status by tossing roses to the sold-out crowd at the Palestra.

Naturally, coaches from across the nation flocked to Philadelphia to recruit the powerful young forward. UCLA, North Carolina, Notre Dame, Michigan, and N.C. State were at the top of Banks' list. Duke, mired in a decade of mediocrity after the retirement of Vic Bubas, was not in the picture.

"I never knew where Duke was," Banks said. "To tell you the honest truth, I had seen a picture of Norm Nixon playing for Duquesne. They had the word "Dukes" on their uniform. But in the picture I saw, Norm's arm was covering up the 'S' so when I first heard about Duke, that's what I thought of."

Gene Banks goes up for a short jumper against Kentucky in the 1980 Midwest Regional semifinals.

He soon learned that Duke was a school in the South, not too far from North Carolina and N.C. State. He met Blue Devil coach Bill Foster at a summer camp, and in a passing encounter Banks was amused by the coach's odd sense of humor.

"Bill left a book about Duke for me," Banks said. "It was about the school, not the team. I was being tutored at the time by William H. Detwhiler—he was my English teacher. I took the book one day when I went to visit him. He didn't follow the games, but he asked me where I was visiting and I told him Michigan, UCLA, North Carolina, [N.C.] State and Notre Dame. He said, 'You've got one more.' I didn't know where I was going to take the last one. I was going to try to take Hawaii, just for the trip. A lot of guys did that before the NCAA cut that out. But [Detwhiler] saw the book and said, 'Well, Duke's a fine institution. You should go check it out.' So I did."

Still, Banks came very close to committing to UCLA during his visit. His mother fell in love with N.C. State coach Norm Sloan. And Notre Dame's Digger Phelps was by far the most persistent pursuer.

"Nobody ever thought Duke had a shot; I didn't even think so until I visited," Banks said. "The visit took me over the edge. [My host] Harold Morrison was great. I met a lot of good people. I met whites and I met blacks—blacks in good positions. The feel was kind of nice. I saw that all the students didn't come from North Carolina. The campus was pretty. But Bill Foster was pretty much the key. He was funny and he made me feel very comfortable."

Banks stunned the Philadelphia sports community when he committed to Duke in the fall of 1977. After all, the Blue Devils were in the process of finishing last in the ACC for the third straight year. Duke had not had a winning season in ACC play since 1971 and had not played in the NCAA Tournament since 1966.

But Banks told his skeptical listeners that Duke offered the best combination of academics and athletics. He also predicted: "I feel like when the smoke clears, I'll make them a national power."

Those words were to prove prophetic.

THE SETTING

In hindsight, it's easy to suggest that Banks was smart enough to see that the Duke basketball team was the perfect fit for his talents. He was joining a group with a brilliant young center (sophomore

Mike Gminski), a proven wing guard (junior Jim Spanarkel), and a pair of promising transfer point guards (Bob Bender from Indiana and John Harrell from North Carolina Central).

The addition of the dynamic Banks at forward—not to mention fellow freshman Kenny Dennard—would, as Banks predicted, transform Duke from an also-ran into a national contender.

But the fact is that Banks didn't know what he was getting into.

"All I knew about Duke was Tate Armstrong," he said, naming the high scoring guard who graduated before Banks' arrival. "I really didn't know about those other guys. The whole thing was really spiritual."

But the addition of Banks (and Dennard) to the Duke roster turned out to be exactly what Foster needed to turn the program around. Banks, who surprised everybody with his unselfishness and his passing skills, shared the scoring load with Gminski and Spanarkel. Dennard was content to play defense and rebound. When Harrell, nicknamed "Johnny Gun," finally got into the lineup just after New Year's Day, he provided stability at the point. When Bender became eligible a week later, he provided flexibility and a spark off the bench.

What followed was a magic carpet ride—the young Blue Devils won 12 of 13 games down the stretch, claimed the ACC title on national TV in Greensboro, and stormed into the Final Four. For Banks, who became the first active Duke athlete to be pictured on the cover of *Sports Illustrated,* the last three wins were particularly sweet—Duke beat Philadelphia powers Penn and Villanova in the East Regionals, and then knocked off Digger Phelps and Notre Dame in the national semifinals.

The incredible run ended in the national title game, when Kentucky's Jack "Goose" Givens shot holes in Duke's zone. Banks, who scored 22 points in both Final Four games, finished his freshman year averaging 17.1 points and 8.6 rebounds.

The Blue Devils had to settle for second place after the 94-88 loss to the Wildcats, but their youthful enthusiasm—which stood in stark contrast to Kentucky's businesslike approach—won over many of the nation's basketball fans. As the Duke players walked out to accept their second-place trophies, fans chanted, "We'll be back."

Only it didn't happen. The wonderful chemistry that characterized the 1978 Duke team broke down over the next two seasons. Banks cited several factors that created the problems: the departure of assistant coach Lou Goetz ("To me, Lou was the balance to Bill; Lou was like the Jewish mother"), and the decision to replace Harrell in the starting lineup with Bender ("He did it without a competition. Johnny Gun was really pissed off and he didn't care any more.").

But Banks accepts some of the responsibility, too.

"On top of all that, we were getting all the publicity—*Sports Illustrated* picked us No. 1 and everybody was kissing our behinds. We were reading all our press clippings," Banks said.

Duke didn't exactly fall apart in 1979, winning 22 games and sharing the ACC regular-season title with North Carolina. But compared to expectations, it was a major disappointment, capped by a disastrous postseason. Injuries (Dennard was out with the sprained ankle) and illness (Bender missed the ACC title game with appendicitis; Gminski played in the NCAA Tournament with a severe case of food poisoning) ruined Duke's chance of returning to the Final Four.

Injuries also played a part in Duke's 1980 slump. Although the Devils climbed to No. 1 in the national polls after an early-season victory over North Carolina, a series of problems cost the short-benched team down the stretch. Duke ended the regular season with a lopsided loss to UNC in Chapel Hill to finish 19-8 and tied for fifth in the ACC.

But that wasn't the worst news from Banks' point of view: he began hearing that Foster was going to leave Duke.

"He kept it quiet for a long time, but the news started to leak out," he said. "Finally, he began to meet with us one on one. I remember, we ate at the old Red Lobster and that's when he told me. My comment to him was, 'You've got a family and you've got to do what you've got to do.' He felt badly about it."

Yet, Foster's decision seemed to energize a team that had just been playing out the string. Or maybe it just took the pressure off a team that could never live up to 1978. For whatever reason, Banks and his teammates began to have fun again. They met North Carolina in the ACC Tournament semifinals and, six days after losing by 25 to the Heels, won by 14—a 39-point turnaround. One night later, Duke edged Maryland in the ACC title game. The Blue Devils were sent to Lexington, Kentucky, for the NCAA Tournament and upset top-seeded Kentucky on its home floor. Purdue stopped Duke one game short of the Final Four, but it was still a satisfying conclusion to a disappointing year and a nice end to Foster's tenure.

But Banks had another year of eligibility and with Foster gone—not to mention All-America center Mike Gminski—the prospects for 1981 weren't stellar. His future became even cloudier when Duke athletic director Tom Butters hired unknown Army coach Mike Krzyzewski to replace Foster.

"I thought [Boston College coach] Tom Davis was going to get the job," Banks said. "I didn't know anything about Coach K. Kenny was in Myrtle Beach and I was in Philly when he was introduced and it was said that we were boycotting (the press conference). But he called us, and Kenny and I came back to Durham and we met with (Krzyzewski) in his office. He said, 'Look, I'm not Bobby Knight.' He basically looked at Kenny and I and said, 'This is what guys have to do.' He gave us a lot of responsibility."

Banks wasn't sure he wanted it.

"I flirted with the NBA thing," Banks said. "They told me I'd go late in the first round. But it always seemed like if I left, I'd be letting my teammates down. My Mom laid a lot of heavy stuff on me. She told me I had a responsibility to my teammates and she reminded me that I'd be the first one in my family to get a college degree."

So Banks returned to anchor Krzyzewski's first team. The all-star forward was joined in the starting lineup by Dennard, a tough, experienced forward (with limited scoring ability) and by junior Vince Taylor, a very talented wing guard from Lexington, Kentucky. Krzyzewski basically filled out his lineup with a number of one-dimensional players—guards Tom Emma (a good ball-handler) and Chip Engelland (a good shooter), forward Jim Suddath (a slender shooter), and undersized center Mike Tissaw.

It was a far cry from the late 1970s, when Duke boasted as talented a starting five as anybody in college basketball. Krzyzewski's first Blue Devil team struggled to survive in a league that featured Ralph Sampson at Virginia, James Worthy, Al Wood, and Sam Perkins at North Carolina, Buck Williams and Albert King at Maryland, and Thurl Bailey and Sidney Lowe at N.C. State.

Duke struggled early, opening 0-4 in the ACC and taking a 7-7 overall record to N.C. State for a game in late January. That's when Banks began to learn what Mike Krzyzewski was made of.

"I found out that he had a little Bobby Knight in him after all," Banks said. "He was tough on the kids. He put pressure on me. He changed the offense several times to get me more shots. The only thing I questioned was his insistence on playing man-to-man defense. I thought, 'Man, we're going to play Ralph Sampson and Sam Perkins and Buck Williams man to man?'"

But Krzyzewski's adjustments appeared to pay off. Banks emerged as the leading scorer in a league of all-stars. His man-to-man skills so impressed the young coach that Krzyzewski called his senior forward "the best defender in the country."

Duke upset N.C. State in Raleigh to remain over .500, then won six of seven to climb out of the ACC cellar. But a heartbreaking 54-52 loss at Clemson in the last week of the regular season left Duke at 14-11 (5-8 ACC) heading into the finale against powerful North Carolina.

THE GAME OF MY LIFE
DUKE VS. NORTH CAROLINA, FEBRUARY 28, 1981
BY GENE BANKS

The thing that touched me most was the realization that this was going to be my last game. I had never thought about that stuff until one night I was walking past the Chapel thinking about the game. That's when it hit me; after four years, this was my last freaking game. I sat there on the Chapel steps and thinking about four years of memories and everything I had gone through. It really hit hard. It never really dawned on me before, but this was it. The Chapel door was open, and I walked into the Chapel and sat in a pew for a second. This was it.

I wanted to do something for the fans, and Milt Mannella (who owned a popular restaurant just off campus) reminded me that I had thrown roses to the crowd in high school. I got four roses, one for each corner. I wanted to show my appreciation for the crowd.

I never had a chance to think about winning or losing. Going out to shoot, I was getting involved with the Cameron Crazies, but I was so numb. I wasn't thinking about playing Carolina, I just kept thinking, 'This is it.'

It was scary. I was so wound up that I couldn't even do my Incredible Hulk thing with Kenny (for four years, during introductions the two forwards would run and jump at each other and smash chest to chest). All I could do was bow my head and say, "God, give me the opportunity to leave these people with a good memory." I didn't pray to win the game. I didn't say, "Let me have a great game." I didn't want to embarrass myself in my last game. It was just, "Give me the strength to give the fans something special."

After I did that, then everything came back to basketball. It was almost like a release.

We went at it. I scored here and there. Vince played very well. The fans were pumping it up. It was close, but then in the second half they opened a can of whup-ass on us (going up nine points). That's when it kicked in to me that I was going to die out there. They were going to have to carry me out before we would lose this game. That's when the reality changed and I said, "We're not going to lose this game."

Sam Perkins went to the free-throw line (with two seconds left) and put them up two. Here's the key—Dean Smith called timeout, not K. They let K set things up. He told us, "[Two seconds] is a lot of time in basketball." He was right. He had us get the ball to half court and call another timeout [with one second left].

He was the coach and I had no questions about his strategy. The only thing that was different was his play call for the last shot. He wanted Chip (Engelland) to take the last shot. Kenny and I broke the play on that one. He wanted me under the basket, which is where I started. Chip was supposed to come off the top and have an open shot . . . hopefully. Kenny and I were sitting next to each other, and we just looked at each other like, "What the hell!"

But like I said before, it was all spiritual. I was down at the bottom, Chip made his move and I just stepped out. Kenny wasn't looking at me. He saw me with his peripheral vision. He didn't throw the ball right to me. He threw it so that as I caught it I was turning into the shot.

I could see Sam's finger right there as I released the ball, so I had to arch it just a little bit to get over him. And it ended up rock bottom.

When that happened, I knew we were going to win the game (in overtime). I've never heard that place so loud. It was amazing. My girlfriend, who became my wife, was there. My Mom was there. It was incredible. I got such a jolt of adrenaline when I made that shot.

How I made the last basket (in overtime) was weird. Vince took a shot and (UNC's Al Wood) was right there. I was behind Al. The ball careened off too quick. It came off his hands and off his shoulder to me. It went blip, blip, and then I put it in, blip. It was that quick.

It was all spiritual to me. They had a hell of a squad and compared to them, we were pretty shorthanded. What we had were guts and determination

THE AFTERMATH

Banks follow shot of Vince Taylor's miss gave Duke a 66-65 victory in overtime. The senior forward played all 45 minutes. He not only hit the game-tying shot in regulation and the game-winner in overtime but also finished with 25 points (on 12-of-18 shooting from the floor) and seven rebounds.

In addition, Banks did a stellar defensive job on UNC All-American Al Wood. Since it was Senior Day, Krzyzewski started walk-on Larry Linney, who was promptly burned by Wood for three quick baskets. But Banks shut the Tar Heel star down, limiting him to 10 points the rest of the way. UNC, playing without sophomore stand-out James Worthy (out with back spasms), got 24 points from Perkins and 12 from point guard Jimmy Black. Dennard scored 16 and Taylor added 14 for the Blue Devils.

That was the last loss for UNC before the national title game. With Worthy back in the lineup and Wood unfettered by Banks' defense, the Tar Heels won the ACC Tournament in Landover, Maryland, then stormed through the NCAA Tournament to finish second to Isiah Thomas and Indiana.

Duke put up a good fight before losing to Maryland by three points in the ACC Tournament quarterfinals. The team's strong finish earned Krzyzewski's first team an NIT bid. But in the opening game, Banks—who was 6-for-6 at the time—suffered a broken left wrist that ended his college career. The Blue Devils managed to scrape out two wins without their star, but in the NIT quarterfinals, Purdue ended Duke's season for the second straight year.

REFLECTIONS ON DUKE

Banks' injury would have serious consequences.

Pro teams, reportedly hearing rumors that the injury would never heal completely, were wary. When Banks dropped to the second round of the draft, he said he was "destroyed." But his despair soon turned to joy when he was drafted by the San Antonio Spurs, which didn't have a first-round pick.

"[Coach] Stan Albeck called me and there was a group of people behind him cheering," Banks said. "Stan's comment was, 'We are the luckiest people in this draft. We got a first-rounder with a second-round pick.'"

Banks became a part of a powerful team—one that featured the scoring of George "Iceman" Gervin and the inside strength of Artis Gilmore. He quickly found a role as the team's defensive stopper, although he still averaged 11-15 points a year and about eight rebounds. After four seasons with the Spurs, Banks went to Chicago for two years and seemed to be headed for a long career before he ruptured his Achilles tendon while playing in a charity basketball game to raise money for inner-city youth in Philadelphia.

But Banks was prepared for life after basketball. He left Duke with his degree, even earning a spot as a speaker at his graduation.

He started the Gene Banks Foundation to help disadvantaged youths, which has sponsored clinics and summer camps all over the Eastern seaboard and in Canada. He coached the women's basketball team at Bluefield State and has appeared in movies such as *Eddie* and *Stargate*.

"I'll be honest, I've been so blessed," Banks said. "I've had tragedy, too; my wife passing, that was one of the toughest things. My legacy is the kids. I have a great relationship with my sons. I live for my daughters. I think I've made a difference for the youth in Greensboro with my basketball camps. My foundation has some big things coming up."

The former Philadelphia schoolboy legend has come a long way.

CHAPTER 7

JOHNNY DAWKINS

Duke's young basketball coach was in desperate need of help when he hit the recruiting trail after the 1980-81 season.

Mike Krzyzewski had won 17 games and earned his team a bid to the NIT Tournament in his first season at Duke, but most of that modest success was due to the efforts of seniors Gene Banks and Kenny Dennard. The 34-year-old coach would still have one more season from Vince Taylor in 1981-82, but the slender swingman from Lexington, Kentucky, was the last quality holdover from the Bill Foster regime.

If Krzyzewski hoped to succeed in a league that was about to produce the next two national champions, he knew he had to find his own talent. But his background at Army didn't prepare him for the world of big-time recruiting. His first foray on the recruiting trail the year before had been nothing less than a disaster. Krzyzewski pursued a number of quality prospects, but while he came close to such future standouts as Chris Mullins, Jimmy Miller, Bill Wennington, and Uwe Blab, the inexperienced Duke coach couldn't close the deal.

That failure would result in one of the worst seasons in Duke history as the Blue Devils finished a dismal 10-17 in Krzyzewski's second season. And with the talented Taylor graduating, more dreadful seasons appeared to be in the offing.

Krzyzewski's response was to return to the recruiting trail with a vengeance. He quickly zeroed in on a number of prime targets—a powerful post player from Southern California, a slim swingman from Chicago, a Larry Bird lookalike from Nebraska, a versatile combo forward from Arizona and a gifted swingman from rural Warren County, North Carolina, just north of Duke's campus.

But very early in the process, Krzyzewski fixated on a painfully slender guard from Washington, D.C.

Johnny Dawkins was blessed with speed, leaping ability, and shooting skills. Although the mercurial guard lived in a comfortable neighborhood on the northwest side of the District of Columbia, he spent 12 hours a day on the inner-city playgrounds, developing the moves that made him a prep All-American. By the time he was a senior at Mackin High School, Dawkins was being pursued by almost every top college program in the country.

So why would he consider a struggling program such as Duke, and a coach with no real record of success?

"I grew up an ACC fan and always saw myself playing in the league," Dawkins said. "I remembered Duke's great teams from the late 1970s, so I knew the school could compete. The academic reputation was terrific, but, ultimately, it was the people who sold me, especially Coach K. He did such a great job of recruiting me as an individual, painting a vision for my future. He was fiery, competitive, and knew where he wanted to go and how to take us there."

Dawkins wrestled with his choice through most of the 1981-82 season. He liked Duke, but he was also interested in Digger Phelps' more successful program at Notre Dame and in the program Dave Gavitt had built at Providence. His indecision put Krzyzewski in a tough spot. The Duke coach badly needed a quality guard in his new class and Dawkins wasn't his only option. He was also looking at highly coveted guard Jo Jo Buchanan, who was ready to choose between Duke and Notre Dame.

Krzyzewski, who had endured so many near misses the year before, couldn't afford another one. He much preferred Dawkins to Buchanan, but could he take the chance to pass up Buchanan and perhaps end up with nothing? Four years later, Krzyzewski talked about his choice.

"It's a little easier for us to pass up on somebody now than it was then," he told reporters in the spring of 1986. "But we did not offer a scholarship to a youngster who ended up being a starter at another

Johnny Dawkins, the foundation of Coach K's dynasty, in a rare moment of repose.

school just so we'd have an opportunity to get Dawkins. That was a big, big recruit."

It was the recruit who would make his program.

THE SETTING

The success that Dawkins and his classmates would bring to Duke did not happen overnight.

Krzyzewski brought in six freshman recruits that season. One— 6-foot-9 Nebraska forward Bill Jackman—played more like Big Bird than Larry Bird and returned home after one season. Another—6-foot-5 Chicago swingman Weldon Williams—struggled on the court and in the classroom. He straightened out his academics and earned his degree in four years, but he never made an impact on the court.

However, the other four recruits all became starters and made a huge impact on the program Krzyzewski was trying to build. Southern California big man Jay Bilas never became much of a scorer, but the 6-foot-9 future broadcaster became a force as a rebounder and defender in the post. Forward Mark Alarie, from sunny Arizona, was a 6-foot-8 dynamo on both ends of the court, who developed into a first-round NBA draft choice. Swingman David Henderson, seen by many as a backup recruit for Krzyzewski after losing hometown prep All-American Curtis Hunter to UNC, turned into a far better college player than his more celebrated prep rival.

Then there was Dawkins, who first displayed his explosive offensive potential on a trip to the West Coast two weeks into his freshman season, when in the space of 48 hours, he scored 28 points against Colorado and 22 more against California. He hit 19 of 29 shots from the floor in the two games and added six assists and eight rebounds.

Unfortunately, Duke lost both games en route to a second straight 17-loss season. As talented as the Blue Devil youngsters were, they were overmatched against their more experienced opponents and somewhat hampered by Krzyzewski's stubborn insistence that they play straight man-to-man defense—no zones, no gimmicks.

"We went after teams that were physically better than us and more experienced, and we suffered for it," Dawkins said of his freshman experience. "But it improved us for the years beyond that. We stuck with what we believed in, knowing that we'd be [at Duke] for three more years. We knew the things we learned would stay with us."

Many Duke fans didn't understand that, leading to demands for Krzyzewski's dismissal.

"You heard the rumbling," Dawkins said. "People were always coming up and asking questions: 'What do you think? Can he do this? Can he coach? Why aren't you guys playing zone?'"

The questions became even harsher when Dawkins' freshman season ended on a horrific note. Ralph Sampson and Virginia routed Duke 109-66 in the first round of the ACC Tournament in Atlanta. Worse, Sampson, who had picked up a foul for elbowing Bilas 11 seconds into the game, complained to reporters that Duke was a dirty team. Coach K was still fuming as the team's coaches and a handful of administrators gathered at Denny's for a late-night dinner. Sports information director Johnny Moore raised his class of water and offered a toast:

"Here's to forgetting tonight," he said.

Krzyzewski response: "No, here's to never forgetting tonight."

The remembrance started at the first day of practice the next season. When Dawkins and his teammates took the court, they saw that the scoreboard was lit up with the score 109-66. But Dawkins believes the real turnaround occurred a few months earlier.

"We went to Europe that summer," he said. "We had a chance to play. It kind of helped ease the pain after the ACC Tournament. The loss we had taken in that tournament was difficult to swallow. I think going and playing in Europe against good competition kind of got our feet wet again. You felt, 'Okay, let's get going.' We were older, more experienced, and we were looking forward to our sophomore season."

Krzyzewski also added a new element to the mix when he installed freshman Tommy Amaker at point guard. The Fairfax, Virginia, product was almost as skinny as Dawkins, but he was a ferocious defender and a superb floor leader. His presence allowed Dawkins to freelance more on offense and together they were to form one of the great backcourts in ACC history.

Almost overnight, it seemed, Duke had become a contender again. The Blue Devils won 14 of 15 games to open the season, including an upset of No. 20 Virginia in Charlottesville. Not only was that sweet payback for the loss in Atlanta, it marked the first of 16 straight victories over Virginia—Dawkins and his classmates would never again lose to the Cavs.

The last remaining hurdle in Krzyzewski's rebuilding effort was North Carolina. The young Blue Devils waged three titanic battles against the top-ranked Tar Heels that season, losing two heartbreakers before finally edging Michael Jordan and company in the semifinals of the ACC Tournament. The effort seemed to drain the energy from Dawkins and the young Blue Devil team. It was almost like a replay of Dick Groat's 1952 Southern Conference experience—after expending everything in a tough semifinal game, the Devils ran out of gas in the title game, losing to Maryland after leading at the half.

Dawkins' junior year also ended in disappointing fashion. Duke won 23 games and finished the season ranked No. 10 in the final AP poll, but injuries to Alarie and Henderson cost the team in the ACC and NCAA tournaments. Krzyzewski's foundation class entered their senior seasons with a solid legacy of accomplishment, but they had failed to lift Duke to the top of the ACC pyramid.

The 1985-86 season would be its last chance.

"Having played in our conference for three years, we knew how tough it was," Dawkins said. "We knew we were one of the better teams in the country, but people don't realize that three ACC teams spent time at No. 1 that season."

Indeed, Duke started the year ranked No. 6 in the nation—but third in the ACC behind No. 1 Georgia Tech and No. 2 North Carolina. The Blue Devils quickly climbed to No. 3 after winning the inaugural preseason NIT in Madison Square Garden over a Final Four that included three eventual NCAA tournament No. 1 seeds (Duke, Kansas, and St. John's) and the 1986 NCAA champion (Louisville).

The success continued through December and January as Duke won a school-record 16 straight games to open the season. That streak ended in Chapel Hill, when No. 3 Duke fell by three points to the No. 1 Tar Heels in the first game ever played in the Dean Smith Center. Three nights later, Duke lost a hard-fought game to No. 4 Georgia Tech in Atlanta. The headline in the Durham newspaper screamed, "Duke's slump continues."

Some slump. Duke would not lose again until the last day of March. And the biggest reason for that late-season streak was Dawkins, who simply refused to let the Blue Devils lose. He became the centerpiece for a weekend TV show that made the Duke star and his teammates familiar faces to the nation's fans.

The show debuted in mid-February when Dawkins led Duke to two narrow victories in less than 20 hours. It started when his two free throws in the final seconds clinched a 72-70 Saturday night victory over No. 17 N.C. State in Raleigh. The next afternoon, a national TV audience watched as Dawkins blocked a potential game-winning shot by David Rivers, as Duke edged No. 14 Notre Dame 75-74.

A week later, another national TV audience saw Dawkins dismantle No. 10 Oklahoma in Cameron Indoor Stadium. And on the final weekend of the regular season, yet another huge TV audience watched as Dawkins cemented Duke's No. 1 national ranking with a 26-point performance in an 82-74 victory over North Carolina.

"It was great," Dawkins said. "We were playing well and actually getting better during that stretch. We were gaining some momentum. The two losses helped harden us. We were battle tested."

But Dawkins and his classmates weren't finished. They still had to find the postseason success that had eluded them for three seasons. It started in Greensboro, where the top-seeded Devils beat Wake Forest, Virginia, and Georgia Tech to give Krzyzewski his first ACC championship. The finale was especially sweet for Dawkins, since it capped a four-year personal duel with Georgia Tech star Mark Price.

"We had both moved up the ladder in the ACC together," Dawkins said. "They had won the ACC Tournament the year before and gone pretty far in the NCAAs, so they had done some things that we were wanting to do."

Dawkins, who averaged exactly 20.0 points in the three ACC Tournament games, earned the Everett Case Award as the Tournament's most valuable player. It was just one of the honors he collected that week. Already named as a first-team All-ACC selection for a second straight season, Dawkins learned on the Tuesday after the Georgia Tech win that he was to receive the Naismith Award, given to the nation's top player.

All the honors, the excitement, and the relief of winning the three-day ACC Tournament marathon for the first time obscured the fact that Duke had to return to Greensboro for the first round of the NCAA Tournament.

But surely that wouldn't be a problem would it? The No. 1 seed in the entire field couldn't possibly lose to little Mississippi Valley State, could it?

THE GAME OF MY LIFE
DUKE VS. MISSISSIPPI VALLEY STATE, MARCH 13, 1986
BY JOHNNY DAWKINS

The ACC Tournament is brutal. People don't realize that tournament can take something out of you. It's the toughest tournament I've ever been a part of. Teams are well prepared. Everyone's fighting for something—whether you're fighting for a certain seed in the NCAA tournament or to get in the NCAA tournament or to win the ACC Tournament or a combination of all of the above.

So it's a tough tournament, then you turn around and play that Thursday game after winning the ACC—it's physically and mentally tough. I would think it's more mental because you have to get back on a horse right away.

I remember that week. It was beautiful weather and everybody was in a great mood. We had accomplished a lot, winning the regular season and the tournament. Those championships meant a lot to us. It was celebratory. It was very upbeat on campus. The week went by so fast that before you knew it, you were leaving for the hotel.

My first reaction when I saw we were playing Mississippi Valley State was realizing that I didn't know anything about them. You hear they are a 16th seed and you know you're the No. 1 seed. I didn't take them for granted. I'd been in that tournament long enough to know, you can't predict who is going to win those games. That's what makes that tournament so great. It's a 40-minute race to the finish.

We prepared for them the way we prepared for everybody else. We had information on their program and their team and a good feel for what they were going to do. That was not the problem. It was just the first game of the tournament and they were an unorthodox opponent. It gave us problems defensively. They pulled our bigs away from the basket. That was unusual at the time. You see that more now with teams that spread the floor with bigger players who can handle the basketball. Except they were all undersized, so their center was maybe 6-foot-6. They were all perimeter players, so offensively they were able to spread us. We had a hard time defending.

There was a good crowd that day. Greensboro is always a great place for us. But I think there was an expectation that we were going to win. The crowd kind of took that attitude—a 1 vs. a 16. They came in expecting a walk in the park, so the energy wasn't there that you would normally have.

They played us well. I can remember the more time that ticked off the clock, the more they were running their tempo. They were pressuring us and picking us up full-court, and we wanted to run our offense and attack. They sped us up a little by picking us up full and forcing Tommy and myself to be ball-handlers and not playmakers. Across halfcourt, the ball wasn't in our hands so much.

We were down at half (40-37) and I can remember thinking in disbelief that we were losing to this team. And we didn't have any real momentum. The first five or 10 minutes of the second half was similar to that. Coach K was good in the timeouts. We were all just trying to get a grasp of what was going on. He knew we weren't playing up to the level that we were capable of. His demeanor was good. It wasn't like he pulled us out and sat us down. We had four seniors in that lineup. It was like, "Okay, these guys know what they need to do."

I sense that as the game was going, we weren't making any inroads. I can remember thinking, "We're not losing this game."

At that point, instead of being the guy who received the basketball in the backcourt, I switched with David (Henderson) and went to halfcourt, so that when the press got broken, they threw it to me, and I was the guy to finish the play. That was a whole different look because you had somebody who was more offensive-minded attacking. That really hurt them because they stayed in that long enough to where we were able get the lead and the momentum.

Growing up as I did and playing in a lot of environments, it was a comfortable game for me. I can remember some really good finishes in that game, being fouled and still finishing. I think that surprised them—they tried to take a couple of good fouls and the bucket still went.

Then, I can remember them at the end of the game. Of course, everybody is congratulating each other on a great game and how hard both teams played, when several of their players came up to me and asked for my autograph. That shocked me.

I'll go down in history saying, I don't think they were a No. 16 seed. I still believe that this day. There were teams that I had seen play that year that made the tournament I know Mississippi Valley State was better than.

GAME RESULTS

In the 22 years since the NCAA Tournament expanded to 64 teams, setting up four matchups each season between No. 1 and No. 16 seeds, no No. 1 has ever lost to a No. 16.

Duke's 85-78 come-from-behind victory over Mississippi Valley State in 1986 remains one of the closest calls any No. 1 has ever faced. The Blue Devils trailed 44-37 with 12 minutes to play before Dawkins rallied the favored top seed.

"Duke has a helluva club, but we didn't take any wooden nickels," Mississippi Valley coach Lafayette Stribling said. "I thought we were just a few things from winning this game."

Actually, Stribling might have said that his Delta Devils were one player away from the upset—Dawkins. The senior guard scored 20 of his game-high 27 points in the second half, including 16 points in one torrid five-minute span.

"We had to have somebody pick us up and Johnny did that today," Alarie told reporters. "We needed some big plays, and that's his style. He's being doing it all year."

Dawkins continued to do it through the 1986 NCAA Tournament as Duke recovered from its first-round fright to storm into the NCAA title game. The Blue Devils blitzed Old Dominion in the second round, knocked off DePaul (as Dawkins outscored future all-pro Rod Strickland 25-15), and then sank David Robinson and Navy in the East regional title game—a victory that was summed up by a play in which the 6-foot-2 Dawkins posterized the All-America center with an in-your-face slam dunk.

"Johnny was always our heart and our drive," Alarie said. "He not only wanted to win more than anybody, he wanted to win big and embarrass people more than the rest of us. When the rest of us were hunched over huffing and puffing in the huddle, he was always able to say something that helped bring the team together."

Dawkins, named the East Regional MVP after averaging 26.2 points in the four wins, attributes Duke's strong run to the lessons learned against Mississippi Valley State.

"Having gone through that game was the best thing for us," he said. "That game was a wakeup call for us. Now the ACC regular season and ACC Tournament were behind us. This NCAA Tournament was its own entity."

Duke's bid for the national title came up inches short. After a hard-fought victory over Kansas in the semifinals, the Blue Devils couldn't quite put Louisville away in the title game. Dawkins contributed 24 points and some brilliant defensive play against the Cardinals, but, ironically, his great defensive effort turned out to be the backbreaker in the final minute. Duke was down one, but the shot clock would force the Cardinals to give up the ball if the Devils could get a stop. Dawkins was defending Louisville guard Jeff Hall as the shot clock wound down. Just as he did against Rivers a month earlier, Dawkins timed his jump to block the shot.

"He had to adjust because of my pressure," Dawkins said. "Hall put more arch on the shot. He put so much that the shot was way short—an air ball. In all my years of playing and coaching, I've noticed that almost every time a player shoots an air ball, the offense gets the rebound. That's what happened to us. Pervis Ellison got the rebound and put it in."

But Duke's narrow loss in the title game was the only disappointment for Dawkins and his classmates. The Blue Devils finished 37-3, tying the national record for victories in a season. They clearly established Krzyzewski's program at the top of the national scene, leaving a legacy that continues to this day.

REFLECTIONS ON DUKE

Dawkins, who saw his No. 24 jersey retired on the day of his home finale against North Carolina, finished his Duke career as the leading scorer in school history. His 2,556 career points were the most ever scored by an ACC player, although league records long listed him as No. 2 behind Wake Forest's Dickie Hemric, who actually scored half his points in the old Southern Conference before the ACC was formed.

It doesn't matter—Duke's J.J. Redick, who was coached by Dawkins for four years, ended up passing both of them. The new Duke scoring leader had nothing but praise for the player he passed.

"He's such a great man and a great coach," Redick said, "and he was probably the best player in Duke history."

That's certainly possible. One thing that's certain is that Dawkins was part of the best recruiting class in Duke—and maybe ACC—history. Not only did Dawkins finish with the school scoring record, but Alarie finished with 2,136 points (fourth on the school scoring list at that time), Henderson scored 1,570 points (13th), and Bilas finished with 1,062 points (25th). Throw in Williams' 126 career points and the 87 points that Jackman contributed before he left the program, and the six-player class ended up with 7,537 combined career points—the most by any single recruiting class in NCAA history.

"That '86 class is the best I've ever had," Krzyzewski said. "They came in when we hadn't won. And the commitment they showed to me, to the program, and to each other is really the foundation upon which we've built everything in our program."

After his senior season, Dawkins took his game to the NBA. A first-round draft pick by San Antonio, he played three seasons for the Spurs and six seasons with the Philadelphia 76ers. He enjoyed considerable initial success, averaging 15 points and more than seven assists a game over a three-year span before suffering a knee injury that would cut his career short.

Dawkins returned to Duke in 1996, and after serving a year as an intern in the athletic department, he joined Krzyzewski's staff before the 1998 season. Although he's had numerous chances to explore head coaching opportunities, Dawkins has said he's content to remain at Duke. He's widely believed to be first in line to succeed Krzyzewski as head coach—a belief that was strengthened when Coach K told reporters that if he were able to choose his successor, it would be Dawkins.

The former Blue Devil star won't respond to that kind of speculation, but he does reflect on his time at Duke.

"The one thing I wanted to do while I was here was I wanted to leave my mark," Dawkins said. "My family always taught me that at any place you are, you want to leave it better than when you arrived. If you try to do that wherever you go, you'll have a lot of success and you'll leave a legacy behind."

Duke is certainly better for its association with Johnny Dawkins.

CHAPTER 8

MARK ALARIE

Even though Mark Alarie was born and raised in the sunny Southwest, his roots stretched back to the nation's basketball heartland.

"My father grew up in Fort Wayne, Indiana," Alarie said. "As early as I can remember, we had a basketball hoop on our carport. Growing up, I really enjoyed baseball, but it seemed like I had a knack for basketball. And it didn't hurt that I was always the tallest kid in class."

Alarie attended Brophy Prep, an academically oriented prep school in Scottsdale, just outside Phoenix. But he first attracted national attention as a prospect during the summer, when he represented Phoenix in the BCI (Basketball Congress Invitational) Tournament in Provo, Utah.

By the time Alarie entered his senior season at the Catholic prep school, he was receiving offers from all over the country.

"There was a lot of pressure on me to stay home at Arizona State or to play at Arizona," he said. "People still ask me why I didn't play for Lute Olson at Arizona. I tell them it was for a very simple reason—Olson wasn't there at that time. It still probably would not have been a consideration. I was a pretty good student and I was looking for the best combination of academics and athletics I could find. I pretty much came down to Notre Dame, Stanford, and Duke."

Duke, struggling through a 10-17 season in coach Mike Krzyzewski's second year at the helm, was definitely the long shot of that trio.

"At Brophy Prep, the ultimate goal for most students was to go to Stanford," he said. "It meant a lot when Stanford offered me a scholarship."

Then there was Notre Dame.

"My father grew up a huge Notre Dame fan," Alarie said. "But my father passed away during my sophomore year in high school."

That left an opening for the aggressive Krzyzewski.

"Duke separated themselves once I met with Coach K and his assistant coaches," Alarie said. "[Notre Dame coach] Digger Phelps came down, but he was a little late to the party. Plus, I didn't believe their basketball program would ever be something great."

Yet, he did believe Duke's could, despite the team's struggles and the unproven young coach.

"Coach K had that quality—he was passionate, he exuded confidence, he had a vision," Alarie said. "You couldn't help believing that what he said was going to happen was going to happen. And I was the fifth recruit that year. They already had Jay Bilas and Bill Jackman and Weldon Williams and Johnny Dawkins. I saw that the class was already ranked in the top five or top 10. I thought I could put us over the top. Then we got David [Henderson] after I signed.

"That was the nucleus of a top club. It helped convince me that I was getting in on the ground floor."

THE SETTING

Alarie can recall just one moment of doubt about his decision.

"One of my first days in North Carolina, a bunch of us went over to Woollen Gym [on the North Carolina campus] to play in the pick-up games there. Their guys were there, including a bunch of pros who had come back in the off-season, plus a bunch of players from N.C. State. I can remember sitting by the wall, waiting for our turn to play and watching guys like [James] Worthy, [Sam] Perkins, and [Michael] Jordan go at it. I was thinking, 'What have I gotten myself into?' I didn't feel like I belonged on the court with those guys."

There were also moments during Alarie's freshman season when it looked like he and his classmates didn't belong in the ACC. Krzyzewski usually started four freshmen at a time in a league that was overpowering.

Mark Alarie soars for a rebound in a victory over St. Joseph's in the Palestra.

"It's not like today where people play a lot of freshmen because the top players go pro early," Alarie noted. "In those days, everybody stayed. The league was a lot better than it is now."

Indeed, during Alarie's freshman season in 1982-83, UNC still boasted All-Americans Michael Jordan and Sam Perkins off its 1982 national championship team; Virginia was led by senior All-American Ralph Sampson; Maryland was loaded with veterans Adrian Branch, Herman Veal, Ben Coleman, and a gifted freshman named Len Bias; N.C. State started three seniors and a junior, who would guide the Pack to the 1983 national championship.

Duke's 11-17 finish that season, capped by a 109-66 humiliation at the hands of Virginia in the first round of the ACC Tournament, was hardly surprising. Neither, according to Alarie, was it in any way discouraging.

"I know we didn't win a lot, but we learned that we could play with those guys," he said. "I came away from my freshman season with the feeling that if we would just keep working, we could get to that level."

The summer before the next season played a big role in that development. Duke took a summer tour of Europe that helped Krzyzewski's young team bond together. In addition, a number of Duke players participated in USA basketball tryouts that off-season.

"That gave guys a chance to develop individually—to learn and to gain confidence," Alarie said. "I proved that I could knock down the 18-foot jumper consistently. That gave me a huge amount of confidence in my shot and in being a scorer."

The results showed up early in his sophomore season as Alarie displayed better skills as a scorer, rebounder, and defender. During his freshman year, he averaged 13.0 points and 6.5 rebounds and shot 49.4 from the floor. But as a sophomore, Alarie upped his averages to 17.5 points a game and 7.2 rebounds, while raising his shooting percentage to 57.5 percent. More importantly, he did it in the context of a winning team. Duke won 14 of 15 games to open the season.

"As I remember, the schedule wasn't particularly difficult," Alarie said. "But that was good. It gave us a chance to fit into our new roles."

Alarie and sophomore guard Johnny Dawkins were emerging as the team's two main offensive weapons, while sophomore Jay Bilas and Canadian junior Dan Meagher did much of the dirty work down low. Sophomore swingman David Henderson accepted the role as sixth man so that freshman Tommy Amaker could take over as point guard.

At first, Alarie wasn't too sure about the youngster from northern Virginia, who appeared to be as slender and frail as Dawkins.

"I had questions about the size of our backcourt," he said. "I wondered if we could guard people. I also wondered why Johnny would want to play the two guard—he always looked like a one guard to me. But after a week of playing with Tommy, I understood the difference between a point guard and a wing guard. With Johnny, he would get you the ball, but if there was an opening, he was going to take it himself. Tommy always looked for the other guy. You knew if you ran the floor and got yourself open, he'd get you the ball."

Alarie's defensive concerns also proved unwarranted.

"Our freshman year, I don't care how much Coach K emphasized the man-to-man defense, it just didn't feel very effective," he said. "A lot of us questioned, 'Is this ever going to work?' By our sophomore year, we all got confidence in our defensive strength. The key was Tommy and the pressure he put on the ball. He made other point guards turn their back on him—if they didn't, he'd steal the ball. That made everything else work. Our defense became a weapon. You just couldn't run plays against us."

That new found defensive confidence was put to the test when No. 1 North Carolina rolled into Durham in late January with one of the most talented teams in ACC history. Not only did the Tar Heels feature junior Michael Jordan, who was en route to sweeping national player of the year honors, but also power forward Sam Perkins was about to become a three-time first-team All-American. In the middle, UNC started 7-foot sophomore Brad Daugherty, who was destined to be the first player taken in the 1986 NBA draft. At point guard, freshman Kenny Smith, another future national player of the year, had just been featured in *Sports Illustrated*. The other forward position belonged to three-year starter Matt Doherty, a future UNC coach, and a holdover from the 1982 national champs. On the bench, legendary coach Dean Smith could call such quality players as guards Buzz Peterson and Steve Hale, or big men Dave Popson and Joe Wolf, who both played in the NBA.

"Yeah, it was a great team from top to bottom," Alarie said. "There were not a lot of weaknesses to exploit."

The first matchup of the season was not expected to be close, even in Cameron.

"The year before, they had very simply kicked our asses," Alarie said. "We were blown out before halftime in both games."

But 1984 was a different story. Duke matched up man to man with the powerful Tar Heels and held their own. Amaker embarrassed

Smith in a battle of freshman point guards, while Henderson kept Jordan under control. Alarie was doing the same to Perkins.

"Defensively, we played a great game," Alarie said. "Offensively, we fell short."

Duke still led most of the way in what became one of the most contentious games in the history of a contentious rivalry. UNC assistant Bill Guthridge chased the officials off the court at halftime, while Krzyzewski called a second-half timeout and spent the entire break staring down one young ref. Smith himself went a little berserk in the closing minutes, pounding on the scorer's table and accidentally hitting a button on the scoreboard controls that gave his team a quick 20 points.

Somehow, Smith escaped a technical foul for his shenanigans, which provoked an angry postgame comment by Krzyzewski that there was a "double standard" in the ACC when it came to dealing with the veteran Tar Heel coach and everybody else. He was bitterly disappointed by his team's narrow 78-73 loss.

"I don't have a strong memory of that first game," Alarie said. "I remember Dean pounding the table and Coach K's double-standard remark. But what I remember taking away from the game was the realization that, 'These guys are good, but not that good.' We felt like if we had executed a little better, we would have won."

Duke got a chance to test that theory a month later in Chapel Hill, where a Duke team that had climbed to No. 15 in the national polls took on No. 1 North Carolina in Carmichael Auditorium. The Blue Devils had lost 17 straight games on UNC's home court, but just as in Durham, Duke led the heavily favored Tar Heels most of the way. In fact, the Devils appeared to be in control when Alarie converted a three-point play with 20 seconds left to give the visitors a 73-70 lead. When Meagher rebounded Hale's missed jumper and was fouled with seven seconds left and Duke up two points, victory was one free throw away.

Unfortunately, Meagher's free throw was long and Perkins rebounded for the Tar Heels. UNC tried to get the ball to one of its stars, but Duke's defense took away Jordan and Perkins. In desperation, Doherty threw up a running one-hander from about 15 feet out . . . and the improbable shot went in to force overtime. The two teams battled into a second overtime before UNC finally pulled away with a 96-83 victory.

"We really felt like we should have won that game," Alarie said. "That game was frustrating, just because of the way it ended—

Carolina fouling Meagher, then Doherty hitting that unbelievable shot. It seemed like the victory was in our grasp, then we lost it due to circumstances that weren't in our control."

Still, Alarie left Chapel Hill more convinced than ever that Duke could beat the mighty Tar Heels.

"We were even more confident than before," he said. "We felt like if we could play them in the ACC Tournament, we'd have an edge because it's so tough to beat a competitive team three times in a row."

Duke entered the ACC Tournament in Greensboro seeded No. 4, setting up a semifinal matchup with the top-seeded Tar Heels.

Of course, before that happened, the Devils had to get past fifth-seeded Georgia Tech in the first round. Bobby Cremins' program was almost a mirror image to the one Krzyzewski was developing at Duke. His young team was built around sophomore guard Mark Price, second-year big man John Salley, and freshman swingman Bruce Dalrymple. And just as Duke had jumped from 11-17 in 1983 to 22-8 entering the ACC Tournament in 1984, the Jackets had vaulted from 13-15 to 18-9.

"In a way, we felt Georgia Tech was more of a rival than North Carolina," Alarie said. "It was just because we had both followed the same path from doormats to competitive. It's funny though, I don't remember much about that game."

Actually, the Duke-Georgia Tech opener was a thriller. The Blue Devils overcame a 30-24 halftime deficit to force overtime, then pulled out the 67-63 victory as Alarie outscored Salley 18-14, and Dawkins and Price cancelled each other out with 18 points each.

The victory was Krzyzewski's first ACC Tournament win in four tries. But there was little celebration. Alarie and his teammates knew that less than 24 hours later, they would get their third chance to knock off No. 1 North Carolina.

THE GAME OF MY LIFE
DUKE VS. NORTH CAROLINA, MARCH 10, 1984
BY MARK ALARIE

After we beat Georgia Tech, we knew as soon as we got to the locker room that we'd be playing North Carolina the next day, but we didn't dwell on that the Friday before the game. As I remember, the one thing Coach K told us was to make sure we got plenty of rest, stay hydrated, and make sure that we ate right.

The prep time for the game was obviously minimal; we didn't need much. We knew who Carolina was and what they did. We knew the matchups. I do remember Coach saying, "After we beat these guys, shake their hands and be sure to walk off the court like we've done this before. I don't want to see any celebrations." That was a real confidence builder. We could just picture ourselves as winners, so going into the game our mental image was very good.

My recollection of the game is that it was fairly nip and tuck. My matchup was with Sam Perkins. I always used to play well against him. I got to know him after this game when we were both in the NBA. I always enjoyed playing against Sam. I made him work on the defensive end. It's a difficult thing for a 6-foot-11 post player. I shot a lot of 18-foot jumpers and ran him off a lot of screens; I had a good shooting game.

I also had one play where I got a fallout pass and had a chance for a lay-up. But Jordan and Perkins were coming, so I spun 180 degrees and put up a left-handed lay-up. I had never done anything like that before or since.

Defending Perkins, it wasn't rocket science. People were always telling me, "You know he's left-handed?" That was pretty obvious. I pride myself on studying a player and learning what they do. I knew where he wanted to set up. I did my best to take away his favorite shots and position myself to keep the ball away from him. I always wiped the sweat off my brow when he didn't get the ball. David's approach to defending Jordan was the same. We figured if you could just prevent them from getting the ball 3-4 times in a game that could cut down 6-8 points.

Also, I wasn't afraid to yell at Bilas or Meagher for help. Of course, that meant leaving somebody else open. But that game, we decided that we weren't going to let Jordan or Perkins beat us. We wanted to make Matt Doherty beat us. I know he hit the shot in Chapel Hill—we wanted to make him beat us again.

I felt we were in control of the last two or three minutes. I felt confident that we had a lead that we could maintain. It didn't feel like a choke situations. This time we held on.

Did we shake hands and walk off the floor like we had been there before, like Coach suggested? That didn't happen—and Coach K was the worst offender. We were all jumping around and he was yelling, 'We did it! We did it!' I was smart. I found a cheerleader to hug.

But seriously, in my career, that was my greatest victory. I can't think of anything else that compares to it.

GAME RESULTS

Duke held on for a 77-75 victory over the Tar Heels, holding off a furious second-half rally by the top-ranked team. The key moment in the game occurred with nine minutes to play, when a Jordan dunk gave UNC—which had been down eight at the break—its first lead of the game.

Krzyzewski called timeout and calmed his team down. Duke came out of the timeout and scored five straight points to regain the lead. The Blue Devils never trailed again, although the game was tied at 69 with two minutes left. First, Dawkins hit a short jumper, and then Alarie converted two free throws to give Duke a four-point lead. Henderson hit four free throws in the final 17 seconds to protect that margin.

"I guess it's human nature that when you're so close to winning something and you fail, it discourages you the next time you try," Alarie told reporters after the game. "The difference with us is that we wanted it that much more each time we played them."

Alarie's advantage over Perkins proved to be the difference in Duke's victory. The Blue Devil sophomore led his team with 21 points, hitting 9 of 13 shots from the floor. He held the UNC senior All-American to nine points on four-of-10 shooting. Perkins was scoreless over the game's final 14 minutes.

"Duke never died on us," the Tar Heel standout said.

But Duke did die 24 hours later, running out of gas in the ACC championship game against Maryland.

"I think the needle went to empty," Alarie said. "We had a big lead early, but we just couldn't sustain it. I know I was a little tired. I also remember that I couldn't shake Herman Veal, and that every time I bounced into the lane, either Ben Coleman or Len Bias was there waiting for me."

Alarie had to wait two years to earn his ACC championship ring. His junior season was successful, but ended on a sour note when a hip injury hobbled him in the postseason. As a senior, he was one of the stars on a team that won an NCAA record-tying 37 games, including the ACC regular-season and tournament titles. Duke finished No. 1 in the final AP poll that season and made it all the way to the NCAA title game before losing a heartbreaker to Louisville.

"There's no question there is a gaping hole in my career because we didn't win the national championship," Alarie said. "You dream of being on that stage and we got there, but we were just outplayed on that night. Now every time I see a game in Cameron, I can't help thinking that we should have a banner up there for 1986."

REFLECTIONS ON DUKE

Alarie was taken in the first round of the NBA draft by the Denver Nuggets and played for five seasons in the league, topping out at a 10.5 point-per-game scoring average for Washington in 1990.

The kid from Arizona briefly tried his hand in coaching, working as an assistant at Navy, but he moved on to pursue a career in money management. He still gets back to Duke for a number of basketball games each season.

"I was fortunate to play for Coach K when he was a nobody—when we were all nobodies," Alarie said. "Now I look and think that only a handful of programs have approached the success he's achieved at Duke. It might have happened without me, but it wouldn't have happened without the class of 1986. We were the cornerstones. Danny Ferry said he came here because he liked the way I played; Christian Laettner came because of Danny Ferry and so on. It's like we're all part of one big family tree.

"I feel fortunate to be a part of it. I can go back to Duke today and feel like I'm one member of a big, happy family."

CHAPTER 9

DANNY FERRY

It was perhaps inevitable that Danny Ferry would wind up as a basketball player. His father, Bob Ferry, was a 10-year NBA veteran who had become the general manager of the Washington Bullets by the time his second son was born.

"I was born with a sort of silver spoon as far as basketball was concerned," Ferry said. "My earliest memories are going to Bullets games as I was growing up. I remember being around the team in practice. It was a fun part of my life. I was exposed to some great teams and great players—those were the days when the Bullets had Elvin Hayes, Wes Unseld, Mitch Kupchek . . . "

Ferry grew up playing on a court that his father built beside their home in Bowie, Maryland. At a very early age, he participated in organized youth leagues at the Boys and Girls Club and later the Catholic Youth Organization (CYO).

"I was painfully skinny," Ferry said. "Around home, my nickname was 'Beans'—from beanpole."

Ferry quickly matured into one of the most renowned young prospects in the Washington, D.C., area. He grew taller than his father (a 6-foot-7 power forward) and his older brother, but what most impressed college coaches who began to notice the young big man was the flexibility of his game. Ferry might have had a center's body, but he had the shooting skills of a small forward and the passing abilities of a guard.

"My father taught me to shoot, and he gave me more depth of fundamentals than most kids get," Ferry said. "A lot of it is just that I came from a very rich basketball environment. I used to ride with my father to scout college games at the University of Maryland and at Virginia and up in the Philadelphia area. I was exposed to a lot of good basketball."

More exposure came when Ferry started hanging around DeMatha High School in Hyattsville, Maryland, where his older brother was playing for the legendary Morgan Wootten. When Danny was old enough, he enrolled at DeMatha, too.

"That was the first time I felt like I was part of something special," Ferry said. "That was due to Coach Wootten's presence."

It was at DeMatha that Ferry was identified as one of the nation's premier prep prospects and became the object of an intense recruiting battle. Maryland's Lefty Driesell put on the hard sell early, trying to land the star who grew up just a few miles from Maryland's College Park campus. But Driesell was fighting an uphill battle from the start.

"I grew up a [North] Carolina fan," Ferry said. "That was the model for the DeMatha program. Coach Wootten and Coach [Dean] Smith were very close."

But Ferry also began to notice that a hungry young coach with black hair and an unpronounceable name always seemed to be in the stands for his games. Duke's Mike Krzyzewski made an impression by outworking the competition. Ferry often saw the Blue Devils play an afternoon contest in Durham, and then would see Coach K in the stands for his game that night.

"As I began to dig into it, I felt Coach K was exceptional," Ferry said. "I also wanted to go where I was needed. His program was just getting off the ground. He had his first great group of players—Johnny [Dawkins], Mark [Alarie], David [Henderson], and Jay [Bilas]. But they were older and there was a question of whether they could sustain success after they were gone. That's where I thought I could help."

So in the end, Ferry—rated by several recruiting services as the nation's No. 1 prospect—picked the Blue Devils.

"It was a combination of Coach K, a high-level program, and the opportunity to be an important part of the program," he said. "I just seemed to fit in there with the coaches and the players. There was just a connection."

Danny Ferry (No. 35) goes up for a shot as teammate Marty Nessley provides a screen.

94

THE SETTING

Ferry found some familiar faces when he arrived on Duke's campus in the summer of 1985. He had played against senior Johnny Dawkins in high school and had been an AAU teammate of sophomore forward Billy King.

But he soon discovered that the transition from high school to college would not be easy.

"That first group—Johnny, Mark, David, and Jay—they established a work ethic . . . a level of excellence that surprised me," Ferry said. "To see them work so hard and do so much extra stuff, it made me think, 'Wow, this is what it's going to take?' Really, they set the tone for everything that's come after them at Duke."

Ferry soon carved a role for himself, even though it wasn't easy.

"There was a transition," he said. "Everybody was just better [than in high school]. That first year, my level of play was clearly as a supporting player."

The freshman big man actually started his first 21 games at Duke, but that was solely due to a preseason knee injury that sidelined senior starter Jay Bilas. When Bilas regained his health at midseason, he moved back into the starting lineup and Ferry became the team's sixth man.

"I didn't like going to the bench at the time," Ferry said. "But it was absolutely the right decision. I was a kid, still figuring out what we were doing, and he was a man. I still got to play a role. I think I still contributed."

Indeed, Ferry became a valuable sub. It was his offensive-rebound basket in the final seconds that helped Duke overcome Kansas in the NCAA semifinal game in Dallas. He ended up playing in all 40 games for the 1986 Blue Devils, averaging 5.9 points and 5.6 rebounds for a 37-3 team.

But when he returned for his sophomore season, it was to a very different Duke team. Coach K's first great class—Dawkins, Alarie, Henderson, and Bilas—had graduated, leaving point guard Tommy Amaker and Ferry as the team's two most experienced players.

"Not too much was expected of us," Ferry said. "Duke wasn't Duke yet and we weren't under the microscope like they are today. That was a fun year and we ended up having a good season. I felt like we had maximized our potential."

Ferry began to emerge that season as a special player. He led the team in scoring at a modest 14.0 points a game, but also added 7.8

rebounds, a team-high 4.3 assists a game, and nearly a steal a game. He was voted second-team All-ACC as Duke won 24 games and reached the NCAA Sweet 16 before losing to the eventual NCAA champions, Indiana.

The strong finish raised the expectations for his junior season.

"We had really established ourselves on paper," Ferry said. "I was put in a position to succeed."

The 1987-88 Blue Devils were an extraordinary defensive team, but Ferry was the key to the team's offensive production. He improved his scoring average to an ACC-best 19.1 points a game, while continuing to dish out four assists a game. He was voted ACC player of the year and earned significant All-America honors. Ferry was the centerpiece of a Duke team that beat rival North Carolina three times head to head, won Coach K his second ACC title in three years, and upset No. 1 Temple in the East Regional title game to reach the Final Four—the second for Ferry in three years.

"That Final Four was special," Ferry said. "My first one was awesome, but that was Johnny, Mark, and David's team. The second one was evidence that we were becoming a great program."

Ferry's second Final Four was almost his last. Although it wasn't reported at the time, the Duke star came very close to jumping to the NBA after his junior season.

"At one point, I was going to do it," he said. "My father had a lot of input—basically giving me information about where I'd be picked and stuff. But he allowed me to make the decision and didn't try to influence me."

Bob Ferry told his son that he'd probably be picked fifth or sixth in the NBA draft.

"In the end, I felt like I'd be missing a lot if I left," Ferry said. "I loved being a part of the Duke program. I felt like I'd be missing a lot of fun if I left. I knew of the great opportunity we had to be a good team the next year. And the only reason to go was money, so I decided to stay. It was one of the best decisions I ever made."

Krzyzewski, who was just about the only person outside the Ferry family who realized how close he came to losing his All-America big man, breathed a sigh of relief. He went about planning for the 1988-89 season, when he'd try to work freshman big man Christian Laettner into a veteran team that featured the likes of Ferry, forwards Robert Brickey and John Smith, and guards Quin Snyder and Phil Henderson. The combination was good enough to earn Duke the preseason No. 1 ranking in the AP poll—the first time that had happened in the Krzyzewski era.

No. 1 Duke—and Ferry—got off to a fast start by routing Kentucky in the Hall of Fame Tipoff Classic in Springfield, Massachusetts, as Ferry scored a game-high 23 points.

But his point production slipped as Duke reeled off four straight home-court victories over a quartet of patsies. There just wasn't any point in churning out big numbers against the likes of The Citadel or East Carolina. Ferry took just seven shots and scored a mere 11 points in a 49-point rout of ECU. He had a different problem against Stetson, picking up two quick fouls and spending much of the game on the bench as Duke coasted to a 38-point win without him.

Ferry was averaging a mere 15.4 points a game as the Blue Devils packed up for a trip to Miami for the team's first true road game of the season. At the time, there were no hints of the offensive explosion that was about to occur.

THE GAME OF MY LIFE
DUKE VS. MIAMI, DECEMBER 10, 1988
BY DANNY FERRY

I had no idea that I would have an especially good night against Miami. I don't remember anything special (in the scouting reports) or in pregame.

Well, there was one thing that was kind of quirky. I had been asking (team trainer) Max Crowder for pancakes before the game. We always had steak and eggs and pasta for our pregame meal. Just once, I wanted pancakes. And that morning, he finally gave in and we had pancakes.

The game started and it was a fast-paced game, but it seemed to be moving very slowly for me. I knew I was having a different kind of game, but I never thought about that. I was able to stay in the moment.

It's easy to get ahead of yourself in a situation like that. You start thinking about how many points you have or scoring the next point and you lose focus on the game. At no point did that happen to me.

I do remember that I was going in at halftime, one of my teammates told me I already had 30 (actually 34) points. That was shocking, but I did a pretty good job of putting that aside. Other than that, I don't think any of my teammates said anything about what was happening. Coach K never mentioned it—he was just frustrated by our defense.

It was a close game until very near the end, and that helped me stay focused on the moment. For the most part I was guarded by (6-foot-6 Eric) Brown, but they played zone, man to man—everything.

I was aware when I got to 50—I'm not sure if they announced it or what—but when it was over and they told me I had 58, my reaction was, "What the hell?" Afterward, I just walked around happy and a little in awe. It was a surreal experience for me.

When we got back to the locker room, Max grabbed me and said, "Well, I guess we'll have pancakes more often!"

THE AFTERMATH

Duke's 117-102 victory over the Hurricanes was overshadowed by Ferry's 58-point performance. Not only did it shatter Dick Groat's Duke scoring record of 48 points, it was one point better than David Thompson's ACC record of 57 points in a single game—a record he had set against Buffalo 14 years earlier.

"Danny was brilliant," Krzyzewski told reporters after the game. "I thought Danny could have a big night scoring because they are not a big team."

But Krzyzewski couldn't have anticipated the full extent of Ferry's big scoring night. His star hit 23 of 26 from the field—just missing the NCAA single-game record for field-goal percentage. Two of his baskets were three-pointers. He also hit 10 of 12 free throws, pulled down six rebounds, blocked two shots, and added three steals.

"I have never seen anything like that," said Miami coach Bill Foster, who had previously coached at Clemson. "He wasn't making gimmies. Some you expect him to make. Some were unbelievable. And we hounded the heck out of him."

Ferry credited his teammates with getting him the ball in the right spots.

"There was a good post exchange," he told reporters after the game. "All I had to do was turn and shoot. I knew I had scored a lot of points, but I was amazed when I heard the total."

Astoundingly, Ferry also passed out seven assists in the game, which was the most impressive aspect of his performance to Miami's Foster.

"I'd like to be one of their other four guys," Foster said. "Everybody is trying to guard Ferry. By the time you think you've got him stopped, he lays it off to somebody else. If he ain't the player of the year, I want to see who is."

Actually, Ferry's penchant for passing cost him the NCAA record of consecutive field goals. After missing his first shot of the game, Ferry hit seven in a row. At that point, he attempted a lob to center Alaa Abdelnaby. But his pass hit the rim and for statistical purposes was counted as a missed shot. Ferry went on to hit his next 12 field-goal attempts before missing a 17-foot jumper with 12 minutes to play. Without the lob pass that counted as a shot, Ferry would have hit 19 straight field-goal attempts—which would have been well beyond the NCAA record of 16 straight set by Kent State's Doug Grayson in 1967.

Of course, no one was complaining about that in the aftermath of Ferry's big game.

"He still didn't outscore me and the rest of the team," teammate Quin Snyder said. "We got 59 and Danny only got 58. As you can see, we beat him by one point."

The big night bumped Ferry's scoring average from 15.4 points a game to 22.5 points a game. He would finish the season at an ACC-best 22.6 points a game, his second straight league scoring title.

"I think there was a carryover," Ferry said. "The game against Miami certainly helped my confidence the rest of the season. I had a good year."

Although Ferry remembered struggling in his next game, he actually turned in another brilliant performance the next time out—he hit 11 of 17 shots from the floor and scored 33 points in a 94-88 victory over Wake Forest. He just missed a triple-double with nine rebounds and nine assists.

That kind of play earned Ferry a second straight ACC player of the year award and consensus first-team All-America honors. He was also selected national player of the year by UPI, the U.S. Basketball Writers, and the Naismith Foundation. Ferry led Duke to 28 wins and a second straight trip to the Final Four—his third Final Four trip in four years.

"Going to the Final Four was an awesome experience," Ferry said. "I'm disappointed we never won it. My freshman year, I thought we were the best team and should have won. The other two years, it was an accomplishment just to get there."

Still, Duke might have turned 1989 into a title year, except for an untimely injury to senior forward Robert Brickey in the first half of the semifinal game against Seton Hall in Seattle. Duke led big early and was up at the half, but without Brickey and with young big man Laettner in foul trouble, the Pirates gained the upper hand.

"I was hot early, but after Robert got hurt, that changed the momentum," Ferry said. "Toward the end, I started to try and do too much, and it kind of got away from us."

Ferry finished with 39 points (his second best career scoring game) and 10 rebounds, but it wasn't enough to save the Devils. Seton Hall's 95-78 victory was the last game of Ferry's collegiate career.

REFLECTIONS OF DUKE

Waiting one year to turn pro had a major impact on Ferry's career.

It didn't hurt his draft position. Instead of the fifth or sixth place his father had projected in 1988, the younger Ferry went second in the 1989 draft, just behind the same "Never Nervous" Pervis Ellison who had helped Louisville beat Duke in the 1986 title game.

Unfortunately, that second pick belonged to the Clippers and Ferry—with his NBA background—understood just how bad an organization that was. Instead of signing with the inept club, the former Duke star elected to play a year in Europe—signing a hefty contract with the Italian team, Il Messaggero. He finally made his NBA debut a year later . . . after the Clippers had traded his rights to the Cleveland Cavaliers.

Ferry never found NBA stardom, although he was good enough to play 13 years in the league. He finally won a championship ring in his final season (2003), serving as a backup for the San Antonio Spurs. The former Duke star remained with the Spurs after his retirement as a player, serving as the team's director of basketball operations. In June of 2005, he signed a five-year contract as general manager of the Cleveland Cavaliers.

Ferry remembers his four years at Duke fondly and is proud of the role he played in sustaining and extending Coach Krzyzewski's program.

"They had a great team when I arrived," he said. "But I was part of turning a great team into a great program. When Johnny and David and Mark and those guys graduated, people wondered what would happen to the program. Going back to the Final Four my junior and senior years was awesome. And that's carried on."

CHAPTER 10

SHANE BATTIER

When Shane Battier arrived at Detroit Country Day School, he found himself in Chris Webber's very large shadow.

The Michigan All-American had graduated from Country Day in 1991, just before Battier's arrival. And Webber was everything Battier was not—a playground legend in Detroit and a powerful, athletic player with a combative edge.

"People were quick to tell me why I'd never be Chris Webber," Battier said. "I was from the suburbs, he was from the city. He was more skilled, more athletic. He was this and that. I kept hearing what I wasn't. That was tough for a 14-year-old."

Battier was already regarded as a promising prospect when he arrived at Webber's old school. He had learned the game in his family's driveway, playing against his father and his brothers and other neighborhood kids.

"I was the anti-playground guy," Battier said. "I was lucky. As I got older, I was always the tallest kid in my class. I was sought after to play on AAU teams at the YMCA. I benefited from a lot of knowledgeable coaches."

But the biggest benefit came from the most knowledgeable coach of all—Country Day coach Kurt Keener, who had previously coached Webber. He told his young project not to worry about the comparisons with Country Day's earlier star.

"He told me to just be myself and not try to replicate Webber's game," Battier said. "He helped me learn early that I'm my own person and that if I did my best, that would be good enough. The funny thing is that while Chris was at Country Day, they won three state titles, he was voted Mr. Basketball in the state of Michigan, and he won the Naismith Award [as the nation's top prep player]. By the time I finished at Country Day, we had won three straight state titles, I was voted Mr. Basketball, and I won the Naismith Award.

"The kid who was never going to live up to Webber, left high school with almost exactly the same accomplishments."

And, like Webber, Battier finished his prep career as one of the nation's top college prospects. With his strong academics and his much-admired game, the Country Day product could have played anywhere in the country, but he narrowed his choices down to five: Michigan, Michigan State, Kansas, North Carolina, and Duke.

But in reality, Michigan (Webber's school) and Michigan State had little chance.

"I wanted to leave the state," Battier said. "I wanted to get out and experience something new."

Duke started out as a long shot.

"Growing up, I didn't like Duke," he said. "I pulled for the Fab Five [the Michigan class that included Webber]. Then in 1994, I started to change my mind. I realized that Grant Hill was pretty good."

In the end, Mike Krzyzewski's recruiting efforts, along with Duke's strong combination of athletics and academics, led him to sign with the Blue Devils. But that decision did not come without a bit of controversy.

"On the day of my announcement, I called the four coaches who had been recruiting me and thanked them for recruiting me and told them I wasn't coming," Battier explained. "All of the coaches were great. When I talked to [UNC coach Dean] Smith, I don't know if I caught him at a weird time or what, but he just said, 'All right . . . good luck.' And that was it."

Somehow, the rumor spread that Smith had hung up on Battier.

"He didn't hang up on me," Battier said. "Later, he wrote me a very nice letter, wishing me luck."

As it turned out, Battier wouldn't bring much luck to the Tar Heel coach. Smith actually retired before the Michigan prep star played a game at Duke, but he remained close to the program. And

Shane Battier slams one home in front of the Cameron Crazies.

he couldn't have been happy to see Battier lead Duke to a 7-3 record over the Tar Heels in his four seasons in Durham.

THE SETTING

Battier arrived at Duke along with two other players who were rated by one recruiting service or another as the number-one player in the prep Class of 1997. New Yorker Elton Brand was a powerful 6-foot-9 forward, whose game looked very much like Chris Webber's. Chris Burgess was a 6-foot-11 center from Utah with a sculptured body and rare athleticism for a player that big.

The fourth member of the class was guard William Avery, who was merely a Parade All-American.

They joined a program that Krzyzewski had been rebuilding since the disaster of 1995, when the team had collapsed in his absence with a back injury. Duke recovered to make the NCAA Tournament in 1996 and won the ACC regular-season title in 1997, but the arrival of the four heralded freshmen promised a return to the top of the national scene in 1997-98.

"One of the best things about the freshman class was that we all thought we could step in and play right away," Battier said. "But there was a lot of talent already there. Our practices were more competitive than a lot of our games."

Battier found his niche as a defensive stopper. He averaged almost 25 minutes a game as a freshman, starting 20 times and averaging 7.6 points and 6.4 rebounds for a 32-4 team. A year later, he upped his scoring average to 9.1 points and started 26 times for a 37-2 team that swept the ACC and reached the national title game before suffering a heartbreaking loss to Connecticut.

Despite his modest numbers, Battier was recognized as an excellent all-around player. He was third-team All-ACC as a sophomore and was named the national defensive player of the year. Significantly, he blossomed as a three-point shooter, exploding for 27 points and hitting 4-of-4 three-pointers in a February victory over Maryland.

The three-point shooting seemed to come from nowhere. Although Battier had won the three-point shooting contest at the 1997 McDonald's All-America game, he had done little from beyond the arch in his first season and a half at Duke. He hit just four-of-24 three-pointers as a freshman and had converted just 12-of-42 attempts in his first 22 games as a sophomore.

But starting with that magical night against the Terps, Battier established himself as one of the deadliest long-range shooters in college basketball. He would finish his second season by hitting 27-of-52 3-point tries in Duke's last 17 games, then would hit 79-of-178 three-pointers as a junior and 124-of-296 as a senior.

But the dramatic turnaround in Battier's offensive game did not happen by chance.

"I was a good shooter in high school, but I knew the form on my jump shot would not hold up in college," Battier said. "It's kind of like Tiger Woods changing his swing after his first major championship. I'm not comparing myself to Tiger Woods, but I did the same thing. The summer after my freshman year, I worked with [former Duke guard and professional shooting coach] Chip Engelland. We had some deep, philosophical discussions about shooting. He's one of the three best basketball minds I've ever been around. He helped me develop a routine and a way to change my shot. It took nine months for that to pay off. That Maryland game was when it clicked."

Battier's newfound three-point prowess would have major consequences in the coming seasons, but it was merely a small addition for that powerful 1999 Duke team, which got most of its offense from Brand, who swept all the national player of the year awards, and from senior All-American Trajan Langdon. In addition, Avery and explosive freshman Corey Maggette were double-figure scorers. Battier and junior forward Chris Carrawell were the team's fifth and sixth scoring options.

"When I look at that roster—1-to-13—the depth of talent was amazing," Battier said. "I knew we had plenty of great scorers. Defense was what I did best. That was my role."

But Battier knew that his role had to change after the 1999 season. Langdon graduated, and Brand became the first Duke underclassman to jump to the NBA. That was expected after his player of the year season. What was not expected were the early entries of Avery and Maggette. And if that was not enough, Burgess—frustrated by his inability to cash in on his enormous potential—elected to transfer to Utah.

Duke's unusual depth of talent was erased in a few short weeks. Krzyzewski was bringing in another strong recruiting class, but Battier was one of just three holdovers with any playing experience, along with Carrawell, and Nate James.

"When all those guys left, the Blue Devil nation was pretty upset," Battier said. "I know this sounds bad, but Chris Carrawell,

Nate James, and I were the most excited guys on campus. We knew it was our time."

The 1999-2000 season got off to a rocky start when Duke lost its first two games in New York—heartbreakers to Stanford and UConn.

"When we lost our first two games, people wrote us off," Battier said. "But I knew we had some talent. I knew that if we played hard, we'd have success at the end."

Indeed, that's just what happened. Duke followed its opening weekend with 18 straight wins. The Blue Devils rolled to a fourth straight ACC regular-season title, claimed a second straight ACC Tournament championship, and finished No. 1 in the AP's final poll.

Both Carrawell and Battier had transformed themselves from role players into stars. Battier not only earned first-team All-ACC honors, but he was named to the Wooden All-America team and was a second-team All-America pick by the AP, the NABC, and the *Sporting News*. He also picked up his second straight national defensive player of year award.

The only disappointment for Battier was the team's ouster at the hands of Florida in the Sweet 16. The loss ended Duke's season at 29-5.

"It was a bad matchup for us," Battier said. "They went on to play in the national title game. Our youth caught up with us. But, you know, I think every champion has to go through something like that. It happened to Michigan State—they lost to us in the Final Four in 1999 before they won it all [in 2000]. And it was going to happen to Maryland—we knocked them out in 2001 and they came back to win it all [in 2002]. Losing like that galvanizes you as a player and a team. Losing to Florida helped us win the next year."

Winning the national championship was very much on Battier's mind as Duke opened the 2000-01 season. Carrawell was gone after a superb senior season, but four starters returned, including gifted sophomores Jason Williams, Carlos Boozer, and Mike Dunleavy. Battier and James, a tough-minded fifth-year senior, rounded out the starting lineup, while freshman guard Chris Duhon provided a spark off the bench.

"I knew we had a great shot at the national title," Battier said. "And we played well. We lost a few and had some close games, but I thought the team was playing well and we generally had a positive feeling. That feeling kind of changed on my senior night."

Duke was 25-3 and ranked No. 2 nationally when Battier celebrated his last game in Cameron against a very talented Maryland team. The Terps had emerged as the strongest challenger to the Blue Devils in the ACC.

"During my four years at Duke, I thought Maryland was our biggest rival," Battier said. "There was a difference between the rivalry with Maryland and the rivalry with Carolina. With Carolina, there was a healthy dislike and distrust, but there was also a level of respect. With Maryland, there was no love lost at all. I consider it one of my proudest achievements at Duke is that I never lost at Cole Field House."

Battier had barely kept that streak alive earlier his senior season when Duke mounted one of the most incredible comebacks in ACC history, erasing a 10-point Maryland lead in the final 55 seconds of regulation and winning in overtime.

The Blue Devils appeared headed for another hard-fought win on Battier's Senior Night in Cameron, but early in the second half, with Duke nursing a narrow lead, Boozer—the team's only proven big man—came down awkwardly on his foot and had to leave the game. Duke collapsed in his absence and Maryland pulled out the 91-80 victory. Worse, Battier and the other Blue Devil players soon learned that Boozer's foot was broken and that he'd be out the next month or more—just as postseason play was about to begin.

"Initially, I had selfish thoughts," Battier said. "It was like, 'You've got to be kidding me. I put in all this time, I've been a model player and this is the way it's going to end for me?' I really felt sorry for myself."

The feeling persisted the next morning at practice. The team Battier prided himself on leading was so unfocused that Krzyzewski threw the players out of practice.

"Normally, I don't get emotional in the locker room," Battier said. "But that day, I was probably as emotional as I've ever been. I realized we could possibly lose our next three games and my college career would be over."

Battier felt better that afternoon, when Krzyzewski revealed to the team his plan for coping with Boozer's departure. Little-used sophomore Casey Sanders would replace Boozer at center, but more significantly, the speedy Duhon would replace the more experienced James in the starting lineup, giving the Devils far more quickness and an improved three-point capability.

"When he inserted Casey Sanders, Coach K told him that his one job on offense was 'Screen for Shane,'" Battier said. "I'd never had a personal screener before."

Battier learned that Coach K was going to turn his team loose from the three-point line. Two days before the Blue Devils were to close out the regular season at North Carolina, he got a taste of what was to come.

"We do this drill where the managers rebound and we all shoot threes for five minutes," Battier said. "This time we made almost 400 threes as a group. Coach blew his whistle and said, 'This is how we're going to play.'"

That's exactly what Duke did to North Carolina that Sunday afternoon in Chapel Hill, burying the Tar Heels 95-81 in a blizzard of three-pointers. Battier, who hit four threes, finished with 25 points, 11 rebounds, four steals, and five blocked shots—including one block of a Joe Forte breakaway that seemed to break UNC's spirit midway through the second half.

"I've never been prouder of a win than that one," Battier said. "The Carolina guys were so full of themselves before the game. They knew we were without Boozer and they were certain of victory."

The decisive win helped boost the team's confidence going into the ACC Tournament in Atlanta's Georgia Dome.

"It had us feeling that even without Carlos, we were the best team in America," Battier said. "We knew we could be good playing that style. It was almost like we were the [run-and-gun] Phoenix Suns before the Phoenix Suns [even were]."

Duke stormed through three opponents in Atlanta to claim a third straight ACC championship. Battier earned MVP honors as he scored 16 in an easy victory over N.C. State, 20 in a thrilling two-point win over Maryland, and 20 more in another rout of North Carolina.

Only the Maryland game—won on a last-second tip-in by James—was competitive, continuing the streak of memorable Blue Devil-Terp classics that season. Afterwards, Battier sought out Maryland star Juan Dixon and told him, "I'll see you at the Final Four."

In hindsight, he doesn't think his remark was particularly prescient.

"It was inevitable," he said. "We knew we were going to be there, and we knew they were one of the best teams in the country. As soon as the brackets came out, we said, 'Ah-ha, we'll have to beat Maryland in the semifinals.'"

That's exactly what happened. Duke took care of business in the East Regional, winning four games by double-figure margins, while

Maryland upset top-seeded Stanford in the West Regional to earn a trip to Minneapolis. And there in the first national semifinal game, Duke and Maryland renewed their bitter rivalry.

For almost a half, it was an unmitigated disaster for the Blue Devils as Maryland opened up a 22-point lead.

"They came and out and . . . wow!" Battier said. "Playing in the Final Four is such an emotional thing. It takes a while to get your bearings. Jason, Carlos, Mike, and Chris had never been to the Final Four before. It was an intimidating scene. We were really bad, but they were making everything. We were in disbelief. We came in knowing we had beaten them two out of three times and we thought we were the better team."

Battier said that Coach K calmed the team down at halftime.

"He told us to just relax and play," Battier explained. "He said, 'What's the worst that could happen—we lose by 40?'"

Duke made a little run to open the second half, cutting the Terp lead to 15. That's when Battier's confidence returned.

"You could see the look in their eyes," he said. "They knew they couldn't put us away. I'm convinced the game in Cole Field House [when Duke rallied from 10 down in the final minute] had a lot to do with that. These guys had cracked before and they knew it was going to happen again. To see them fighting among themselves and passing up shots . . . we were down 15, but I knew we were going to win."

Duke did just that that, pulling away in the final minutes for a 95-84 victory. Battier had 25 points, eight rebounds, and four blocked shots in the win. Duke also got major contributions from Williams (23 points) and from Boozer, who returned to action and came off the bench to score 19 points in 25 minutes.

"I'll never forget the two different feelings I had in that game— the embarrassment when we were down 20 points in the first half and the confidence I had in the second half, when we were down 15," Battier said.

But the Duke senior didn't have too much time to reflect on the satisfying victory over the Terps. Less than 48 hours later, he had to take the court against Arizona in the national title game. Battier had already endured a heartbreaking national title game loss in 1999, when he was a supporting character on one of the most talented teams in Duke history. Now it was his Duke team, and his final college game—win or lose.

THE GAME OF MY LIFE
DUKE VS. ARIZONA, APRIL 2, 2001
BY SHANE BATTIER

I thought Arizona was the most talented team we had played that season. When you looked at their roster, you see all these future pros—Richard Jefferson, Gilbert Arenas, Jason Gardner, Michael Wright, and Luke Walton.

We knew it would be a tough game, but we never felt any doubt that we would win. We may have felt some doubt before the Maryland game, but there was no doubt before we played Arizona. We started the game calmly.

I was guarding (7-foot-1 center) Loren Woods. I was giving up four or five inches on him, and in the beginning, they did a good job of exploiting that. There was not a lot I could do—he was just turning and shooting over me. Luckily, they didn't go to that much.

Some were concerned when Jason [Williams] got a couple of early fouls, but Chris [Duhon] did a good job of running the team while he sat out and Mike Dunleavy decided he was going to have a great game.

Michael was my roommate and my best friend, but he had not been shooting well in the tournament. But it's a funny thing, just before the championship game, his mother told Heidi—my girlfriend at the time, now my wife—that Mike was going to have a good shooting game. She called it as only a mother can.

(Dunleavy helped Duke to a 10-point lead early in the second half when he hit three three-pointers in 45 seconds, the last one set up by a remarkable defensive play by Battier on Arenas.)

It happened so fast that I didn't think about it at the time, but there was some similarity between that play and the one I had against Forte in Chapel Hill. But it was just instinct at the time. When I look at the tape to this day, I don't know how I did it—not just blocking the shot from behind, but saving the ball and getting it to Mike.

Arizona came back, but I was able to make three really athletic plays in a row that kept us in front. That's kind of remarkable because I wasn't that kind of player. People who know me know I'm not a high flyer. I like to say my game's not 10 feet and above the rim . . . it's six inches between the ears.

But those three plays . . .

The first play was a Jason Williams miss. Nobody blocked me out and I was able to catch it off the rim and slam it back in. I was lucky

112

that the ball bounced right to me, but I also think Loren Woods was shocked I got up that high.

The second one was when we missed a tough shot around the rim and I jumped for it. But I got tangled up and twisted around so that all I could do was tap it with the back of my hand. I was just trying to keep it alive when luckily, it went in. I've since seen an overhead picture of that play, and you can see me surrounded by four Arizona players. That play was just unexplainable.

The third play . . . Jason was dribbling and Loren Woods turned his head for an instant. Usually, in that situation, I'd step back for a three. But something in my head said, "You have to dunk this . . . you have to dunk it!" So instead of stepping out, I broke for the basket. Jason got me the ball and I went up and was able to dunk it.

It's kind of funny to end my career with three very athletic plays. But that's the way it happened, and it was enough to give us the title.

My reaction was just unbelievable exultation. It was almost like I had a moment of clarity in which I understood everything: "This is why I put so much time into preparation. This why I made sure to eat right, why I got my rest, why I watched all that film . . . "

It's kind of hard to talk about, but at that moment, I understood everything that I had done was to prepare for that moment.

THE AFTERMATH

Duke's 82-72 victory over Arizona in the title game was the third national title for the school and Krzyzewski. But it was the first for Battier, who earned Final Four MVP honors with his 18-point, 11-rebound, six-assist effort against the Wildcats.

That honor merely capped a brilliant senior season. Strangely, Battier only shared the ACC player of the year award with UNC's Joe Forte, but he swept the national player of the year awards and earned consensus first-team All-America honors. In addition, he claimed his third straight national defensive player of the year award and was voted academic All-America for the second year in a row.

"I have just one regret about my college career," Battier said. "My sophomore year, I got very sick just before we played Fresno State in the Great Alaskan Shootout. I had a temperature of 102 degrees, and Coach K made me stay in the hotel room and watch on TV.

"At the end of my career, I ended up tied with [Kentucky guard] Wayne Turner as the player who appeared in the most victories in

NCAA history. If I had it to do all over again, I'd have dressed out for that Fresno State game, then gone out there for a minute at the end of the game to get on the books. With that victory, I'd have beaten him by one."

As it was, Battier was a key player on teams that finished 32-4, 37-2, 29-5, and 35-4. More remarkably, his first three Duke teams finished 15-1, 16-0 and 15-1 in ACC play. To this day, no other ACC team has won as many as 15 regular-season ACC games.

Battier was the sixth player taken in the 2001 NBA draft, picked by the Memphis Grizzlies. He played there for four seasons, earning all-rookie honors in 2002, before being traded to the Houston Rockets.

He's established himself as one of many former Duke players who have emerged as successful NBA players—including his Duke contemporaries Brand and Boozer and Duhon and Dunleavy, not to mention blossoming youngsters like Luol Deng and veterans like Grant Hill.

"Not too bad for a program that supposedly can't produce NBA players, huh?" he said. "When I was drafted, I had to defend the alumni from my alma mater. But that stuff goes in cycles. Now it's easy to see that Duke turns out plenty of successful pro players."

REFLECTIONS ON DUKE

No matter what Battier accomplishes in the NBA, he'll always be regarded as the consummate college player—maybe the closest thing in modern times to the NCAA's perfect student-athlete. He's still the only consensus national player of the year to also be an academic All-American since Bill Walton in 1974.

Battier appreciates being a part of the program Krzyzewski constructed at Duke.

"Those guys will always have a special part of my life," he said. "Their words and encouragement mean so much. You see, that's what makes the program special. When you get there as a freshman, you are taught by the seniors and the other upperclassmen what it means to be a Duke basketball player—how to work, how to prepare, even how to carry yourself.

"By the time you are an upperclassman, you're expected to teach the young guys."

Battier theorizes that the reason Duke struggled somewhat in 2007 was a break in that continuity. Without a senior and with just one junior, who had been injured much of his career, there was no one to pass on the lessons of the past.

"I know that I wouldn't have gotten where I was without Steve Wojciechowski, Trajan Langdon, Roshown McLeod," he said. "That collective experience is what makes Duke great."

And Shane Battier remains a very important part of Duke's collective experience.

CHAPTER 11

CHRISTIAN LAETTNER

Christian Laettner looked like a prep school product.

With his finely chiseled looks and his long sideburns, Laettner resembled a character off the set of the then-popular show *Beverly Hills 90210*. His appearance and his background at The Nichols School—an exclusive, academically oriented college preparatory school in Buffalo—created the impression that the future Duke standout was a soft, upper-middle class finesse player.

But looks can be deceiving.

Laettner was not a child of privilege. Instead, he grew up in the blue-collar suburb of Angola, 20 miles south of Buffalo. His father was a printer for the *Buffalo News* and his mother was a schoolteacher. Laettner attended local parochial school through the eighth grade. His mother, concerned that her son was not excelling in the classroom, wanted him to repeat the eighth grade. To do that, he had to transfer to The Nichols School, a small, private prep school that was located on the north side of Buffalo—just across the street from the Buffalo Zoo.

The campus was a 45-minute commute from Angola—in good weather. Laettner would have to rise every morning at 6 a.m. and ride in with his father, who would drop him off just south of the city. He'd ride the rest of the way with classmate Rick Torgalski, a future baseball player at Duke.

"His was the longest day of anybody—maybe 6 a.m. to 9 p.m.," Torgalski said. "He'd have to get up an hour early to get to where I picked him up. Then I'd drop him off and he'd have to wait for his father to pick him up and take him the rest of the way home."

Laettner played four years of varsity basketball for The Nichols School, first displaying his legendary toughness in games against the inner-city teams from Buffalo and New York City.

"It was always like, 'The preppies are coming to town,'" Torgalski recalled. "Going to a private school, people are always going to resent you and try to test you. You had to stay mentally tough."

Nichols coach Jim Kramer points to an early game against South Park High, which tried to intimidate the frail-looking prep school kid.

"They wanted to brawl with us," Kramer said. "They came in real cocky, thinking they would intimidate us. When the teams lined up to shake hands before the game, they'd spit in their hands. They were in your face on every dead ball."

Laettner responded to the taunts and the cheap shots in the same way he would so often do at Duke—by ratcheting his game to another level. He led Nichols to an easy victory and left the reigning New York west regional champions in disarray.

"They weren't used to somebody putting up with it and dishing it back," Kramer said. "All of a sudden they were down 20 points in the third quarter and they couldn't handle it."

A string of dominant performances such as that one turned Laettner into a nationally prominent prospect. Kramer, who was also the director of college counseling at The Nichols School, helped the family trim a long list of suitors down to three finalists: Virginia, North Carolina, and Duke.

"The family liked all three, but they felt [Virginia coach] Terry Holland did his best job with average talent," Kramer said. "North Carolina had a lot of top big men at that time. While Christian knew he could play with them, he also knew there would be more competition for playing time.

"Besides, he just decided he liked Duke best."

THE SETTING

Laettner joined a Duke program that was coming off its second Final Four trip in three years. As it turned out there was as much competition in Durham as there would have been in Chapel Hill. He

Christian Laettner rips down a rebound in traffic against Kansas in the 1991 NCAA title game.

found himself battling for playing time up front with senior All-American Danny Ferry, junior Alaa Abdelnaby (a future NBA lottery pick), two-year starter John Smith, and veteran Robert Brickey.

Not only was the competition formidable, but Laettner also needed to adapt to the demands of college basketball.

"Your freshman year at Duke, it's a whirlwind," he said. "Everything comes at you 100 miles per hour. It was rough, but I loved everything I was doing. I loved everything Coach K threw at me."

Laettner displayed a steep learning curve. After playing just six minutes in Duke's opening win against a probation-riddled Kentucky—and not attempting a shot from the floor—he moved into the starting lineup on Christmas Eve, scoring 20 points in a lopsided victory over Cornell. Ferry remained Duke's big gun as Laettner averaged 8.9 points and 4.7 rebounds as a freshman. Significantly, he hit 72.3 percent of his shots from the floor—an indication of things to come.

There were other indications as well.

In late February, the freshman big man had 12 points and 10 rebounds in just 21 minutes of action against No. 2 Arizona in the Meadowlands. Although Laettner was 6-for-6 from the field in that game, he missed a crucial free throw late that cost Duke a chance to force overtime. Afterwards, he was consoled in the locker room by Duke Law School graduate Richard Nixon, who knew a thing or two about bouncing back from failure.

Laettner was determined to learn from his shortcomings against Arizona. Although it was reported at the time that he vowed he would never miss another pressure free throw at Duke, he doesn't remember making that claim.

"I don't know if I said that, but I was going to try my best not to," he said. "So I prepared in case I was in that situation again. I practiced more than anyone on pressure free throws."

Laettner's chance for redemption would come. He would emerge as the greatest clutch player of his generation—and maybe the greatest in college basketball history. He certainly figured in more pivotal NCAA Tournament moments than any other player.

It started his freshman year, when Duke faced top-seeded Georgetown in the East Regional title game on the same Meadowlands court where Laettner had come up short a month earlier. He was matched against Georgetown's fearsome center Alonzo

Mourning, who had just dominated the Big East Tournament and made the Hoyas the betting favorite to win it all.

"I had been playing against Alonzo [in summer camps] since my freshman year in high school," Laettner said. "He had always been a nemesis. He was a great player, but I thought I had a better team around me."

The key moment in the game occurred 90 seconds after the opening tip. Laettner put up a short shot in the lane, only to have Mourning swat it back in his face. Instead of being intimidated by the blocked shot, Laettner calmly retrieved the ball and put up another shot—this one arching over Mourning's outstretched fingers.

His second try went in—as would every other shot he attempted that afternoon. Laettner finished with 24 points, hitting his final nine shots after that opening block, to go along with nine rebounds and a defensive job that limited his rival Mourning to 11 points and five rebounds. Duke proved its superiority with an 85-77 upset of the Hoyas, giving Laettner his first trip to the Final Four.

"I played better—not because I was a better player, but because I was part of a better team," Laettner said. "I knew Alonzo was special. We had to attack him. We overcame him with our system."

Although an early injury to Brickey combined with Laettner's foul trouble kept the 1989 Blue Devils short of a national title, that year's NCAA Tournament demonstrated that Laettner was going to be more than just a supporting player.

He proved that in 1990, upping his averages to 16.3 points a game and 9.6 rebounds. He earned second-team All-ACC honors, but took another step toward NCAA immortality in the 1990 East Regional title game—back on the same Meadowlands court Laettner knew all too well. This time the opponent was top-seeded Connecticut, enjoying what was then the greatest season in its history under new coach Jim Calhoun.

The hard-fought game moved into overtime when Abdelnaby missed a potential game-winner at the buzzer ending regulation. In the extra period, UConn's Nadev Henefeld gave the Huskies a 78-77 lead when he sank two free throws with just seconds remaining. Blue Devil coach Mike Krzyzewski called a timeout with 2.6 seconds left and designed a play for senior guard Phil Henderson.

But as the Blue Devils lined up for the inbounds play in front of the Duke bench, Krzyzewski noticed that UConn was not guarding the inbounds passer—who happened to be Laettner. Coach K screamed, "Special!" switching the play he had just designed to a "special" situational play the Devils had practiced. Laettner's pass went to his roommate Brian Davis, who gave it right back to the unguarded inbounder.

Laettner had time to launch and sink a 15-footer as the buzzer sounded.

"It was a really lucky shot," Laettner said. "It was a short shot, but I had to double clutch to avoid a defender. That's what made it a lucky shot. I'll never forget the pandemonium that followed on the floor. It was one of my great memories."

It was followed a week later by one of his worst memories as Duke was routed in the 1990 NCAA title game by UNLV. Laettner had a solid 15 points and nine rebounds, but with freshman point guard Bobby Hurley battling an intestinal disorder, the Blue Devils couldn't compete with the powerful Runnin' Rebels, losing by a record 30 points.

"I remember thinking, 'I'd love to play that team again with a healthy Bobby . . . a Bobby Hurley who was a sophomore,'" Laettner said.

As it happened, Laettner got his wish. This time it didn't take any heroics in the regional finals to get Duke to the Final Four. The 1991 Blue Devils breezed out of the Midwest Regional, beating Northeast Louisiana, Iowa, Connecticut, and St. John's by an average of more than 15 points each.

But all that did was earn Duke a rematch with No. 1 undefeated UNLV in Indianapolis. If anything, Jerry Tarkanian's Runnin' Rebels were even more intimidating in 1991 than they had been the year before.

"All I was concerned about was that they beat us by 30 and I didn't want to let that happen again," Laettner said. "I knew we were a much better team my junior year. And Coach K did a great job of convincing us we could win. He had us play against seven defenders in practice because there were times when UNLV's five players seemed like seven."

UNLV's Tarkanian complained before the game that he didn't have a player capable of matching up with Laettner. At the time, his concern was dismissed as poor-mouthing, but as it turned out, he had pinpointed what would turn out to be his team's primary problem. Laettner abused a number of UNLV defenders for 28 points and seven rebounds. With the game tied and just 12.7 seconds left, Laettner rebounded Thomas Hill's missed shot and was fouled before he could put up the follow shot.

Tarkanian called timeout to ice Laettner and let the Blue Devils star think about the two foul shots to come. But this wasn't the nervous freshman who had missed a clutch free throw against Arizona. Whether Laettner really vowed never to miss another key free throw or not, he had prepared himself for just this situation. He calmly sank both free throws, then dropped back to defense and prevented UNLV All-American Larry Johnson from attempting a game-winning three-pointer.

Two nights later, Laettner contributed 18 points and 10 rebounds as Duke edged Kansas, giving the school its first national championship. The title capped a superb junior season for the "preppie" from New York—second-team All-American, first-team All-ACC and the Final Four MVP. He averaged 19.8 points and 8.7 rebounds, and in a February game, he absolutely humiliated LSU's Shaquille O'Neal, the consensus national player of the year.

Was it the right moment for Laettner to turn pro?

"I thought about it . . . maybe for a minute," Laettner said. "It made me feel good to know I could turn pro. But I still had more to accomplish at Duke. I loved playing for Coach K and learning from him. I was in no hurry to leave."

Laettner's decision to stay—along with the return of Hurley at point guard and gifted forward Grant Hill—guaranteed Duke the No. 1 spot in the preseason polls. The national spotlight would turn up the heat in Durham.

"It changed everything; it took everything up a notch," Laettner said. "At Duke, you always get everybody's best shot. But [in 1991-92] teams were even more focused, more intense when they played us. To me, it just made the whole atmosphere better . . . more fun. And with all the things people threw at us, it made us a more resilient team."

That would pay off one March afternoon in Philadelphia.

For the most part, Laettner's senior season was a triumphant campaign, marred by a series of serious injuries to his teammates. Hurley was out for a month with a broken foot. Grant Hill suffered a high ankle sprain that hobbled him late in the season. Freshman big man Cherokee Parks was lost for a good part of the year. Even Laettner missed the opener with an ankle problem—the only game he would sit out in his four-year career at Duke.

Yet, through it all, Duke kept winning against an impressive slate of opponents. Laettner had 26 points as the Devils routed No. 7 St. John's in the ACC/Big East Challenge, and then poured in 24 points in a overtime victory at No. 18 Michigan, against what would come to be known as the Fab Five. Laettner scored 29 to beat Notre Dame, and then had 22 points and 10 rebounds to beat No. 22 LSU and O'Neal in Baton Rouge. Duke topped the Tigers without the injured Hurley as Laettner broke the game open with back-to-back three-pointers. He had 29 points and 13 rebounds when Duke traveled to UCLA and smashed the No. 4-ranked Bruins.

Duke held the No. 1 spot in the polls all season, despite losing two games. The first was a bloody battle with No. 9 North Carolina in Chapel Hill. The second was a narrow loss to unranked Wake Forest in Winston-Salem. It went unnoticed at the time, but a key play in that game came with Duke down two points and just seconds remaining. Grant Hill attempted a length-of-the-court pass to Laettner, but his football-like throw curved to the left and Laettner stepped out of bounds as he brought it in.

"I remember walking off the court and saying to Grant, 'Throw me a good pass next time and maybe we'll win,'" Laettner said.

Just as Duke got a second chance against UNLV, Laettner and Hill would get a second chance to execute the play they called "home run."

Duke completed the regular season at 25-2, and then added three more victories in the ACC Tournament—Krzyzewski's third ACC title—to enter the NCAA Tournament at 28-2. The Blue Devils pushed it to 30-2 with early-round victories over Campbell and (for the second straight year) Iowa. That earned the team a return to the East Regional semifinals—not in the familiar New Jersey Meadowlands this time, but in the dark, dirty Philadelphia Spectrum.

Duke's easy road to the Final Four in 1991 would not be repeated in 1992. With the national spotlight focused tightly on the defending champs, the Blue Devils endured a tense, difficult game against Seton Hall in the third round.

"It was a hard game for us," Laettner recalled. "They had a pretty good defensive team. Nothing came easy. We had to work very hard to beat them."

Laettner didn't have one of his better games against the Pirates. He scored just 16 points on 6-of-13 shooting. Hurley, facing the emotional hurdle of battling his younger brother, also struggled. It took major contributions from the two Hills—Grant and Thomas—and from Brian Davis for Duke to survive with an 81-69 victory.

The final score was deceptive. Laettner and his teammates knew they'd have to play a lot better in the regional championship game to get past Rick Pitino's Kentucky Wildcats.

THE GAME OF MY LIFE
DUKE VS. KENTUCKY, MARCH 28, 1992
BY CHRISTIAN LAETTNER

Kentucky raised a lot of concerns. Seton Hall was a good defensive team. Kentucky could outscore you. It was a whole different beast. Seton Hall wanted to score 62 points and win. With Kentucky, it was a race to score 100.

I was really concerned. They were a hard team to stop. We were going to have to outscore them to win. And they were really a hot team.

I was worried, but maybe that helped my focus.

As the game got going, I never realized that I was playing in a classic. If you play basketball for the right reason, none of that hits you. I remember parts of the game where I thought we had it under control, then the next thing I knew, it was a tight game.

We were playing classic Duke basketball—hard-nosed defense and taking advantages of our opportunities on offense. They stayed hot and we stayed hot.

We came down to the end of regulation with the score tied and Coach K drew up a good play. Bobby (Hurley) had the option to penetrate and shoot or to kick it out to somebody else. He had a good shot. We almost won it right there. It just didn't go down.

I kind of joked to myself, "Jeez, why didn't Laettner get it? What the heck's going on here?" I told Bobby he should have dumped it to me. But you can't always demand the ball for the last shot. It's a team game, and Bobby got a great shot. I forced myself to move on to the next play.

(With the game tied in overtime and the shot clock running down, Laettner hit a shot from the left side of the foul line that was very much like the one he hit two years earlier to beat Connecticut.)

It was just a little closer and I thought I got fouled on the play. I felt the contact, so I just threw it up. But the ref didn't call the foul, and luckily the ball went in. That was my lucky shot of the day.

(Jamal Mashburn converted a three-point play at the other end to give Kentucky a one-point lead, but with 15 seconds left, he fouled Laettner.)

My confidence level as I went to the free-throw line was very good. I remember thinking if I make these, we go back to the Final Four.

I was shocked when Sean Woods made that shot (to give Kentucky a 102-101 lead). The only thing I know is that I didn't warn Bobby of the pick soon enough. I jumped out on Woods and made him take a tough shot. He banked it in from straight on—just over my outstretched fingers.

The smartest thing we did was call timeout right away. The clock didn't stop on a made basket in those days. But if you look at the tape you can see Bobby and I calling for a timeout just as the shot goes in. That gave us a chance (with 2.1 seconds left).

I was shaken. I was mad. But I knew it was not over. We had been involved in a lot of crazy things during my career. When we got to the huddle, Coach K instilled us with his confidence. That's what a leader's supposed to do.

We all knew we had practiced a play for this situation. We called it the "Home Run Play." As we broke the huddle, I told Grant, "Don't throw a curve like you did last time. Let me get a shot off." He threw a great pass this time.

I would have defended it like Kentucky did (with no defender on the inbounds passer, but two defenders on Laettner). I would have made those two guys play better defense. They didn't contest the pass or the shot. They didn't want to foul. I guarantee you that the last thing their coach said as they broke the huddle was, "Don't foul!"

I remember saying to myself that with two seconds left, I didn't have to catch it and fling it up there. Two seconds was enough time to set my feet, get my balance, make a little fake . . .

(Duke assistant coach Pete) Gaudet and I worked all the time on drills for last-play situations. At the end of practice, I would always run to the end of the court, run back and take the final shot. I was prepared for that situation.

When it went in, there was unbelievable pandemonium. The very first thing I thought as I turned around and started screaming was, "I can't believe God is good enough to allow me to make another shot like this to go to the Final Four. For God to allow me to be that successful . . . I never wanted anything more than to be in big games and to hit the big shot."

I knew God was good. I didn't know he was *that* good.

THE AFTERMATH

Laettner's performance that Saturday in Philadelphia is the stuff of legends. He finished with 31 points, hitting 10 of 10 shots from the floor (including a three-pointer) and 10 of 10 from the foul line.

He also added seven rebounds, three assists, two steals, and a blocked shot.

"I saw Bill Walton play in the game when he hit 21 of 22 shots from the floor [in the 1973 national title game against Memphis]," Laettner said. "That was a great individual accomplishment. But the Kentucky-Duke game was better. There were so many lead changes, so many incredible shots. When I watch the tape, I forget I was there. I see Mashburn. I see Sean Woods. Then I pop up."

Laettner's performance was not without controversy. Midway though the second half, he reacted to a hard foul from Kentucky's Aminu Timberlake by putting his foot on the chest of the fallen Timberlake in a gesture that has come to be characterized by Kentucky fans as "Laettner's stomp." But the gesture was hardly that—Timberlake bounced off the floor laughing and clapping as Laettner was assessed a technical foul.

The 103-102 victory propelled Duke to the 1992 Final Four in Minneapolis, making Laettner the first (and still only) player in college basketball history to start in four Final Fours. The Blue Devil star couldn't match his Philadelphia heroics against Indiana in the semifinals or against Michigan in the finals, but he doesn't find that surprising.

"That's what happens when you have a game like that," he said. "The next time out, the team you're playing is going to focus on shutting you down. I was double- and triple-teamed against Indiana and Michigan. That's why I had so many turnovers, trying to get the ball to my open teammates.

"Minneapolis showed the strength of our team. Other guys stepped up."

Indeed, Hurley was named the Final Four MVP, although it's interesting that Laettner—despite all the defensive attention—was Duke's leading scorer against Michigan with 19 points as the Blue Devils became the first team since UCLA in 1973 to successfully defend its national title.

Individual accolades poured in for Laettner. He was the consensus national player of the year and won the McKelvin Award as the ACC's best athlete. He finished his career with 2,460 points—the second highest total in Duke history at the time and still the sixth highest total in ACC history.

He capped his collegiate career with a singular honor—he was the sole college player accepted to play on the 1992 U.S. Olympic Dream team. He joined Michael Jordan, Larry Bird, Magic Johnson, Karl

Malone, Patrick Ewing, and Charles Barkley on the gold medal-winning team in Barcelona.

REFLECTIONS ON DUKE

Laettner was the third player taken in the 1992 NBA draft—just behind the two centers he had bested in college matchups—LSU's Shaquille O'Neal and Georgetown's Alonzo Mourning.

His career got off to a great start as he made the all-rookie team in 1993 after averaging 18.2 points, 8.7 rebounds, and 2.8 assists for the Minnesota Timberwolves. He averaged between 16 and 18 points in each of his first six seasons, eventually reaching the all-star game in 1997, when he averaged 18.1 points and 8.8 rebounds for the Atlanta Hawks.

His career suffered a setback the next off-season when he tore an Achilles tendon—an injury that never really healed. Laettner played another eight seasons (13 in all), but never regained his all-star level of play. Ironically, he ended his career in 2005 as a backup frontcourt player for the Miami Heat—sharing time with O'Neal and Mourning, his two college rivals and the two players drafted ahead of him in 1992.

Laettner's post-NBA career involves a series of economic ventures in partnership with Brian Davis, his roommate at Duke. Their enterprise includes several projects in Durham, along with efforts to purchase a number of sports franchises—including the NBA's Memphis Grizzlies. The two former players have also been prime benefactors of the Duke basketball program, contributing $2 million to endow a scholarship and help fund the construction of a new practice facility.

Laettner remains one of the most recognizable players ever to perform for the Blue Devils. He's also the Duke star opponents most love to hate—a feeling that persists to this day. Just last March, when Laettner was introduced to the crowd at the St. Pete Forum in Tampa, Florida, during the 2007 ACC Tournament, he was greeted by a chorus of boos. Typically, Laettner responded by blowing a kiss toward the booing fans.

He doesn't mind playing the villain.

"You have to know where it's coming from," he said of the boos. "If the people at Duke didn't love me after spilling my heart and soul for them, then that would bother me. If the boos are coming from the

Kentucky people, the UConn people, the UNC people, that's okay. I was trying to make them hate me. It was my job to beat them."

It's safe to say that few Duke players have been as loved and admired by Blue Devil fans as the "preppie" from the blue-collar neighborhood in New York. And it's equally safe to suggest that the hatred Laettner's name evokes from Duke's rivals is evidence of how much he tortured them.

CHAPTER 12

JIM SPANARKEL

It's unlikely that any other great player at Duke University arrived on campus with such little fanfare.

Jim Spanarkel grew up in Jersey City as the son of a cereal salesman, the middle child of a large family. He was a successful athlete at Hudson Catholic High School, starting for four seasons on both the varsity basketball and baseball teams. But he was not a prep All-American like his Hudson Catholic teammate Mike O'Koren, who was a year younger, two inches taller, and far more coveted by college coaches.

"Mike and I went back a long way," Spanarkel said. "We had competed against each other since the fifth grade and played together [at Hudson Catholic] for three years. We have a special bond. Even when he went to [North] Carolina, we were friendly competitors."

The two future rivals had grown up together on Jersey City's playgrounds and in the city's excellent CYO leagues. O'Koren was a natural with the physical gifts that would make the 6-foot-7 forward one of the nation's premier recruits in 1976. Spanarkel lacked O'Koren's physical explosiveness. He didn't jump particularly well. He was slow and he ran with a peculiar pigeon-toed gait. Few coaches could look at the awkward 6-foot-5 Spanarkel and see a college star.

Luckily for Duke, coach Bill Foster proved to be the exception. Trying to rebuild a program that had fallen to the bottom of the ACC in the mid-1970s, Foster was desperate for talent. He also got a chance to see Spanarkel in the summer camp he ran with former Temple coach Harry Litwack in the Pennsylvania Pocono Mountains. It was there Foster realized that, although Spanarkel's foot speed was suspect, his hand speed was extraordinary. He saw a fundamentally sound player with a rare combination of intelligence and toughness.

Spanarkel had scholarship offers from Ohio University, Holy Cross, and William & Mary. Wake Forest was also interested, but Foster had a Hall of Fame ace up his recruiting sleeve.

"I played four years of high school baseball, and at the time, it was a tossup whether I liked baseball or basketball better," Spanarkel said. "Duke's good academics also helped, but what really sold me was that Duke offered me the chance to play both sports. The most interesting part is that I got to play for Enos Slaughter."

The Hall of Fame outfielder, most famous for his dash from first base to score the winning run for the St. Louis Cardinals in the 1946 World Series, had retired after his playing days to his Roxboro, North Carolina, farm—just about half an hour north of Duke's campus. When former Pittsburgh Pirate relief pitcher Tom Butters gave up the coaching job to join the school's administration (eventually becoming Duke's athletics director), he lured Slaughter out of retirement to coach the Blue Devils.

Spanarkel, a right-handed pitcher of considerable promise, ended up playing two springs for Slaughter's Diamond Devils. It was easy for him to make the transition from basketball to baseball when the hoops season ended in the first week of March. It was only when— thanks to his help—the basketball team began extending its season deep into the spring that Spanarkel gave up his baseball dreams.

THE SETTING

Spanarkel didn't really understand just how far Duke basketball had fallen in the years before his arrival.

Less than a decade after Vic Bubas' glory days, the Blue Devils had become an ACC punching bag. In 1973, Duke suffered its first losing season in 46 years under former Bubas assistant Bucky Waters. Foster, brought in after successful stints at Rutgers and Utah, managed to squeeze out a 13-13 record in 1975, but that was an illusion created by a soft nonconference schedule. His first Duke team was a pitiful 2-10 in conference play and had little going for it beyond talented guard Tate Armstrong.

Jim Spanarkel shows off his shooting form—and his modest elevation—against North Carolina.

"You've got to understand, that was before cable and the game of the week," Spanarkel said. "I didn't really think about the program when I signed. Maybe I was a little naïve, but I wasn't thinking about going to a school to lead them to a championship or anything like that. I was just grateful at that time to be going to school."

And Foster was grateful to have Spanarkel in the backcourt with Armstrong. Even the Blue Devil coach was surprised by how well his unheralded recruit played as a freshman in the ultra-competitive ACC. Spanarkel averaged 13.3 points and shot 54.8 percent from the floor and was voted the inaugural ACC rookie of the year. Unfortunately, the backcourt combo of Armstrong, who averaged 24.2 points a game, and Spanarkel wasn't enough to lift Duke out of the ACC basement.

Spanarkel knew he had to get better.

"My freshman year, I was carrying 15 pounds of baby fat," he said. "Always growing up, I had been big and chunky. Bill Foster and George Lehmann [a former ABA star who traveled the country as a part-time shooting instructor] told me that if I had aspirations of getting better, I had to lose weight. I had never thought about conditioning to get better. I lost that extra weight and it not only made me quicker, but I had better stamina."

The new-and-improved Spanarkel would play on a better Duke team in his sophomore season. Foster had added another piece to the puzzle, landing 6-foot-11 Mike Gminski out of Monroe, Connecticut, to provide an inside anchor to balance his two gifted guards. For a time, it looked like the Duke program had turned the corner. The young Blue Devils followed a tough loss to Wake Forest in the opener with 10 straight wins, including an upset of No. 15 N.C. State in Greensboro and a stunning 81-78 victory in Knoxville against a ranked Tennessee team featuring Bernard King and Ernie Grunfeld. On a cold, stormy night in January, Duke traveled to Charlottesville, Virginia, and upset Virginia in overtime to improve to 11-3 on the season.

However, that proved to be a costly victory. Late in the game, Armstrong fell and broke his wrist, and the senior guard, who was averaging 28 points a game, would not play again for the rest of the season.

"That was a turning point in terms of my development," Spanarkel said. "Tate was playing very well and losing him was terrible from the team's perspective. It turned out to be good for me individually. I handled the ball more and had to take over the backcourt. It made me a better player."

Spanarkel finished the season as a second-team All-ACC pick after averaging 19.2 points and 5.4 rebounds. But Duke struggled down the stretch without Armstrong, losing a series of heartbreaking games to finish 14-13 and 2-10 in the league. It was the team's first winning season since 1972, but it was hardly the turnaround that Foster or Spanarkel had hoped for after that torrid start.

But help was on the way. The night after a gut-wrenching loss to Maryland, Foster received a verbal commitment from Gene Banks, a Philadelphia schoolboy star who was as celebrated as Spanarkel was obscure. Within 48 hours of Banks' public announcement, Duke sold out season tickets for the 1977-78 season.

"Getting Gene gave us some hope," Spanarkel said. "It showed people we were moving in the right direction."

Indeed, that was obvious to the most casual observers. Although Duke had finished last or tied for last in the ACC for four straight seasons, the 1977-78 Blue Devils were picked to finish second in the media's preseason poll. And with Banks joined in the starting lineup by fellow freshman forward Kenny Dennard—a fun-loving bruiser from tiny King, North Carolina—Duke suddenly had the biggest, most talented frontline in the ACC. Spanarkel, playing the best basketball of his career, anchored the backcourt, sharing time with a pair of transfers—John Harrell from North Carolina Central University and Bob Bender, who owned an NCAA championship ring as a member of Indiana's 1976 title team.

After a promising early-season performance, the Blue Devils caught fire as February turned into March.

"Now, when I do NCAA Tournament broadcasts [for CBS], I always point out that the teams that do best are those that get hot just before the tournament," Spanarkel said. "That's what happened to us."

Duke won five of six to close the regular season, losing only a thriller to No. 8 UNC in Chapel Hill on Phil Ford's senior day. The Blue Devils won three games in Greensboro to claim the school's first ACC title since 1966, then stampeded through the East Regionals to reach the Final Four in St. Louis.

Spanarkel, Gminski, and Banks all scored 20-plus points as Duke edged Notre Dame in the semifinals, then repeated that feat in a hard-fought 90-86 loss to Kentucky in the title game. The defeat was disappointing, but hardly crushing for a team that started two freshmen (Banks and Dennard), two sophomores (Gminski and Harrell), and one junior (Spanarkel). As the Blue Devil players accepted their second-place trophies, Duke fans in the Checkerdome chanted, "We'll be back."

But it wasn't that easy. Although Duke started the 1978-79 season as everybody's No. 1 team, the senior captain felt that something was missing.

"We may have gotten caught up a little bit in what we did before," Spanarkel said. "We had such great chemistry my junior year. I'm not sure we ever got that back, especially after New York."

New York was the site of one of the most disastrous weekends in Duke basketball history. The Blue Devils arrived at Madison Square Garden just after Christmas unbeaten and ranked No. 1 in the nation. But in the opener of the ECAC Holiday Festival, Duke blew a big lead and lost in overtime to Ohio State. The next night, Duke once again blew a big lead and fell to St. John's.

The two nightmarish defeats cast a pall over what had been expected to be a magical season. Even though the team fought back to win 10 of its next 11 games, the aura of invincibility was gone. A loss to North Carolina in Chapel Hill left the Devils chasing their rivals in the ACC regular-season race. Late losses at home to unranked Pittsburgh and on the road to Maryland and Clemson, seemed to indicate that the season was coming apart.

The loss to the Tigers in Littlejohn was especially disconcerting. Clemson, whose coach was also named Bill Foster, seized an early lead, then spread the floor. The big, strong Blue Devils—more comfortable in a zone than chasing a three-guard lineup all over the floor—never even made a run at the Tigers.

The lopsided 70-49 loss left Duke at 19-6 and 8-3 in the ACC heading into the regular-season finale against No. 4 North Carolina (21-4, 9-2 ACC) in Cameron Indoor Stadium. It would be the third meeting of the season for the two old rivals—Duke had beaten the Tar Heels 78-68 in Greensboro to win the Big Four Championship back in December, while UNC had won 74-68 in Chapel Hill. A Duke victory would not only give the Blue Devils a share of the ACC title, but would go a long way toward erasing the frustration that had haunted the team since New York.

"It's been building and building like a snowball," Spanarkel told reporters during the days leading up to the showdown. "Nothing could make it any bigger."

Not even the fact that it was to be Spanarkel's last game in Cameron? That circumstance was very much on the mind of UNC coach Dean Smith, who recalled Phil Ford's heroic performance in his Senior Day game a year earlier.

"He better not do to us what Phil Ford did to them," Smith told reporters. "Tell Jimmy not to be a hero."

THE GAME OF MY LIFE
DUKE VS. NORTH CAROLINA, FEBRUARY 24, 1979
BY JIM SPANARKEL

Walking the campus in the days before the game, you could tell that everybody was ready for the game. On Thursday, 70 hours before tip off, the fans were ready. It really gave us a charge. The buildup was special. That was the game when the camp-out routine (students erecting tents outside Cameron to get the best seats) really started.

For me, there was a real buildup of emotion. Being recognized by the students and the ones up above makes Senior Day really special. I did a lot of reflecting on my career. My family was there—my parents, my three brothers, and my sister Sharon had driven down from New Jersey. My other sister, Mary Beth, was in Duke Medical School, so she was there for all my games. I had a handful of buddies from Jersey who came down, and that was very special for me.

Cameron is such a special place. I used to come out early before the official warm-ups and just shoot around and interact with the students who would be in there. I loved to be in that building. I loved all the student antics. I always got a kick out of the fans. On that particular day, a charge ran through my body when I realized, "This will be the last time I run out on this floor for a game."

We expected a normal game. We had no suspicion before the game that they would hold the ball. When we realized what was happening, it was kind of like a mixed reaction. I respect Dean Smith and understand that when he held the ball, he was trying to take momentum from us. But I would think when you're No. 4 in the nation, you'd want to lace it up and play.

They only took two shots [in the first half] and both were air balls. I like to believe that's when the "Air Ball!" chant began. The frustration level of our fans was really something, and when we went in at half up 7-0, there was even more craziness.

I understand that they didn't want to play against our zone. The one thing we had established was our matchup zone. Because of our size and our quickness on the wing, we were able to create a lot of turnovers and run out of it. I can understand trying to pull us out of it, but we had the lead. I think that's where Dean's strategy backfired. It's not like we were leading by 20 points at the half. We were just up seven, but because it was 7-0, it was like they were shocked.

In the second half, they came out and played 20 minutes of normal basketball, head to head. We were dead even. Who knows what it would have been like if they'd played from the beginning.

Both teams scored 40 in the second half. I couldn't tell you how many points I scored. The real satisfaction was winning. The final stats meant nothing. If it had ended up 7-5, I would have been satisfied as long as we had the seven.

After the game, I remember some fans picking me up, but it's really all just a blur. I do remember thinking at the time, it was the biggest rush I'd ever had.

I also recall that after the game somebody asked Mike O'Koren about Smith's strategy, and he said they could have played with us, but Coach Smith was the guy who ordered the delay. O'Koren told me that the next day at practice, Coach Smith handed him ankle weights and a weighted vest and said, "I make the decisions, your job is to play basketball." Then he had him run the steps.

AFTERMATH

Although Spanarkel wasn't worried about stats, he ended up as the game's leading scorer with 17 points on eight-of-nine shooting. Just two of those points came in the all-important first half, but he also made a couple of important defensive plays.

Duke was leading 2-0 after freshman Vince Taylor scored the opening basket. That's when UNC first unveiled its stall tactics. The Tar Heels held the ball for 13 minutes before Spanarkel intercepted a Rich Yonaker pass. Gminski hit one of two free throws at the other end before UNC resumed its stall. When Yonaker air-balled a 10-foot jumper with four minutes left in the half, Duke converted it into a fast break that was capped by Spanarkel's feed to Gminski for a dunk. Moments later, Spanarkel helped trap Yonaker in the corner and the ill-fated UNC center threw the ball away. Duke then held the ball against UNC's zone for the final three minutes of the half before Spanarkel capped the scoring with a short jumper with three seconds left. Dave Colescott's midcourt heave at the buzzer missed everything.

"We thought the frustration of the Clemson game would make them chase us," Smith told reporters. "But they didn't choose to chase. The zone is the strength of their defense and we wanted them to play man-to-man."

Although the second half ended up 40-all, leaving Duke with a 47-40 victory, it wasn't really that close. The Blue Devils built a 15-point lead early in the half and were never threatened down the stretch.

After the game, Spanarkel gave credit to Foster for countering Smith's tactics.

"Our game plan was to get the lead so they couldn't go to Four Corners," he told reporters. "When we got the first basket, I said, 'Heck, I'll take a 2-0 win.' But they stuck with [the delay]. I think Coach Foster was the key. It was his decision to sit back. It was a gusty move on his part here before the home crowd. He's underrated as a coach."

Duke and North Carolina were fated to meet again exactly one week later in the ACC Tournament championship game. Unfortunately for the Blue Devils, hours after their semifinal victory over N.C. State, starting point guard Bob Bender had to be rushed to the hospital with acute appendicitis. The short-handed Devils lost 71-63 in a tournament title game unmarred by any stall tactics.

It appeared that the two rivals were headed for yet another meeting—it would have been the fifth that season—when the NCAA Selection Committee unexpectedly seeded UNC No. 1 and Duke No. 2 in the East Regional. But the potential showdown was spoiled on what has come to be known as "Black Sunday," when in front of a partisan Tobacco Road crowd in N.C. State's Reynolds Coliseum, Penn upset North Carolina, and St. John's—for the second time that season—edged Duke.

REFLECTIONS ON DUKE

The loss to St. John's in Raleigh was a sad end to Spanarkel's Duke career, but it couldn't tarnish his four-year accomplishment. The little-known prospect from New Jersey had been the centerpiece of Duke's basketball revival under Bill Foster.

"When I look back on what I was trying to accomplish, I knew I wasn't as physically gifted as some other players, so I had to try and outprepare and outwork them," Spanarkel said. "I think the Duke fans recognized that it didn't come as easily for me as for others and they appreciated that. I think that game against Carolina my senior year brought all four of my years at Duke together. I thought about where we had been and how far we had come.

"The Carolina rivalry was special. I played against guys like Phil Ford, Mitch Kupchak, Walter Davis, Al Wood, Dudley Bradley—a bunch of pros. Carolina guys were always great players. And while we didn't establish the rivalry with Carolina, we did our share in keeping the rivalry going."

Indeed, Duke lost 16 of 17 games to its rival between 1972 and 1977. But starting in 1978, the Blue Devils won three of Spanarkel's last six games against the Tar Heels. He played on teams that were 28-28 in his first two seasons and 49-15 in his final two. Nobody enjoyed Duke's hard-won success more than the kid from Jersey City.

"I think before you can enjoy winning, you have to understand the pain of losing," Spanarkel said.

The once unheralded recruit ended his career as the first 2,000-point scorer in Duke history, although he'd be passed by teammates Gminski and Banks in the next two seasons. He was the 16th player picked in the 1979 NBA draft, going to Philadelphia in the first round. A year later, he was selected by Dallas in the NBA expansion draft and enjoyed his two best seasons for the Mavericks, averaging 14.4 and 10.1 points in successive seasons.

The former Duke star retired from the NBA after five seasons, but has remained close to the game through a variety of broadcast jobs. His fulltime occupation is as an investment advisor for Merrill Lynch.

CHAPTER 13

MIKE GMINSKI

Mike Gminski, who would become one of the youngest stars in Duke basketball history, actually got a late start playing organized basketball.

Growing up in suburban Connecticut, the future "G-man" was plagued by allergy issues as a child and didn't take to the hardwood until he was an eighth grader. Five years later, he would be starting—and starring—in the ACC.

"I played some basketball in the park as I was growing up—just pickup ball," Gminski explained. "I was a much better baseball player as a kid. But I just kept growing and I was 6-9 by the time I was a freshman in high school. That was kind of pushing the envelope for baseball."

But it made the youngster a prime basketball prospect, especially when coupled with his innate intelligence. Gminski quickly blossomed into a basketball prodigy, averaging 15 points as a freshman at Masuk High School, then 30 as a sophomore, and 41 as a junior.

"Monroe was a small town and we played in a small league," Gminski recalled. "The competition wasn't that great. We never lost a league game."

Still, Gminski's spectacular stats and his obvious physical skills marked him as a top prospect from a very early age. Many college coaches saw Gminski as a major recruiting target in the prep Class of 1977. What they didn't know was that they were shooting at a moving target—Gminski wasn't going to wait for his high school class to graduate.

"I made the decision before my junior year that I'd benefit more from a year as a college freshman than as a senior in high school," he said. "All I had to do to graduate early was to accelerate a couple of English courses."

Gminski didn't consciously keep his plan secret, but only a handful of college coaches found out that he was planning to graduate in the spring of 1976 and not a year later. Maryland's Lefty Driesell always bemoaned the fact that he didn't know Gminski was coming out early—although Gminski remembers Driesell as one of the six coaches he told about his plans.

"I picked six schools that I really liked," Gminski said. "Duke wasn't originally on that list. I contacted North Carolina, South Carolina, William & Mary, Davidson, Maryland, and Notre Dame."

Duke coach Bill Foster, trying to rebuild the shattered Blue Devil program in the mid-1970s, got lucky.

"I went to the Maryland camp in the summer after my sophomore year," Gminski said. "Terry Chili [a little-used Duke center] was a counselor. I happened to have a great camp and he talked to me about Duke. I agreed to let them get in the process."

Even then, Gminski considered himself a strong lean toward Digger Phelps' Notre Dame program. Frank McGuire also offered a strong lure at South Carolina.

"Coach McGuire was so charismatic," Gminski said. "If I had just liked Columbia better . . . "

In contrast to Columbia, Gminski liked the Duke campus at first sight.

"I visited in October, during homecoming," he said. "I fell in love with Duke that weekend. I was there on the same weekend with Mike O'Koren and Jim Graziano. Jim was a much higher rated center and it wasn't easy to commit knowing he might come. But I do a lot of things by feel and Duke just seemed like the right place for me.

"Twenty-five years later, I can look back and say it was one of the best decisions I ever made."

THE SETTING

Gminski arrived on campus in the fall of 1976 at a low point in Duke's basketball fortunes. The Blue Devils were coming off a 13-14

Mike Gminski launches a foul-line jumper over Wake Forest center Larry Harrison.

season and a last-place ACC finish. The glory days of Vic Bubas seemed very far in the past—Duke hadn't finished with a winning ACC record since 1971 and had not been ranked in the final AP top 20 since 1968.

But Gminski did find a couple of quality players on campus—senior guard Tate Armstrong, who earned first-team All-ACC honors on that last-place team in 1976, and sophomore swing man Jim Spanarkel, the inaugural ACC rookie of the year.

"Jimmy was a big reason I came," Gminski said. "It proved to me that Coach Foster could recruit."

The addition of the 6-foot-11 Gminski to balance the backcourt of Armstrong and Spanarkel would give Foster an impressive foundation to build upon. Of course, nobody expected the 17-year-old Gminski to be the immediate force he was in fact to become.

Actually, to be accurate, it wasn't quite immediate. Making his debut against Wake Forest veteran Larry Harrison in the Big Four Tournament, Gminski showed his youth in a loss to the Deacons.

"It was a disaster," he said. "I was awful."

But one night later, he provided evidence of what was to come. He scored just eight points, but pulled down 14 rebounds and blocked five shots as Duke edged No. 15-ranked N.C. State 84-82. A week later, Gminski was a force as Duke traveled to Knoxville and upset No. 15-ranked Tennessee—the team led by Bernard King and Ernie Grunfield, which had taken N. C. State's spot in the rankings.

Duke reeled off 10 straight wins as Gminski blossomed in the middle, while Armstrong and Spanarkel provided the firepower on the perimeter. The Blue Devils lost a hard-fought game at No. 5 North Carolina, but bounced back for an overtime victory at Virginia that snapped a 27-game ACC road-losing streak.

Gminski scored 20 points that night in support of Armstrong, who poured in 33 of his own. Unfortunately, the senior guard suffered a broken wrist late in the game and wasn't able to play again that season.

"I really believe that my freshman year could have been really special if Tate had not gotten hurt," Gminski said. "I'm still heartsick the way it worked out."

The loss of Armstrong proved too much for Duke to overcome. While his scoring was missed, his role as the team's primary ball-handler proved even more irreplaceable. Junior Steve Gray, a fine athlete who was offered a number of football scholarships on the West Coast (and the uncle of future Pitt standout Aaron Gray), tried to step in at point guard, but he couldn't cope with the demands of the job.

"Steve was playing out of position," Gminski said. "And without Tate, it was just too much for me and Jimmy to overcome."

Duke ended the season with a 3-10 tailspin, once again finishing at the bottom of the ACC standings. Gminski averaged 15.3 points and 10.7 rebounds, becoming stronger and stronger as the season progressed. He ended the year on a personal high note—convincingly outplaying future pro Wayne "Tree" Rollins in the first round of the ACC Tournament loss. Gminski had 21 points and 16 rebounds in the loss (compared to eight points and nine rebounds for the 7-foot-1 Rollins). Spanarkel added 23 points, but no other Duke player scored more than five points. Clemson put five players in double figures to pull out an 82-74 victory.

Clearly, Gminski, and Spanarkel needed help. And, luckily, it was on the way. Foster struck recruiting gold that spring, landing 6-foot-7 Gene Banks of West Philadelphia High School, the nation's top recruit and that city's top-rated prospect since Wilt Chamberlain.

"Gene was probably the most heralded player Duke had ever recruited," Gminski recalled. "That was a reason to hope and look forward."

More reinforcements were also on the way, including ebullient freshman forward Kenny Dennard from tiny King, North Carolina, and two transfer point guards—former prep All-American Bob Bender, who left Indiana after playing on the Hoosiers' 1976 national championship team, and unheralded John Harrell, a Durham native who had started as a freshman for Division II North Carolina Central University. That summer Gminski got to know his future teammates in a series of pickup games.

"I remember the scene," Gminski said. "I don't think we knew how good we could be, but as I looked around, I remember thinking, now we can compete with N.C. State, Maryland, and North Carolina."

Competing with the Tar Heels was the ultimate goal for the Blue Devils of that era. Whereas Duke had finished either last or tied for last in the ACC for four straight seasons, UNC was working on a streak of 11 straight years of finishing either first or second in the league. Dean Smith's juggernaut had recorded 10 straight top 20 finishes and had beaten the Devils 15 of the last 16 head-to-head meetings, including the last seven in a row.

"We had not been competitive [with UNC] for a long time," Gminski said. "It was just brutal."

Early in the 1977-78 season, UNC made it eight straight (and 16 of 17) in the rivalry, dominating the second half to beat Duke 79-66 in the Big Four Tournament in Greensboro. Gminski and Spanarkel combined for 46 of the team's 66 points, but neither Banks (nine points), Dennard (four points), nor Bender (not yet eligible) were ready to contribute. Harrell played 25 minutes at the point, but he had four turnovers, no assists, and just two points.

Clearly, the young Duke team had a lot of growing up to do.

That process started one night after the UNC loss, when the Blue Devils knocked off No. 18 Wake Forest in the Big Four consolation game. It continued throughout December as Duke suffered a bitter loss at Southern Cal (on a mistaken officials' call that resulted in a letter of apology from the Pac-10 director of officials), and then rolled up a number of lopsided wins. Foster's burgeoning team opened the New Year with an impressive win against Virginia Tech in Roanoke, followed by a 10-point victory over Maryland in College Park.

The team was coming together as evidenced by a stunning 107-85 victory at Clemson as Gminski (28 points), Banks (23 points), and Spanarkel (20 points), all clicked, along with the newly eligible Bender, who teamed with Harrell to give Duke a combined 19 points from the point guard position.

"Bobby had played in the national championship game," Gminski said. "He brought a lot of intangibles. He had been a scoring point guard in high school, but he sacrificed a lot of that to fit in. He wasn't the only one. That team had a lot of upperclassmen who sacrificed. My backup, Scott Goetsch, did that. Harold Morrison was a senior forward who lost his starting job [to Banks]. The upperclassmen were great—they really pushed up in practice. The chemistry was good. I guess while you're winning, those things are going to be good."

Duke was winning. The Blue Devils, downtrodden so long, returned from Clemson with an 11-3 record—exactly the same as the 1977 team posted before its collapse.

And waiting back in Durham was No. 2 North Carolina, hoping to send the Blue Devils into yet another tailspin.

THE GAME OF MY LIFE
DUKE VS. NORTH CAROLINA, JANUARY 14, 1978
BY MIKE GMINSKI

That Clemson win was a big confidence builder. We knew how tough it was to win on the road in the ACC. And Clemson was tough in Littlejohn (Coliseum). They were a terrible road team in those days, but really tough at home. They were big and athletic. Beating them there was a big step on our learning curve.

I don't remember thinking about Carolina on the bus ride back, just that the (five-hour) ride went a lot faster after the win.

But back on campus there was a lot of anticipation. We felt we really had the opportunity to beat them. That may have been the first time students were sleeping outside Cameron. They didn't have tents in those days, but they were lined up for days, waiting to get in and get the best seats.

As I think back, I remind myself of how lucky I was that I got to play in Cameron. The more away from it I get—and the more places I broadcast from—the more I appreciate it. I never worried about getting up for a game at home. All I had to do was walk out for the pregame shootaround and the crowd would get you up.

I think there were three levels of intensity in Cameron: non-conference games, conference games, and the Carolina game. The intensity level would get so high that I'd have to bring myself down a bit to keep from getting over hyped. There were times when I almost felt like I had played a half before the game even started.

We didn't have any special game plan for Carolina that day. There was a sense that we couldn't stop (UNC All-America point guard) Phil (Ford), but we had to keep everybody else quiet.

UNC used Jeff Wolf and Geff Crompton at center against me. (The 6-foot-11, 350-pound) Crompton was the most talented, but he wasn't in very good shape. Really, if it was just a half-court game, he would have been one of the best big men ever. He was amazingly quick for a guy that size. He just had troubles getting up and down the court.

I did most of my scoring down low, although I remember hitting a couple of baseline jumpers. Both teams shot incredibly well in the first half. Both were over 60 percent. It was a close game (UNC led 47-46 at the break). The locker room was calm. We had a sense that we had to tighten up defensively in the second half.

Coach Foster could be emotional, but he could also be very subtle. I remember a game against LaSalle in the Spectrum. After the halftime warm-ups, I like to go over and sit on the bench for a minute or so and gather myself. He was standing there reading a stat sheet. I had played well offensively, but I had just one rebound. He looked down at me and said very quietly, "One rebound . . . you're having a hell of a game."

But he didn't need to say much (at halftime of the Carolina game). We knew what we had to do. It was a pretty close game for 30 minutes, and then we grabbed control at the 10-minute mark, maybe a little later.

What really stands out in my memory are the last two minutes. We had control, we were going to win, and the anticipation of the crowd was incredible. They just wanted the final seconds to tick off so they could celebrate. The noise! That's the loudest I can ever remember Cameron being.

It seemed to reach a crescendo as I went to the foul line. I just took a second to look around and enjoy the moment. It was an afternoon game and the sun was coming in through the windows (which were painted over in Cameron's 1987-88 remodeling) in these long shafts. It was a surreal scene. The only thing that could have been cornier was if the windows had been stained glass.

I have never forgotten that moment.

When the final buzzer sounded, I saw Bobby (Bender) sprint across the floor and slide into Coach Foster. Students rushed the court. Their exuberance was fun. Most of us lingered on the court awhile to enjoy it. Then we took it into the locker room.

It was a great feeling, but I remember thinking we still had a long way to go. We didn't want to be a flash in the pan. We wanted to validate the win over the rest of the season.

I think that's what we did. That Carolina game was a statement that we were back where we needed to be. Every young team—every new team—has a game where that realization takes place. That was ours.

THE AFTERMATH

Gminski enjoyed one of his greatest individual performances in Duke's 92-84 victory. The 6-foot-11 sophomore scored 29 points, pulled down 10 rebounds, and blocked four shots. He hit 12 of 15 from the floor and all five of his free throw attempts.

Spanarkel added 23 points, Banks had 15, and Bender contributed 11 points and four assists as Duke found the balance that was missing six weeks earlier. The Blue Devils also seemed to find the perfect chemistry that would carry the 1978 team to unimaginable heights.

"Everybody talked about how young we were—and we were young," Gminski said. "But we did have a lot of upperclassmen on that team who didn't play a lot. They did a lot to make the chemistry work. I remember the first time we got ranked, the upperclassmen really pushed us in practice. The second unit just wore us out. When we returned to the locker room, Harold Morrison had written on the chalkboard, 'Duke White [the starters] No. 10, Duke Blue [the subs] No. 6.' I've always believed that great teams were great practice teams."

And after the victory over North Carolina, Duke did become a great team, winning 12 of 14 down the stretch, losing only to what Gminski described as "superhuman" efforts down the stretch by UNC's Ford and Kentucky's Jack "Goose" Givens.

Ford scored a career-high 34 points in his senior-day game to give UNC an 87-83 victory in the rematch game, which was the regular-season finale for both teams. But that close loss did little to slow Duke's momentum. The Blue Devils knocked off Clemson, Maryland, and Wake Forest the next week in Greensboro to claim the school's first ACC title in 11 years. After a close call in the NCAA opener against Rhode Island in Charlotte, Duke defeated Penn and Villanova in the East Regionals in Providence, Rhode Island, to reach the Final Four.

The magical run lasted one more game in St. Louis as Gminski (29 points), Banks (22 points), and Spanarkel (20 points) were all sharp in a semifinal victory over Notre Dame. The Devils' big three all topped 20 points again in the championship game, but that wasn't enough to overcome a 41-point performance by Kentucky's Givens, who shredded Duke's 2-3 zone with a barrage of medium-range jump shots.

Even after the loss, Gminski and his teammates weren't crushed by the defeat.

"We were so young, we thought it was our birthright to be back," he said. "We didn't have that sense of immediacy that Kentucky had. They felt like they *had* to win that game."

But Gminski and his young teammates were to learn that success is never guaranteed. The 1978-79 Blue Devils boasted five returning starters off the NCAA runner-ups, but never recaptured the magical chemistry that made the '78 Blue Devils so special.

"Going through a season like that changes you," Gminski said. "We were ranked No. 1 in preseason. We were THE game for everybody we played. Privately, we might have read our press clippings too much."

It wasn't a bad season—nothing like the horrid years before 1978. Duke beat UNC in the regular season finale to win a share of the

ACC regular season title. Gminski, who averaged 18.8 points and 9.2 rebounds a game, was voted as the league's MVP. The Blue Devils reached the ACC title game against North Carolina, but on the morning of the title game, Bender was rushed to Duke Hospital with a case of appendicitis. The Tar Heels broke open a close game late and pulled away for a 71-63 victory over the shorthanded Devils.

Duke was even more shorthanded a week later when the Devils opened NCAA play against St. John's in Raleigh's Reynolds Coliseum. Not only was Bender still sidelined, but also Dennard had suffered a sprained ankle in a late night pickup game and was on the bench in street clothes. Even worse, Gminski was suffering from a mild case of food poisoning, and though he played, he was not near 100 percent.

Duke's 80-78 loss to St. John's that afternoon, coupled with UNC's loss to Penn in the first game of the doubleheader, entered ACC lore as "Black Sunday."

"I talked about the frustration of my freshman year, when Tate got hurt . . . I felt the same thing [in 1979]," Gminski said. "If we had just gotten by that game and gotten healthy, I would liked our chances in the Final Four that year. I would have liked to compete against Magic [Johnson] and [Larry] Bird."

Gminski's senior year was also a frustrating experience. Although Duke climbed to No. 1 in the polls after a 12-0 start that included wins over No. 2 Kentucky and No. 6 North Carolina, the season began to unravel as the Devils were staggered by a series of key injuries. Duke lost four straight games in early February and ended the regular season with a 25-point loss to North Carolina in Chapel Hill.

But just when it looked like Duke basketball was about to return to the mediocrity of the pre-1978 years, the Devils found a spark and on successive nights in the ACC Tournament in Greensboro, knocked off No. 3 seed N.C. State, No. 2 seed North Carolina (the 14-point win coming one week after the 25-point loss—a 39-point swing in a six day span), and then edged No. 1-seeded Maryland 73-72 on Gminski's follow shot in the closing seconds.

Duke followed up that three-day run with a strong showing in the NCAA Tournament. After beating Penn in the first round, the Blue Devils took on No. 4 Kentucky on the Wildcats' home court in Lexington, Kentucky, and beat Sam Bowie, Kyle Macy, and company 55-44. Gminski, who had 17 points and eight rebounds, thoroughly outplayed Bowie (two points, three rebounds).

Unfortunately, Duke's second magical postseason run in three years ended two days later, when Purdue's Joe Barry Carroll outplayed

Gminski, and the Boilermakers earned the ticket to the Final Four with a 68-60 victory in the regional title game.

Nevertheless, Duke's strong finish left Gminski with a much better feeling about his final year at Duke.

"Yeah, it salvaged the season," he said. "If we had not finished that way, I think it would have left a bad taste in my mouth."

REFLECTIONS ON DUKE

Gminski finished his career as the leading scorer, rebounder, and shot blocker in Duke history. Although he's since been passed by Johnny Dawkins, Christian Laettner, and J.J. Redick in career scoring, and by Shelden Williams in rebounding and blocked shots, the G-man still ranks No. 7 in ACC history in career points (2,323), No. 7 in rebounds (1,242), and No. 6 in blocked shots (345).

Gminski also became just the second Duke player to have his jersey retired when his No. 43 was raised to the rafters in a ceremony before his final home game on February 20, 1980.

Up to that point, Dick Groat was the only Duke player to be so honored. Former Blue Devil athletic director Eddie Cameron had blocked Vic Bubas' attempts to retire the numbers of his greatest players. But Cameron was gone in 1980, and the new AD, Tom Butters, approved Foster's request to retire Gminski's number. That opened the door for new coach Mike Krzyzewski to honor his future stars and to go back and give belated honors to Bubas-era superstars Art Heyman and Jeff Mullins.

Gminski is more proud of his part in restoring Duke's basketball legacy than in any individual honors. His Blue Devil teams served as the bridge between Bubas' brief dynasty in the 1960s and Krzyzewski's long reign in the last quarter-century. For three seasons, Gminski and company made Duke basketball matter again.

He takes special pride in reviving the great Duke-North Carolina rivalry. The Tar Heels won 16 of 17 in the series before Gminski's landmark game in 1978. UNC would win eight of nine games from Krzyzewski before he got his program off the ground. But in between those two runs, Gminski's Duke teams split 10 games with the Heels evenly—five wins apiece.

"I like to think we re-established the rivalry," he said. "When you played in that game, regardless of the talent level, both teams elevated their game. But there had been an overwhelming talent disparity between Carolina and Duke. We felt [with that 1978 win] that for the first time we were as talented as they were."

Gminski's talent was recognized in the 1980 NBA draft, when he became the No. 7 pick of the New Jersey Nets. The former Duke star would play 14 seasons in the NBA.

"I never thought I'd play 14 years," he said. "My only disappointment is that I never got to the finals. We came close a couple of times in Philadelphia. That's when I got to play with Buck Williams and Charles Barkley. I was a good fit with those guys—I was a high-post center who allowed them to operate down low."

Gminski averaged 11.7 points and 6.9 rebounds for his pro career. He still ranks among the NBA's top 250 all-time scorers and top 100 rebounders. After retirement, he joined the broadcast team for the Charlotte Hornets and spent eight years working NBA games.

Gminski, who still lives in Charlotte, has become the top college basketball analyst for Fox Sports. His job brings him back to Cameron several times each season, and he's seen his former team play some memorable games in that time.

But that first victory over North Carolina in 1978 retains a special place in his memory.

CHAPTER 14

DICK GROAT

Ironically for a young athlete who starred in baseball and basketball, it was a football coach who paved Dick Groat's way from the Pittsburgh suburb of Swissvale to Duke University.

"I wanted to attend Duke because I read an article in *Sport Magazine* that said they played big league baseball at Duke," Groat said.

The Duke baseball coach at that time was Jack Coombs, a former Major League pitcher who had won 31 and 28 games in back-to-back seasons for Connie Mack's Athletics before World War 1. Groat couldn't find a connection to Coombs, but Groat's brother was good friends with Pittsburgh Steelers coach John Michelosen, who was very close to Duke football coach and athletic director Wallace Wade.

"Coach Michelosen contacted Coach Wade and was told, 'We don't give baseball scholarships,'" Groat said. "Coach Michelosen said, 'He plays basketball, too.' Coach Wade asked, 'Is he any good?' [Michelosen answered], 'His brother says he is.'

"Now, I often tell people about that and I wonder out loud if Dean Smith or Mike Krzyzewski ever offered a player a scholarship because his brother said he was good."

It's a good story, but Groat admits that Duke was a bit more careful with its scholarship money than his tale makes it sound. What really happened is that Michelosen's endorsement was enough to earn Groat a tryout. He came to Durham and spent two days scrimmaging against the Blue Devil varsity before head coach Gerry Gerald decided to offer him a scholarship.

Gerard had inherited the Duke program from Eddie Cameron after the 1942 season and he led the Blue Devils to Southern

Conference titles in 1944 and 1946, as well as runner-up spots in 1943 and 1945. It's safe to say that Duke, boasting the finest arena in the Southern Conference, was the league's premier program—until 1947.

That's when Everett Case arrived in Raleigh and changed the basketball landscape on Tobacco Road. His Hoosier Hotshots immediately wrestled basketball superiority from Gerard's Blue Devils. In addition, Case personally changed the plans for N.C. State's new basketball arena, expanding what had been a near carbon copy of Duke's Indoor Stadium into a 12,400-seat monster that would, for many years, be the biggest arena in the South.

When Groat arrived on the Duke campus in the fall of 1948, Case's assault on Southern Conference basketball had just begun. Nobody could foresee the Gray Fox's coming dominance; he would win nine league titles in the next 10 years. Gerard was hoping that Groat would be the weapon that would help him restore the Blue Devils to the top of Tobacco Road's basketball pyramid.

THE SETTING

Under the rules at the time, Groat was not eligible to play varsity basketball (or baseball for that matter) in his first season. He played for Duke's freshman team as junior Corren "Creep" Youmans led the Duke varsity to a 13-9 record with a scoring average of 11.5 points a game. As a sophomore in 1950, Groat shared the scoring load with Youmans and averaged 14.5 points for a 15-15 team.

A black cloud hung over the Duke basketball program during the 1949-50 season. The popular and respected Gerard was diagnosed before the season with cancer. It was understood at the time that he was dying, but he remained at his post. The school administration prepared for the worst by bringing in a coach with professional experience to assist Gerard and to be in place to take over the program when the worst happened.

That coach was Arnold "Red" Auerbach.

"He came to Duke to become head coach," Groat said. "While he was here, he also taught P.E. He picked me out of a gym class one day, not knowing I was a scholarship athlete. We used to work out

Dick Groat takes it to the basket hard in a homecourt victory over Temple.

every day. I learned more basketball from him in two and a half months than I learned the rest of my time at Duke."

Auerbach left before the start of the 1949-50 season.

"Red said he couldn't stand to sit around and watch Coach Gerard die," Groat said.

Instead, Cameron, who had replaced Wade as Duke's athletic director, brought Harold Bradley, a successful small-college coach at Hartwick (New York) College, in to guide the Blue Devils. He built his first team around Groat and the junior responded with his first great season—a national record (at that time) 831 points, a 25.2 scoring average, and All-America honors. He led Duke to a 20-13 record that included a remarkable victory over Tulane in the consolation championship of the Dixie Classic in Raleigh. Groat rallied the Blue Devils from 32 points down in the second half to a 74-72 victory that still stands as the greatest comeback in NCAA history.

The season ended with a heartbreaking 67-63 loss to N.C. State in the Southern Conference title game. It was Duke's sixth straight loss to Case's juggernaut.

That state of affairs bothered Groat as he led the Duke baseball team to the Southern Conference title that spring. He couldn't help looking ahead to the next basketball season, when talented sophomores Rudy D'Emilio and Bernie Janicki would join him in the starting lineup and finally give Groat the supporting cast he'd need to help carry Duke past the Wolfpack.

Duke got off to a shaky start against a challenging schedule. Losses to Columbia and Southern Cal in the Dixie Classic over the holiday break plunged the team's record to a so-so 8-4. And when the Blue Devils dropped a double-overtime game at home to N.C. State in the first week of January, the record dipped to 9-5, and all the great expectations Groat had for his senior season appeared to be slipping away.

But Duke followed the loss to Case's Wolfpack with a stunning upset of No. 13 NYU in Madison Square Garden, then routed Temple in the Palestra. Duke returned to North Carolina and promptly knocked off Big Four rivals Wake Forest and North Carolina to improve to 13-5. One night after winning in Chapel Hill, Groat exploded for 46 points against Southern Conference foe George Washington—a record for Duke Indoor Stadium.

But a record that would stand for less than a month.

The victories kept coming—William & Mary, an overtime win at powerful Navy, and, most satisfying of all, a 71-58 rout of N.C. State in front of more than 12,000 fans in Reynolds Coliseum.

"I can still see it like it was yesterday," Groat said. "I was sitting on the bench, watching their fans file out while the game was still going on. They were angry. They weren't used to losing. It was a sweet feeling."

That sweet feeling continued as February played out. All the pieces had come together. Janicki had emerged as a powerful rebounding machine, while D'Emilio was providing the secondary scoring threat that Bradley needed to take some of the pressure off Groat, who was playing the best basketball of his life.

The winning streak reached 12 straight on the night of February 26, when Groat scored 26 points to help overcome a seven-point deficit in the third quarter (games were played in four 10-minute quarters that season) and pull out a 58-50 win over Davidson. The team drove home in a sleet storm to prepare for the regular-season finale against North Carolina on Friday night in Duke Indoor Stadium.

The Duke-UNC rivalry had not reached the epic levels it has achieved in the last 20 years, but the two neighbors were still fiercely competitive.

The Tar Heels were struggling in Tom Scott's final season at the helm. Duke had already beaten UNC twice that season. The first Blue Devil win, an 18-point shellacking back in December, came in a non-conference game staged at Duke as a benefit for Gerry Gerard's children. Duke added a hard-fought 73-66 win in UNC's Woollen Gym in late January and was favored to take the third matchup of the season on the night of February 29.

THE GAME OF MY LIFE
DUKE VS. NORTH CAROLINA, FEBRUARY 29, 1952
BY DICK GROAT

I was emotional before the game. As much as basketball meant to me, the thought that I'd never play again in Duke Indoor Stadium really made me sad. Playing there was always sensational. It was a very special place to play—then and now.

We were ready to start the game, but it was delayed for some reason. It's not like today, when TV runs everything and you always start on the minute. I didn't know what the delay was all about. It turned out that my father and mother and two sisters had driven down for the game and my father had fallen in the parking lot and hurt his knee. It didn't turn out to be serious, but they delayed the game until he was checked out in the hospital and released.

There was no special plan for me to score a lot. I took a lot of shots, but I also thought it was important to get my teammates involved. One thing I am most proud of was that I led the nation in assists. Every year I talk to the kids at Pitt (where Groat works as a radio broadcaster) and I tell them I'm a firm believer that if you are a scoring point guard, you should lead the team in assists. The more you give it up, the more your teammates will bust their butts to get it back to you.

I had some very good teammates. Bernie Janicki pulled down 31 rebounds in that game. That's still a Duke record.

I didn't realize that I was having such a big night. Carolina made a run at us in the third quarter. Things were not going well, but then I got lucky enough to hit some shots in a row. I've since read that I scored 22 of my 48 points in the final quarter. I don't think I forced anything.

I did shoot a lot of jump shots, but I was more of a driver than anything else. I always started way out and I practiced getting the ball up and spinning it off the glass over the big guys inside. I worked many hours alone in the gym perfecting that shot. I used to leave a window open so I could get in and practice alone at night.

Coach Bradley pulled me with 15 seconds left. Fred Shabel (later an assistant coach under Vic Bubas) came in for me. I knew it was all over. I can remember the tears streaming down my face. I had kind of a sick feeling. One of the things I remember vividly is the players on the Carolina team coming by after I came out. The whole Carolina team came over to shake my hand. I thought that was a classy act.

My father came in the locker room afterward and saw me crying. He said, "Christ, Richard, you didn't want to come down here and now you don't want to leave."

I was sorry that my career was ending.

THE AFTERMATH

Groat was carried off the court by delirious Duke students after completing his record-setting 48-point night in the 94-64 victory.

"He's sensational," UNC coach Tom Scott told reporters afterward. "His performance against us tonight was a fitting close to an outstanding career. Even though it happened against us, I was happy to see him break the Duke gym scoring record."

Groat was 19 of 34 from the floor and 10 of 11 from the foul line. He also added seven assists.

The next week, Groat was named the Southern Conference player of the year for the second straight season. The Associated Press, the United Press, and the Helms Foundation also named him national player of the year.

Groat's achievement, as great as it was, was soon overshadowed by the Southern Conference Tournament, which started the next Thursday at N.C. State's Reynolds Coliseum. That event was foremost on Groat's mind, even in the aftermath of his spectacular home finale. He spoke briefly to the swarming crowd after his victory ride, taking the P.A. microphone to tell the fans, "We'll do our best to win the Southern Conference championship for you."

But Duke and Groat were the victims of some bizarre bracketing for the postseason event. The Southern Conference regular-season standings ended with West Virginia at 14-1, N.C. State at 12-2, and Duke third at 13-3 in league play. Somehow the brackets for the tournament set up a semifinal matchup between No. 1 West Virginia and No. 3 Duke, while No. 2 N.C. State ended up playing No. 5 George Washington in the semifinals.

"We had to open with a tough Maryland team coached by Bud Milliken," Groat said. "He was a disciple of Hank Iba and they held the ball on us. We were down six with five minutes left, but I hit three field goals quickly and we were able to pull it out. That game took a lot out of us. The next night, we played West Virginia and we beat them 90-88 on a shot by Dick Johnson. I thought West Virginia was the best team in the country."

That set up a third straight Duke-N.C. State championship game. But Groat, who scored 31 in the victory over the Mountaineers, believes the title game was decided before it even started.

"They had two easy games in the first two rounds and they were able to coast," he said. "We were up four at the half, but I remember sitting in the locker room and looking at my teammates and knowing how I felt, thinking, 'We've got nothing left.'"

Indeed, Duke did not have enough. Groat scored 27 points, but fouled out on a charging call with more than three minutes left, and Duke fell 77-68.

That victory earned N.C. State the league's sole bid for the NCAA Tournament, but Groat left Raleigh hoping to play in the NIT—an event that was far more prestigious in 1952 than it is now.

"The NIT was a bigger tournament than the NCAA in those days," Groat said. "But Duke turned down the bid without giving us a chance to choose or even know about it."

A similar decision by the school's administration had ended Groat's 1951 baseball season prematurely. The team won the Southern Conference title, but Duke refused a bid to the NCAA Tournament. That changed in 1952, only because the school was forcing the venerable Coombs out of his coaching job.

"Because it was his last year, they let us go to the NCAA in 1952," Groat said. "We beat Florida State and some other teams in the regionals in Kannapolis (North Carolina) and became the first Duke team ever to play in the College World Series."

REFLECTIONS ON DUKE

In the immediate aftermath of Groat's 48-point game against North Carolina, the two-sport star told reporters that his future was on the baseball diamond.

"I don't think I'll play pro basketball," he said. "I'm going to try my hand at baseball."

Groat did just that, signing a free agent contract with the Pittsburgh Pirates. Not only were the Pirates his hometown team, but the choice allowed him to jump straight to the Major Leagues. He played 95 games for the Pirates in 1952, hitting a solid .284 and finishing third in the National League's Rookie of the Year voting—just ahead of future Hall of Famer Eddie Matthews.

But Groat wasn't through with Duke. He still needed one more semester of work to complete his degree and as soon as the Pirate season was over, he returned to Durham and enrolled in classes. He also arranged with his friend Carl Sapp to form a barnstorming basketball team known as Dick Groat's All-Stars.

"We played 18 games against teams from all over the state," Groat said. "While we were doing that, the Pistons asked me to fly in and play in an exhibition game on a Saturday night. As it happened, a guard fouled out and I scored 11 points in the last six or seven minutes and they wanted to sign me to a contract. They wanted to fly me in for weekend games. But one night I got caught when my flight was grounded and I couldn't get back to Duke in time for my classes the next day."

That created a major problem since under university rules at the time, students were allowed just three cuts a semester. Groat reluctantly told the Pistons that his part-time playing days were over.

"My father would have killed me if I didn't graduate," Groat said.

But the NBA team was determined to keep the Duke star on its roster.

"The Pistons offered to up my salary to beyond what the Pirates were paying me," Groat said. "And they agreed to hire a private plane to fly me to games. It got so I'd go to classes on Monday, play that night with the All-Stars, then fly to New York for a game Tuesday night in Madison Square Garden, then be back in Durham for my Wednesday classes. I was having a ball. I kept it up until I graduated, then I went in the service."

Groat ended up averaging 11.9 points and 2.7 assists in 26 games for the Pistons in the 1952-53 season. When he finished his two-year Army stint in 1955, he rejoined the Pirates and concentrated on his baseball career.

That turned out remarkably well. Groat was the centerpiece of the rebuilding efforts by Branch Rickey, who in his last baseball job laid the foundation that would turn the worst franchise in baseball into world champions in 1960. Groat made the all-star team for the first time in 1959, and then a year later won the batting title and was named National League MVP as he helped the Pirates reach the World Series.

He was traded to St. Louis in 1963 and hit .319 for the Cardinals that year and finished second in the MVP voting. A year later, he was a veteran anchor for a team that edged the Phillies in a memorable pennant race, and then knocked off the Yankees in the World Series.

Amazingly, Groat was not the first Duke basketball All-American to earn a world championship ring in the Major Leagues. Bill Werber, who became Duke's first basketball All-American in 1930, was the starting third baseman for the 1940 world championship Cincinnati Reds.

Groat retired in 1967 after playing 14 seasons with a career average of .286 and five all-star appearances. He returned to his hometown of Swissvale, where he bought and operated a golf course. He also became the radio voice for the University of Pittsburgh basketball team.

"Basketball was always my first love and still is," Groat said.

And despite his long association with the Panthers, he remains a Blue Devil at heart.

"They recently published a book—*The Legacy of Duke Basketball*," Groat said. "Coach K sent me a copy and he wrote, 'There would not have been a legacy of Duke basketball if it were not for you.' I appreciated that."

CHAPTER 15

FRED LIND

Fred Lind didn't come to Duke to sit on the bench.

A highly regarded prep star from suburban Chicago, Lind turned down offers from dozens of top schools to come to Durham and play for Vic Bubas.

"I thought Duke was the best combination of athletics and academics available," Lind said. "I initiated contact with them."

The Illinois prep star was the son of a college basketball player. His father, Cliff, was also a prep star from Chicago and played his college ball for a young coach named Ray Meyer at DePaul. He was a senior when Hall of Famer George Mikan first played for the Blue Demons as a sophomore.

Lind credits his father for instilling his love of basketball and teaching him the game.

"He coached me and showed me different things—helped me work on a jump shot, stuff like that," Lind said. "When I went to Highland Park High School, I also participated in cross-country, baseball, and golf, but basketball was always the main thing."

Lind was good enough to attract attention from almost every school in the Big Ten and every academically oriented school in the country. The University of Illinois made a big recruiting push, as did Vanderbilt and Davidson. Lind also got letters from a young North Carolina coach who was trying to rebuild the Tar Heel program in the wake of probation and the point-shaving scandals in the early 1960s.

"A few years ago, my folks were in Pinehurst, and my mom saw Coach [Dean] Smith," Lind said. "He sort of kidded her, saying, 'Fred wouldn't even answer my letters.'"

Lind's final choices came down to Stanford, Northwestern, Harvard, and Duke.

"I kind of was interested in Duke from my sophomore year in high school," Lind said. "My minister and his wife were both Duke alums and their son went to Duke. My backdoor neighbor, Mike McLaughlin, was—I think—the first baseball player to be on full scholarship at North Carolina. But even though he went to Carolina, he'd come back and say, 'Yeah, Carolina plays good basketball, but they're having a few bumps in the road. He told me Duke was the best team down there."

When Lind was in high school, Duke played in its first Final Four—losing to Loyola of Chicago in the semifinals. The Blue Devils returned to the Final Four in 1964, finished in the top 10 in 1965, and made a third trip to the Final Four when Lind was a freshman in 1966.

So Lind knew he was joining a program with good players—players who would battle him for playing time. He just never guessed he'd have to wait so long for that playing time to come.

THE SETTING

Lind's freshman class included three players from Illinois: Lind; guard Dave Golden from Pekin, and a talented guard from Lind's prep league named Gene Bromstead.

"Gene had a serious accident about halfway through his senior year," Lind said. "He got shot and had half his face blown off. He came back and played again. He was a heck of a player. Great defense—he guarded Pete Maravich when we played them (Maravich's prep school played the Duke freshmen three times) and he held Maravich to 27 points . . . well under his average of 39 a game."

Bromstead flunked out before his sophomore season. He ended up playing at Marquette, where he shared the backcourt with Dean "The Dream" Meminger.

"He had the best college boards of all of us, but he refused to study," Lind said.

Fred Lind beats UNC's Bill Bunting (No. 31) for a rebound during his memorable game against the Tar Heels.

The class also included Steve Vandenberg, a powerful 6-foot-7 forward from Crespatown, Maryland, and C.B. Claiborne, a slender 6-foot-3 guard from Danville, Virginia.

Claiborne was significant because he was the first African-American player at Duke. He was just the second black player in the ACC, arriving a year after Maryland's Bill Jones broke the league's color line. Lind, who roomed with Golden as a freshman at Duke, was Claiborne's roommate when the team traveled—a pairing that the Midwest-raised big man never considered controversial.

Lind was more concerned with his game, which didn't show up well in his first weeks with the Blue Imps (as the Duke freshman team was called). He didn't even start his first game.

"I started out real poorly my freshman year," Lind said. "I was out of shape. I got kicked out of practice twice. But by the end of the year, I was playing pretty well and we almost beat Carolina. We lost that last game in overtime."

That game was a foreshadowing of what would become Lind's greatest day at Duke. At the time, even playing close to the 1966 UNC freshman team was a significant accomplishment. That Tar Heel class would form the foundation of Dean Smith's program at UNC. It was a perfectly balanced team with a true center (Rusty Clark), a power forward (Bill Bunting), a small forward (Joe Brown), a point guard (Dick Grubar), and a wing guard (Gerald Tuttle).

The next season, three of those players—Clark, Bunting and Grubar—would start with UNC holdovers Larry Miller and Bob Lewis to give Smith his first ACC championship team. That trio of players started all three years as the Tar Heels won the ACC regular-season and tournament titles each year, also making three straight trips to the Final Four.

Two of Lind's freshman classmates (Golden and Vandenberg) soon became starters too, but Lind couldn't find a role with the Blue Devil varsity. He languished at the end of the bench, playing in just six games and scoring a total of 11 points his entire sophomore season. He did get one start, but it was under bizarre circumstances. Bubas suspended nine of 16 players for a curfew violation, and Lind, who called himself the 14th man on a 16-man team, was one of five scholarship players left to start a game against Penn State on January 3, 1967. He played well—mostly as a defender and rebounder—as All-American Bob Verga scored 36 points in an 89-84 Duke victory.

But the return of star center Mike Lewis and of veteran forwards Bob Reidy, Tim Kolodziej, and Joe Kennedy returned Lind to the bench. The strong play of Vandenberg and Warren Chapman, a powerful Texan who battled knee problems, also kept Lind off the court.

"There were a lot of good players ahead of me," Lind said. "I thought I would have gotten more of a chance. I was actually thinking of seeing Coach Bubas about redshirting at one point, then he put me in a game," Lind said. "If I had been smart I would have said something."

Lind's situation did not improve in his junior year. Reidy had graduated, but Lewis was the starting center and on his way to an All-America season, while Vandenberg, Kennedy, and Kolodziej also saw extensive action up front. Chapman played when his knees allowed, leaving precious few minutes for Lind, except in a mop-up role. Going into the final regular-season game of the year, he had played in just 12 of 22 games and scored a mere 12 points.

At that point, it would be fair to characterize Lind as a failure as a college basketball player.

"I had a lot of garbage time," Lind said. "I was discouraged. I guess my attitude wasn't that good. If I hadn't started playing by the end of my junior year, I decided that instead of playing basketball my last year, I'd try football. I used to run pass patterns with some football players and thought with my size, I could be a receiver."

But everything changed on a warm, spring-like day in March of 1968. Fred Lind, Duke's forgotten man, was about to have his day of destiny.

The landscape on Tobacco Road had changed radically in the three years since Lind refused to answer Dean Smith's recruiting letters. Smith, thanks to a head-to-head recruiting victory over Bubas for Larry Miller, a tough-as-nails forward from Aliquippa, Pennsylvania, had seized the high ground in ACC basketball circles. Miller, supported by high-scoring senior Bob Lewis and three standouts from Smith's 1966 recruiting class, had swept three games from Duke in 1967, including the ACC championship game in Greensboro.

Four starters returned for Smith in 1968 and the Tar Heel coach replaced Lewis with an even better all-around talent—Charlie Scott. UNC's first black player—and the ACC's first African-American superstar—helped the Tar Heels make it four straight wins over the Blue Devils with a scintillating performance in Chapel Hill.

"We're doing a pretty good job of containing Larry Miller and Scott is tearing us apart," Bubas said after the loss. "I'm thinking we're covering Superman, and Zorro is killing us."

Duke wasn't the only team to suffer against Smith's juggernaut. The Tar Heels lost an early game at Vanderbilt, but reeled off 20 straight victories to clinch the ACC regular-season title with two weeks to go before the tournament. Ex-UNC coach Frank McGuire, who was building a new powerhouse at South Carolina, engineered a stunning 87-86 upset of the Heels on February 26, as skinny young guard Bobby Cremins converted 16 of 17 free throws down the stretch for the Gamecocks.

Still, UNC was 22-2 and ranked No. 3 in the nation when the Tar Heels made the eight-mile drive from Chapel Hill to Duke Indoor Stadium.

The Duke team they would be facing was no pushover. Bubas had a legitimately great player in Lewis, a bruising 6-foot-8 center from Missoula, Montana. His backcourt of Dave Golden and Ron Wendolin lacked the explosive offensive firepower that Verga had provided, but both were tough, experienced players. Bubas also employed a strong rotation of forwards, including the 6-foot-6 Kennedy, a defensive specialist, and the offensively minded Vandenberg.

Not a lot had been expected from the Blue Devils before the season as Duke started out unranked. But a series of impressive performances, including road wins at Michigan and Alabama, a home victory over Princeton and a tough, one-point loss at No. 3 Vanderbilt all combined to push Duke into the rankings.

Duke was 19-4 and ranked No. 10 nationally when UNC arrived for the traditional regular-season finale. The home fans knew the visitors were favored, but it was not like the Blue Devils were hopeless underdogs. If Lewis could have a big game against Clark . . . if Kennedy could shut down Miller . . . if Vandenberg could score inside . . . if Golden's erratic jump shot was on . . . .

Many Duke fans envisioned ways their team could win. It's not likely that Fred Lind figured into any of those visions.

THE GAME OF MY LIFE
DUKE VS. NORTH CAROLINA, MARCH 2, 1968
BY FRED LIND

We were at practice a day or two before the game and Coach Bubas said, "Fred, I may have a little job for you Saturday. Get ready."

I thought, "Oh, sure, if Mike fouls out with three minutes left in the game." But he definitely had me in the plans a little more.

We were all keyed up. When you play Carolina, it's such a big game. Everybody kind of has his game face on. The crowd was really psyched up.

I got in a lot earlier than I usually did. Mike got his third foul and I came in and played six or seven minutes in the first half. I think I scored three points in the first half. I remember making a left-handed hook and grabbed a couple of rebounds and blocked a shot. So I felt like I contributed.

I wasn't afraid to try some stuff because, I thought, "Somebody's got to do something." I caught a pass to the left side of the key and had a kind of driving, left-handed sort of half-hook, half-layup. I had worked on that shot a lot in high school. My high school coach, Fred Dickman—a former player at Bradley—had worked me and worked me on that shot. He would literally kick me in the seat because I was not that aggressive in high school. He made me understand that if you try for something, you might get it.

I was getting kind of pumped up and the crowd was yelling.

I was played against Rusty Clark. Rusty was a big guy—6-foot-11, maybe 7 feet tall and fairly agile for a player that big. He had some good games against us.

(Lind tied the game with two free throws in the final minute.)

I just felt real good at the foul line. I didn't swish 'em—I remember one kind of bounced around, but I had the right touch and it went in.

Bunting had a couple of free throws that could have won it (in the first overtime). But he missed both shots and I rebounded the second one. I came down and was lucky enough to tie the game. It was a lucky shot. I knew there wasn't much time left and I had to shoot. I don't recall seeing the basket. I just shot and luckily it went in.

(Lind scored the go-ahead basket in the third overtime, then protected the lead with two blocked shots, the first versus Clark, the second on Grubar.)

On Clark's shot, I thought I might have fouled the lad. I hit him with the body a little. I wouldn't have been surprised if they had called the foul. I remember blocking (Grubar's) shot clean. I was just standing there under the basket, and it felt like I got up there pretty high.

It was an exciting game. I had never played in a close game before. It kind of built my confidence up. When the game was over, Coach

Bubas came up and gave me a bear hug and lifted me up a little bit. After that, it was kind of a blur, there was so much excitement. What I do remember is that it was a nice day, and when I came out after the game, I saw all these people there and I almost took a picture. I had my camera. I wish I had taken a picture of those people there. They lifted me up and carried me for a few feet. It was kind of neat.

AFTERMATH

Lind ended up with 16 points, nine rebounds, and at least four blocked shots in his 31 minutes of work. He had more points against UNC than he had scored all season to that point. He had forced overtime with two free throws, forced the second overtime with his running one-hander. In the third overtime, he not only scored the go-ahead basket, but protected the lead with two blocked shots, then secured the game-clinching rebound.

Duke had a lot of other heroes. Kennedy limited Miller to 15 points and Lewis had 18 points and 18 rebounds before he fouled out. Golden, Vandenberg, and Kennedy also scored in double figures for the Blue Devils.

But Lind's contribution—coming as it did out of nowhere—marked the victory forever as the "Freddie Lind Game." It snapped Duke's four-game losing streak to UNC and allowed the Blue Devils to finish the regular season a solid second in the ACC standings. In the next week's AP national poll, Duke climbed to No. 6 in the rankings.

"I couldn't be prouder of our team," Lewis told reporters after the game. "Fred had a lot of pressure on him and he came through with a great performance. He played like he was the starter all season."

Bubas told reporters that he "had a hunch" that Lind would play well against the Tar Heels.

"The bench, the bench, the bench," Bubas said. "It was fantastic bench play, and it was led by Fred Lind. I just can't give him enough credit. I'll have to say we'll probably try him again next week in the [ACC] tournament."

Bubas was ecstatic with his team's strong regular-season finish, especially in a year when little was expected from the Blue Devils.

"This game concludes the greatest regular season a team of mine has had for playing up to its ability," the Duke coach said. "No team that I have had has accomplished as much as this one."

Under modern rules, Duke would have been an NCAA Tournament lock after beating the Tar Heels; the Blue Devils would have entered the playoffs as a second or third seed if today's format had been used.

Instead, the NCAA allowed just one team per conference in the playoffs in 1968. And in the ACC, that was the team that won the league's postseason tournament.

Bubas told reporters after the UNC win that his team had as good a chance as any to win the tournament. But he didn't anticipate running into the coldest deep freeze in ACC history. Norm Sloan, his one-time teammate at N.C. State, held the ball for 40 minutes and derailed Duke in a freakish 12-10 game in the semifinals.

"That was the only game I started my junior year," Lind said. "I think the reason I started was that Coach Bubas had heard there was going to be a slowdown and he put me in to jump center. I think I controlled the tap both halves, but we still ended up losing."

REFLECTIONS ON DUKE

Fred Lind enjoyed a solid senior season. He became a starter on what was to be Bubas' last team. He played well, averaging 10.5 points and 7.9 rebounds in 28 games.

He was especially good against North Carolina, helping Duke to a second straight regular-season ending upset of the Tar Heels in Cameron, and then added 13 points and nine rebounds as the Blue Devils nearly stunned favored UNC in the ACC Tournament title game. Duke led 43-34 at the half when the Tar Heels' Scott single-handedly rallied UNC to victory, scoring 25 of his 40 points in the second half.

"I was trying to guard him at times," Lind said. "You can imagine, that was a mismatch."

Even though Lind proved to be something of a nemesis for the Tar Heels, he later forged a strong relationship with Dean Smith.

"We were getting ready to play Carolina at home, and right before the game [a Carolina manager] came over and said Coach Smith wanted to talk to me after the game," Lind said. "I thought he might be jerking me around."

Instead, Smith wanted to ask Lind to join an all-star team that he was putting together for after the season. The Duke big man joined future pro Bob Dandridge and Tar Heel rivals Bill Bunting and Dick Grubar for the first Aloha Classic in Hawaii.

"We had a lot of fun and I got a nice vacation after that," Lind said. "Later, I worked in his camp four summers. Coach Smith has always been real good to me."

The exposure Smith gave Lind in Hawaii helped him get drafted by the Phoenix Suns. He spent two seasons playing exhibition basketball in the NBA, but never made it past the final cut. He also considered football again—his plan was to put on some weight and try out for the Chicago Bears.

Instead, Lind got an internship with a law firm in Hillsborough, North Carolina. He returned to Chicago and earned a law degree at DePaul University. He came back to North Carolina and now serves as the assistant public defender in Greensboro, North Carolina—about an hour's drive west of the Duke campus.

Lind's athletic interest today is focused on his daughter Caroline, a world-class rower who won the national pairs in 2005 and was a member of Princeton's NCAA championship eights in 2006.

But the most improbable star in Duke history hasn't forgotten his own moment of glory. In fact, the public defender often references his matchup with UNC's Rusty Clark—a doctor who now prefers to be known as Dr. Franklin Clark—by pointing out to juries how much the two look alike.

"What I do in my cases to argue mistaken identification to the jury is say, 'Members of the jury, some of you are old enough to remember Rusty Clark, who used to play basketball for North Carolina. I wish I had a dime for each time I was misidentified as him.' One time the jury was 11 for guilty and one for not guilty and the not guilty vote was from [a big UNC fan]. He said, 'Yeah, I can understand that.'"

CHAPTER 16

BILLY KING

Billy King did not grow up a Duke fan.

"I hated Duke," the future Blue Devil defensive ace said. "I was a big Albert King fan and a big Maryland fan. That game Maryland lost to Duke [in the 1980 ACC Tournament finals], that destroyed me. I still joke to Kenny Dennard every time I see him about how he undercut Buck Williams on that final play."

It was natural that King, growing up in the small Washington, D.C., suburb of Bailey's Crossing, Virginia, should follow the Maryland Terps. He found basketball at a very young age, when his first grade school teacher encouraged the awkward boy to take up the sport. That teacher, Eunice Rankin, paid for his way to Wes Unseld's summer basketball camp and it was there that King first showed signs of becoming an exceptional player.

King was playing in another summer camp when he first met Mike Krzyzewski, and his hatred of Duke began to abate.

"It was at Red Jenkins' camp at George Mason," King recalls. "Coach K was there to watch Tommy Amaker. I was just a rising soph, but one time I was getting some water and I saw him watching me. I was intrigued by him. I had never heard of him at that time, but Coach Jenkins said he was going to be a great coach. Three days later, I got a letter from him, talking about how much he liked my game. I knew he was at Duke and I hated Duke, but that didn't matter. He could have been at any school—there was an instant connection."

Two years later, King was one of the top prospects on the East Coast, attracting interest from Maryland, Virginia, Syracuse, and

Kansas, which had just hired Larry Brown as head coach. Still, King's other suitors had to overcome that connection he had long forged with Duke's Krzyzewski.

"Everybody assumed I was going to sign with Duke," King said. "But the week before I was to visit Duke, I went to Kansas. I was really impressed by Coach Brown and I got to know Danny Manning. After the visit, I was going to Kansas. But my coach had warned me not to commit on a visit, so I came home and made the trip to Duke the next week."

That trip would change King's mind and make him a Blue Devil for life.

"The first night, I stayed at Coach K's home," he said. "They put me in Lindy's room. She was 11 years old at the time and she had made me a poster that said, 'Come to Duke, Billy.' The next night, I stayed in the dorm with Tommy Amaker—I had known him for 12 years—and Marty Nessley. We stayed up and watched *Saturday Night Live,* then they threw a pillow and a blanket on the floor and I slept there. The thing that impressed me was how normal they treated me. It was like I was already a part of the team."

The next morning, King had breakfast with Krzyzewski and assistant coach Chuck Swenson. He felt so at home that he ignored the good advice of his prep coach.

"Coach K was giving me the hard sell when I interrupted him and told him, 'I'm coming,'" King said. "The funny thing was that Coach Swenson had gotten up to pay the bill or something and he didn't hear me. Somehow in the confusion, Coach K never told him that I had committed. Coach Swenson drove me to the airport, then flew back with me, and he was recruiting me the whole time. He didn't find out until the next day that I had already committed."

King signed with Duke in the fall of 1983—just before Krzyzewski's program was about to take off.

"I guess that's how naïve I was," King said. "I never realized that the program was struggling. After I signed, one of my friends pointed out that Coach K might be fired. That's when I checked and saw that he had just had back-to-back 11-win seasons. Luckily, they turned it around [and won 24 games] that season and everything was fine from then on. But looking back on it, the thing that surprises me

---

Billy King gets some last second instruction from Duke coach Mike Krzyzewski.

was that there was no negative recruiting [toward Duke] from any of the other schools I was considering."

THE SETTING

King had to wait his turn before seeing significant action at Duke. He played 10 minutes a game as a freshman and upped that to an average of 15 minutes in 1986, when he was the seventh man on a team that finished 37-3 and reached the national title game.

Defense was the ticket that earned King increased playing time.

"I never thought that I would be a defensive guy," King said. "I scored 1,800 points in high school."

But there were early hints that defense would be King's strong point. He first attracted attention as a defender at the Five-Star camp in the summer before his senior year of high school when he shut down Georgetown-bound Reggie Williams during one scrimmage.

"I didn't realize what I had done until afterwards, when a coach came up and said, 'Nobody had stopped Reggie all summer.'"

King possessed a unique skill set. He was blessed with extraordinary quickness, especially for a player of his size. He combined that with good strength, good instincts, and an exceptional work ethic. Once he began to see himself as a defensive stopper, he began to put in hours of preparation time, studying the players he would be guarding.

King was also an above-average ball-handler, but he was a below-average shooter. He attempted just one three-point try in his career and finished with a dreadful career 47.9 free-throw percentage. His career field-goal percentage of just over 50 percent was a testament to his ability to get dunks and lay-ups—usually off defensive pressure.

Those skills—and shortcomings—became obvious in 1986-87, when King moved into the starting lineup, where he put the finishing touches on his defensive prowess by watching Amaker, the team's senior point guard.

"The whole basis of Coach K's defense was ball pressure, and Tommy did it better than anybody," King said. "He had the ability to force the opposing point guard to turn his back to protect the ball, and after that happens, he can't see what's happening."

King took over the primary ball-pressure role as a senior—often frustrating opposing playmakers with his size and reach. One of his greatest games came against Notre Dame's All-America point guard

David Rivers, when King harassed the Irish star into a 3-of-17 shooting performance. But King also guarded wing scorers and occasionally 6-foot-9 post performers. He was the wild card on a team that was exceptional defensively.

"[Point guard] Quin [Snyder] was good defensively," King said. "Kevin [Strickland] went out and guarded people. Robert [Brickey] was a shot-blocker. We went out and guarded people. We all played defense. Danny [Ferry] was our offense."

And King was the anchor for that defense.

"We all believed in it," he said. "I was like the middle linebacker. I made it a point to make sure everybody was in the right position. I would watch film all the time, staying up nights to try and pick up things."

The hard work and the commitment to defense paid off. Duke spent most of the year in the top 10. Best of all for Blue Devil fans, the 1987-88 team won the so-called "Triple Crown"—sweeping archrival UNC three times, including the ACC Tournament title game. It was Duke's first season sweep of the Tar Heels since 1966. King's usual assignment against UNC was junior point guard Jeff Lebo, who shot a combined 10 of 33 with 11 assists and 10 turnovers in the three Tar Heel losses to Duke.

The Blue Devils' 1988 ACC title was enough to earn them the No. 2 seed in the NCAA East Regional. That was a mixed blessing. On one hand, it meant that the Devils got to play first- and second-round games on UNC's home court in Chapel Hill—which infuriated the hated Heels, who were sent to the West Coast. On the other hand, it meant that Duke was in the same bracket with Temple, the nation's top-ranked team.

Of course, both Duke and Temple had to get to the regional finals before that became an issue. That wasn't a problem for the Owls, who stormed past Lehigh, Georgetown, and surprising Richmond to reach the East title game in the Brendan Byrne Arena at the New Jersey Meadowlands with a 32-1 record. Duke (27-6) had little trouble with Boston University and SMU in Chapel Hill, but faced a formidable threat from Tom Pender's Rhode Island team in the East semifinals.

Before the game with Rhode Island, King's growing defensive reputation was confirmed when Pender's two star guards argued about which would be defended by King. As it turned out, King took out shooting guard Tommy Garrick, rather than playmaker Carlton Owens, holding the Rams' top scorer to 14 points on seven-of-19 shooting. That was just enough to help Duke pull out a 73-72 victory. It was a costly win as junior forward John Smith broke his hand when he punched a basket support and was lost for the Temple game.

At least this time there was no doubt which player King would be guarding. Temple was similar to Duke in one respect—the Owls were a strong defensive team (although relying on John Chaney's tough matchup zone rather that Coach K's pressure man to man). But they had one great offensive weapon—6-foot-5 guard Mark Macon. The national freshman of the year scored just over 20 points a game for a team that averaged less than 70.

Duke's chances of returning to the Final Four for the second time in three years very much depended on King's ability to control Macon.

THE GAME OF MY LIFE
DUKE VS. TEMPLE, MARCH 26, 1988
BY BILLY KING

The night before the game, everybody—Danny, Quin, Alaa (Abdelnaby), Robert—was hanging out in my hotel room, And they all said, "Okay, Billy, you've got to stop this guy."

I had watched Temple beat UNC in Chapel Hill earlier that season. Mark Macon had a big game and I remember thinking, "This guy is real good."

I watched a lot of film and saw that he liked to go left to shoot the jump shot. He never went right. I saw they ran a lot of high screens for him. We decided to switch on the screens. That would put me at a disadvantage against their big men, but we saw on the film that he almost never dumped it down after a switch.

Standing there before tip off, I wasn't thinking about what the game meant—about going back to the Final Four or anything like that. All I was thinking was, "Force him to go right, force him to go right."

Mark was not making a lot of shots, but he was going to keep shooting. That worried me. Even though he was missing, he was such a good player that I figured eventually he'd get hot and start making shots.

I didn't talk to him. That's one thing I never did. I didn't want to talk to the guy I was guarding. I figured there was no need to say anything and wake him up. Mark didn't say anything either. He showed no emotion. He just kept playing.

Offensively, we were struggling against their zone (falling behind 27-17 and then 28-25 at the half). In the second half, they put me at the point of the zone. Because of my size, I had better vision and I was able to penetrate to the dotted line and lob it over Tim Perry to our big men. That opened things up.

We were leading when Kevin (Strickland) hit a couple of big three-pointers late. I remember thinking, "Now we're in control here."

I was overcome by emotion as the buzzer sounded. I broke down and cried. It was like we had won the tournament. I remember going over to (CBS commentators) Billy Packer and Jim Nance at midcourt and shaking their hands. I was just amazed that we were going back to the Final Four.

GAME RESULTS

Duke's 63-53 victory over No. 1 Temple was a stunning surprise. At that point in Krzyzewski's career, the Blue Devils had not yet established themselves as a perennial Final Four team. Indeed, 1988 would be the first of five straight Final Fours for Duke, capped by national titles in 1991 and 1992.

"We feel great," Krzyzewski told the assembled media. "I'd use some other adjectives if we were in the locker room."

Much of the postgame attention was given to King, who was voted to the all-regional team, despite scoring three points in the title game. It was hard to ignore the defensive job he did on Macon. The Owls' scoring star managed just 13 points on six-of-29 shooting. He missed seven of eight three-point tries and never went to the foul line.

"He got by me and missed some easy shots," King said after the game. "I can't take all the credit."

The distraught Macon, who showed so little emotion during the game, was overcome in the aftermath, hiding in the training room after the game and refusing to talk to reporters.

King's euphoria lasted for a long time—too long, he now believes.

"I didn't handle success very well," King said. "It was like 'Mission Accomplished' just getting to the Final Four again. Nobody expected us to get there and looking back, I think I was satisfied with what we had accomplished. And as a senior captain, I think my atti-

tude may have trickled down. We didn't have the same fire and determination in Kansas City as we had before."

Duke also ran into a very hostile reception in Kansas City, where
the nearby University of Kansas was boosted by a huge show of public support. For the first time at a Final Four, the host arena was
packed for NCAA's open Friday practice sessions.

"They were turning thousands of people away," King said. "We
were booed when we worked out. Then on Saturday, Kansas came out
and jumped all over us."

A week after King shut down the celebrated Macon, unheralded
Milt Newton burned Duke's defensive ace for 20 points on eight-of-
14 shooting as the Jayhawks eliminated Duke 66-59 and ended Billy
King's college career.

REFLECTIONS ON DUKE

The National Association of Basketball coaches honored King
with the Henry Iba Corinthian Award, given annually to the nation's
top defensive player. The award was created in 1987, and King was
just the second recipient, following in the footsteps of ex-teammate
Tommy Amaker.

Duke's defensive superstar took a couple of stabs at pro basketball, despite going undrafted by the NBA. He tried out as a free agent
for the brand new Charlotte Hornets but was cut after three days.
Later that summer, he got a call from Sacramento coach Bill Russell,
perhaps the greatest defensive player in NBA history, asking King to
try out for the aptly named Kings.

When that tryout also fizzled, King explored a career in broad-
casting. He auditioned for the job as the radio color analyst for the
Hornets, but lost the job to former Wake Forest big man Gil
McGregor, who still holds that job almost 20 years later. He worked
briefly for Raleigh TV station WRAL and became an analyst for
ESPN, which assigned him to follow the Ohio Valley Conference.

Before King could become a threat to Dick Vitale, he was lured
into coaching by former Duke guard Bob Bender. King joined his
staff at Illinois State, but when Bender moved on to Washington,
King didn't want to follow. Instead, he got an offer to work for Larry
Brown, the coach he almost played for out of college. He joined
Brown with the Indiana Pacers and then followed him to
Philadelphia.

King moved off the bench and into the management side with the 76ers. He started as the assistant general manager, moved up to general manager, and recently became president of the organization.

"It's kind of ironic that I live and work in Philly," Brown said. "People up here are sick of hearing me talk about how great Duke is. You don't know how many times I run into people who remind me about that game against Temple and tell me I ruined their best chance to go to the Final Four."

King said that not long ago, he ran into Macon at the Temple gym.

"He had his little boy with him," King said. "When he introduced me, he said, 'Son, this is Billy King. I used to score tons of points against him when we played against one another.' I didn't say anything. I just smiled."

King could afford to be magnanimous. He knows and Macon knows that when they met with the Final Four on the line, it was the Duke star that shined brightest.

CHAPTER 17

SHELDEN WILLIAMS

A funny thing happened to Shelden Williams during his high school career in Oklahoma.

"Every school I went to changed from a football school to a basketball school after I got there," Williams said.

That would be hard to explain—Oklahoma is, after all, a football-crazy state—if the reason wasn't so obvious: The arrival of Williams invariably transformed his new school into a basketball power.

"Football was my first sport," Williams said. "I loved football. I was a pretty good tight end. I would have loved to keep playing football, but as basketball became more important, it became a year-round thing."

Actually, basketball was the last sport that the future Duke star tried. He was 10 years old when he first took the court. Almost from the beginning, Williams excelled—even though he usually played with older kids.

"My Dad never let me play with my age group," Williams said. "He always wanted me to be the best in everything I did."

By the time Williams was a junior at Midwest City High School in Oklahoma, he was recognized as one of the nation's premier high school big men. He was the two-time Oklahoma prep player of the year. Williams earned the nickname "The Landlord" for his domination of the lane. Naturally, he became the focus of an intense national recruiting battle. Some of the biggest names in the sport—Duke, North Carolina, Kansas, Illinois, and Oklahoma—vied for his services.

"It really came down to Illinois and Duke," Williams said. "Bill Self [the coach at Illinois at that time] had begun to recruit me when he was at Tulsa. I had a really good relationship with him. But I just couldn't pass up the chance to play at Duke."

Williams committed to the Blue Devils in the fall of 2001, just months after Mike Krzyzewski's team had won its third national championship. He was the final piece of a renowned recruiting class—one that also included prep All-Americans J.J. Redick from Roanoke, Virginia, Michael Thompson and Sean Dockery of Chicago, and Shavlik Randolph of Raleigh, North Carolina. It also included Lee Melchionni of Germantown, Pennsylvania, the son of former Duke star Gary Melchionni.

THE SETTING

The class—dubbed "The Super Six" was due to arrive on campus in the fall of 2002. That should have been the senior years of Jason Williams, Carlos Boozer, and Mike Dunleavy—three standouts who anchored Duke's 2001 title team. But it was widely known that Williams and Boozer would be turning pro after their junior seasons.

However, Sheldon Williams did expect to play a season with Dunleavy.

"He called my phone [during the recruiting process] and told me he wanted to play with me," Williams said. "Then he went pro."

Dunleavy's unexpected decision to bolt—he became the third player taken in the 2002 NBA draft—left Krzyzewski with a painfully young team in 2002-03. When the season opened, three freshmen were in the starting lineup: Redick, Randolph, and Shelden Williams.

Williams admits that he struggled to adjust to the new level of competition.

"It was a new system, a new style of play," he said. "In high school, our team was so talented that we could turn it on and off. At Duke, everybody was talented. If you didn't have it one day, it would show up. I was always my own biggest critic, especially starting my freshman year. I didn't play well for a three game stretch and it made me think about a lot of things."

Shelden Williams converts an alley-oop as UNC's Tyler Hansbrough backs off.

The young big man was still trying to find his way when Duke played Maryland in January of 2003. That was Williams' first exposure to a true rivalry game.

"I went in kind of wide-eyed," Williams said. "I had never been exposed to that kind of rivalry. Back home, there was Oklahoma-Oklahoma State and Oklahoma-Texas in football, but I had never seen anything like that in basketball."

The Duke-Maryland rivalry was at its high point when Williams arrived in Durham. North Carolina's program was going through a brief slump under coach Matt Doherty and the Terps were enjoying the best years in their school's basketball history. Duke and Maryland had engaged in four incredible games in 2001. Both teams reached the Final Four that season, but Duke rallied from a 22-point first-half deficit to defeat the Terps in the semifinals before winning the national title two nights later.

The following season, the new rivals split their two games on the court, each winning at home. Maryland claimed the ACC regular-season title, but Duke won the ACC Tournament championship. Then the Terps trumped the Devils by winning the 2002 national title.

So the rivalry was at its highest point when Duke and Maryland met in College Park on January 18, 2003. It was, in fact, too much for the young Shelden Williams. He started, but soon got in foul trouble and ended up with just three points and one rebound in Duke's 87-72 loss.

"I really struggled," Williams said. "The biggest reason I didn't play well was that I had not been exposed to that atmosphere. My parents had come up to watch me and my mind was on that and not on the game. Afterward, I told myself I had to get back at them and redeem myself."

Williams did a better job in the rematch in Durham a month later. He had 13 points, 11 rebounds, and six blocked shots as the Blue Devils secured a 75-70 win. That was part of a strong finishing kick that lifted Williams' freshman stats to 8.2 points, 5.9 rebounds, and almost two blocked shots a game. It was a solid freshman season for a young team that won the ACC Tournament and reached the NCAA Sweet 16.

His sophomore season was even better. The Blue Devils reached the Final Four in San Antonio and very well might have won the national championship if Williams had not fouled out against Connecticut with Duke up six and three minutes to play. He improved all his stats—up to 12.6 points and 8.5 rebounds a game. He also led the ACC with 3.0 blocked shots a game.

There was one sour moment for Williams in 2004—the Blue Devils appeared to be on their way to a sixth straight ACC championship. But in the championship game with Maryland—in what proved to be a preview of the Final Four—Williams was sidelined with foul trouble and the hated Terps rallied to win in overtime.

That only added fuel to the already heated rivalry.

Williams thought long and hard about going pro after a spectacular junior season. He averaged 15.5 points, an ACC-best 11.2 rebounds and again led the league in blocked shots with 3.9 a game. He helped Duke claim another ACC championship and play into the Sweet 16 for the third straight time in his career. The junior big man was voted the National Defensive Player of the Year—the eighth time a Duke player had claimed that honor since it was instituted in 1987.

Most importantly, "The Landlord" was projected to be a first-round draft pick.

"A lot of players I played with in high school were going to the league," he said. "[Playing pro basketball] is something I really wanted to do. But everybody has his own path. I told my parents that I came to Duke to get my degree. My parents had taught me that when you start something, you finish it."

Williams returned to Duke to partner with Redick on a team that spent most of the 2005-06 season ranked No. 1 in the nation. Much of the national attention focused on Redick's spectacular scoring sprees. But Krzyzewski kept reminding the media that Williams' defense and rebounding were just as vital to Duke's success. That should have been obvious against Memphis in the championship game of the preseason NIT. Redick was held scoreless in the second half, but Williams poured in 30 points, hitting 11 of 13 field goals, and added eight rebounds and three blocked shots as Duke pulled out a 70-67 victory. When Redick captured the spotlight with a 41-point explosion against No. 2 Texas, few noticed that Williams backed him up with 23 points, six rebounds, and five blocked shots.

Yet, even as Williams continued to deliver a succession of dominant performances, critics began to wonder just how good his defense was. If Williams was the nation's best defender, some observers wondered, how did so many opposing big men have big scoring games against him? At Indiana, Marco Killingsworth scored a career-high 34, Virginia Tech's Coleman Collins hit a career-high 25, LaMarcus

Aldridge led Texas with 21, and N.C. State's Cedric Simmons scored a career-high 28.

What the critics misunderstood was Williams' role in Duke's defensive scheme.

"I usually played sort of a one-man zone," Williams said. "A lot of my blocks came when I came off my man. I was playing a roaming zone to try and help out my teammates."

Other ACC coaches understood Williams' value.

"When you look at defense, I think you guys have a tendency to look at how many points someone scores against somebody else," Virginia Tech coach Seth Greenberg said. "If somebody is quick to help, he needs someone to help him. Maybe that's why his man is scoring some. You don't play against Shelden Williams, you play against the Duke defense. Coleman Collins [didn't score 25 points] against Shelden Williams. He was the recipient of some excellent playmaking and he scored those points against the Duke defense."

Still, there were a few rare occasions when Williams was outplayed in the middle. One of those times came when Duke traveled to Winston-Salem to meet Wake Forest in early January. The Blue Devils pulled away in the second half for an easy 82-64 victory, but that didn't hide a subpar performance by Duke's senior center. Williams managed just 10 points, four rebounds, and one blocked shot.

It was not a very promising lead-in to the renewal of Duke's bitter rivalry with Maryland.

GAME OF MY LIFE
DUKE VERSUS MARYLAND, JANUARY 11, 2006
BY SHELDEN WILLIAMS

I knew it was going to be the last time I would get to play Maryland in Cameron. My family was there and that was a special thing—a chance to get my revenge in front of my mom.

We knew we had to come out really aggressive against them. That wasn't a problem—we had people who weren't afraid to take their shots. We got on a roll and jumped to an early lead. I got most of my stuff off the defensive end.

I wouldn't say it was easy playing against them. I was a lot stronger than their big men. (Ekene) Ibekwe was athletic. (Travis) Garrison was not as physical. He would spread the floor and shoot jumpers. He didn't challenge me inside. He knew I liked to block a lot of shots.

As the game went on, I knew I was getting close to a triple-double. I used to keep a little tally of my rebounds and my blocks as we were playing. I knew I had a certain amount.

But there were a few times before when I thought I had a triple-double, but when I looked at the stat sheet, they didn't credit me with enough blocks. I always wanted to make sure.

When I saw that I had done it, it was a great feeling. It was a great feeling because it was against Maryland. That was a very personal thing for me then.

THE AFTERMATH

Williams finished the nationally televised game with 19 points, 11 rebounds, and 10 blocked shots. He also had three assists and two steals as Duke coasted to a 76-52 victory. It was just the third triple-double in Duke history and the first against an ACC opponent since Art Heyman did it against Virginia 45 years earlier.

Ironically, it came on a day when Magic Johnson, the king of NBA triple-doubles, was in the stands.

"Meeting Magic Johnson today, and knowing the success that he had in college and the NBA, playing point guard and getting a lot of triple-doubles, it's great to have a triple-double in front of him," Williams said after the game. "Having great company like that watching you, it's a great feeling, and fortunately I did well and had a triple-double in front of him."

Amazingly, the Duke big man almost repeated his feat a month later when the Blue Devils faced Maryland in College Park. This time, Williams had 26 points, 13 rebounds, and seven blocks as Duke defeated the Terps 96-88. The win allowed Williams to complete his Duke career with a 5-4 record against Maryland.

"The Landlord" continued to excel as Duke completed the regular season with a 25-3 record. He averaged 19 points, 11 rebounds, and almost four blocked shots as the Blue Devils earned another ACC championship—the third in Williams' four seasons. And he was Duke's top scorer in three NCAA games as the Devils reached the Sweet 16 for the ninth year in a row, including all four years with Williams. During the team's postseason run, Krzyzewski was effusive in his praise for his superstar big man.

"The guy on our team who is, I think, as good a player as I've ever coached, has been Shelden," Krzyzewski told reporters after the ACC title game. "Shelden is our pillar of strength. He fights for us, he hits big free throws, he makes big buckets, he makes big blocks. We have him down the court when we need to inbound the ball. We have him up there because he's just so damn good.

"He'll never get the credit because (K's voice faded, then resumed) . . . But for me, I just want him to know it. That's why I'm saying it right now. I love Shelden. There's no kid I enjoy more. He really doesn't want anything, he just wants to help everybody. That's the spirit that helps permeate through our team. He's been our guy. All these guys will say the same thing that the success we're had would not be obtained without that kid, that man I should say. Sorry, Shelden."

Williams ended his senior season as the top rebounder and shot blocker in Duke history. He not only repeated as the National Defensive Player of the Year, but earned consensus first-team All-America honors to go with it.

REFLECTIONS ON DUKE

Williams did what he set out to do—he earned his Duke degree on time in the spring of 2006.

His one-year delay in entering the NBA didn't hurt his status. Williams was the fifth pick in the first round by the Atlanta Hawks. He returned to Durham midway through his rookie year to see his No. 23 jersey raised to the rafters.

"When I left I knew it was a possibility, but it was never official," Williams said in a press conference before the ceremony. "When I first found out, I was ecstatic and I told my parents and my family, and they were very happy and proud of me. I felt truly blessed."

Williams said he cherishes the memory of his years at Duke.

"At Duke, they taught me to play at a certain level night in and night out," he said. "I learned that there are a lot of talented players out there and you have to keep working hard if you want to succeed."

Williams considers his two National Defensive Player of the Year awards as his top individual achievement.

"I'm very proud of that," he said. "I didn't think I'd be able to achieve so much. There are just so many great players in the nation."

But not that many who were as good as "The Landlord."

CHAPTER 18

BOBBY HURLEY

Growing up the oldest son of one of New Jersey's most successful high school basketball coaches, Bobby Hurley was destined to be a point guard.

"I can remember him taking me to practice when I was real young—maybe five or six years old," Hurley said. "I was always around it and I always looked up to his players."

Hurley polished his own game in the youth league, but his real training ground was a series of one-on-one games with his father.

"He was pretty good and he never took it easy on us," Hurley explained. "He used to beat me and my brother down. I beat him for the first time when I was in the seventh grade. It was exciting to finally beat him. As I got bigger and stronger, I started beating him all the time."

The younger Hurley put his growing skills on display as a ninth grader at St. Anthony's High School in Jersey City. Midway through his freshman season, he was promoted to the varsity, and when an older player was hurt, the coach's son was forced into the starting lineup.

Hurley played with some exceptional players at St. Anthony's. He was one class behind guard Terry Dehere and forward Jerry Walker, who would start as freshmen on Seton Hall's 1989 Final Four team. He was a class ahead of his younger brother Danny, who would also start for the Pirates.

Sometimes Hurley would lead a group of players from St. Anthony's across the Hudson River into New York City, where they would cruise the playgrounds, looking for the best competition they could find.

"We traveled all over the city—the projects, everywhere," Hurley said. "We'd do our best to take a court and hold it. Yeah, we went to some tough places, but I never felt threatened, even though a lot of times I was the only white face there. People knew who I was, plus, in those places, if you were a good ballplayer, people respected you."

Hurley earned so much respect as a senior, when he guided St. Anthony's to a No. 1 national ranking, that he found himself as a nationally rated recruiting target. He was generally ranked as the No. 2 point guard prospect in the nation—just behind New York City rival Kenny Anderson.

Coincidentally, a similar cast of schools was recruiting both prep playmakers. North Carolina was considered the favorite to land Anderson, but Hurley's father went to UNC coach Dean Smith and promised that his son would commit to the Tar Heels, if Smith would commit to their son and stop recruiting Anderson.

"When I grew up, I watched Carolina a lot," Hurley said. "I was really into Carolina as a kid. But when my dad went to them, Coach Smith told him that Kenny Anderson was their top target."

Hurley had to look elsewhere. At first, he strongly considered Seton Hall, where his former teammates Dehere and Walker had excelled.

"I had grown up with those guys," he said. "Turning down Seton Hall was my toughest call."

While Hurley was watching UNC in his formative years, he had seen plenty of the Tar Heels' biggest rival. Duke was a surging program under coach Mike Krzyzewski, reaching the Final Four in 1986, 1988, and (after Hurley signed) in 1989. When Bob Hurley Sr. made Krzyzewski the same offer that Smith had turned down—Bobby would commit if Coach K would back off Anderson—it was an easy choice for the Blue Devil coach. He was a longshot to land Anderson anyway and after missing on consecutive point guard targets Darrick Martin (who picked UCLA) and Chris Corchianni (who picked N.C. State), he was happy to lock up the nation's No. 2-rated point guard prospect.

"The funny thing is my dad made the same offer to Duke and Georgia Tech and they both said the same thing," Hurley said.

Bobby Hurley launches a jumper against Michigan in the 1992 NCAA title game.

It was funny, too, because Georgia Tech, after finishing second to Duke in the Hurley race, pulled a major upset and beat out UNC for Kenny Anderson.

THE SETTING

Hurley stepped in as Duke's starting point guard in his first day of practice as a freshman.

"I kind of felt like I was the guy, even though they didn't tell me that point blank," Hurley said. "I'm not sure how much I felt in full control of the team that season. I deferred to the upperclassmen. I struggled with that. I struggled with my emotions. I struggled with a lot of things."

Actually, Hurley had a productive freshman season. He started all 38 games and led the team in minutes played. He averaged 8.8 points and 7.6 assists. Of course, he also averaged 4.4 turnovers and shot a disappointing 35.1 percent from the field.

His first season was marked by some impressive ups. He twice held his own against the more celebrated Anderson in leading Duke to a pair of regular-season victories over Georgia Tech. However, he also had some down moments, such as an embarrassing 10-turnover performance in a loss to North Carolina in Chapel Hill.

"That was my first game [against UNC], and it introduced me to what the rivalry was really about," Hurley said. "It taught me what I needed to bring to the table in a game like that."

Hurley applied those lessons as Duke entered the 1990 NCAA Tournament.

"My first year, growing up a college basketball fan, I was so excited to be in the tournament," he said. "I was so hyped up that somebody needed to control me."

It didn't help that Duke had to play the East Regionals in the Meadowlands—just a few minutes' drive from his home in Jersey City.

"It was real comfortable for Duke in the Meadowlands, but for me, it was a distraction," Hurley said. "That was the first chance I had to go home and I had all these friends and family stopping by."

Duke was a big underdog in the regional finals against No. 2-ranked Connecticut, the top seed in the East. The Huskies, enjoying their first great season under Coach Jim Calhoun, played a scrambling, trapping defense.

"Coach K told me that my most important job was to handle their pressure," Hurley said. "I didn't have a real good offensive game, but I think I did that."

Indeed, Hurley scored just three points in Duke's overtime win, but he committed just two turnovers in 43 minutes against the UConn press and balanced those two mistakes with eight assists and four steals.

The win earned Duke its third straight trip to the Final Four and its fourth in five years under Krzyzewski. The first opponent in Denver was Arkansas, which like UConn, featured a full-court press defense that Razorback coach Nolan Richardson labeled, "40 minutes of hell."

It was hell for Hurley—not because of the Arkansas pressure, but because he arrived at the Final Four battling an intestinal disorder.

"I wasn't feeling great," he said. "It had nothing to do with being nervous. I just got a virus."

At one point in the first half, Hurley had to leave the bench and return to the locker room. Yet, he still played 36 minutes and passed out six assists in Duke's 97-83 victory. But he was in bad shape after the game.

"I was exhausted," he said. "After the game and all the interviews afterward, I had to go back to the hotel and get an IV. I didn't even attend the shootaround the next day. I was just doing what I could do to get better."

Yet, Hurley insists that his illness had nothing to do with what happened in the title game.

"I was good to go by tip off," he said. "I was in bad shape after the game Saturday, but by Monday night I felt fine. That was no excuse for what happened."

What happened was that No. 1 UNLV dominated Duke en route to the most lopsided NCAA championship game in history. Jerry Tarkanien's Runnin' Rebels led Duke by 12 at halftime, then blew the Devils away in the second half for a 103-73 victory. Hurley couldn't cope with the Vegas pressure. He had as many turnovers (five) as he did points (two) and assists (three) combined.

"It was one of those games where it seemed like they were a step faster than us on every play," Hurley said. "I'd see a pass to Alaa [Abdelnaby] and by the time I threw it, the passing lane would have closed. I'd drive the lane and nobody would rotate back on defense, so they'd end up getting an uncontested basket at the other end. They were really a great team and they deserve a lot of credit, but we just didn't show up."

Even though Duke finished his freshman season at 29-9 and NCAA runner-ups, the 30-point loss to the Rebels left a sour taste in Hurley's mouth.

"There was nothing satisfying about it to lose like that," he said. "It kind of put a damper on the season. That was a pretty good season, but the way it ended kind of knocked me back. I did something I never did: I put the balls away for two weeks and got away from basketball. It took me a long time to get that game out of my system."

Hurley came back determined to erase the pain by making himself—and Duke—a better team in 1990-91. One of the first things he worked on was his on-court demeanor. Assistant coach Pete Gaudet helped by preparing a videotape showing Hurley's reaction to negative plays, especially officiating calls that went the other way.

"When you do it, you don't think you're doing the stuff you do," Hurley said. "I think what happened was that I wanted to be like my Dad and when I played for him, he was always yelling at the refs. Coach K is mild compared to my Dad. Once I saw what I was doing, I learned not to behave that way. Some of it came with maturity."

Hurley's role on the team increased going into his sophomore year. Senior starters Phil Henderson, Robert Brickey, and Alaa Abdelnaby had graduated, leaving Hurley and junior Christian Laettner as the team's two most experienced players. But there was plenty of talent on hand, especially with freshman Grant Hill joining the roster.

"Christian and Brian Davis had very strong personalities," Hurley said. "They were very vocal. Come game time, I was the guy who orchestrated everything on the court. The roles were clear."

It took time for the young Duke team to find any consistency. However, there were signs of what was to come. Just before Christmas, the team traveled to Oklahoma and snapped the nation's longest home-court winning streak.

"It was important to show toughness on the road," Hurley said. "Coach K told us they were the kind of team we might face in the NCAA Tournament and it did a lot for our confidence to win that game."

But there were also some setbacks as well. After an early January loss at Virginia, the team bussed home, then went straight to practice.

"That was a brutal practice," Hurley recalled. "For those of us who played big minutes at Virginia, followed by a four-and-a-half-hour bus ride . . . we get off the bus and Coach K says, 'Get taped up.' The guys were shocked.

"I think that was a reinforcement of the UNLV game—Coach was telling us he was not going to tolerate that kind of effort."

The effort got better, and so did the results as Duke won the ACC regular-season title and went into the ACC Tournament with a 24-6 record. But the title game against UNC turned out to be a mini-repeat of the Vegas debacle of the year before. The Tar Heels—a team the Blue Devils had swept in the regular season—dominated the ACC finals, coasting to a 96-74 victory.

"It was rough, but in a way it gave us a boost because it reminded us of what we had to bring to the table every time out," Hurley said.

The loss cost Duke its "comfortable" spot in the East Regionals and led to the No. 2 seed in the Midwest. But after a slow start in the opener against Northeast Louisiana, the Blue Devils began to click—reeling off lopsided victories over Iowa, Connecticut, and St. John's.

"That first half of the first game, we were still kind of shaken from the UNC loss," Hurley said. "But after that, we put it together and no one challenged us. We were getting better and better with each game."

When Duke cut down the nets in the Pontiac, Michigan, Silverdome, it meant that the Devils were heading back for their fourth straight Final Four and fifth in six years. That was a great achievement, but none of the previous Duke teams had ever converted a Final Four appearance into a title. In fact, Duke had never won a national title—the great Vic Bubas was also 0-3 in Final Fours, and Bill Foster lost his one NCAA title game appearance in 1978.

Now Mike Krzyzewski, 0-4 in turning Final Four appearances into NCAA titles, was going to try for the fifth time. Standing in his way was a formidable obstacle—the same UNLV team that had routed Duke in the 1990 title game. Tarkanian's unbeaten and No. 1-ranked team featured All-Americans Larry Johnson and Stacy Augman, along with the brilliant backcourt of Anderson Hunt and Greg Anthony. The Rebels were being compared with the great teams in history.

Almost nobody gave Duke a chance in the rematch. The national attitude before the Saturday semifinal game was summed up by San Francisco columnist Art Spander, who wrote:

"Just send out the Rebels, then send in the clowns."

THE GAME OF MY LIFE
DUKE VS. UNLV, MARCH 30, 1991
BY BOBBY HURLEY

We weren't excited to see UNLV in the semifinals—we wanted to play them in the finals.

I'd say we had a measure of confidence. I felt like we were a different team (than the team they beat in 1990). We played differently and we were better. We were peaking. Grant was more assertive. Brian Davis and Thomas Hill were coming on strong. We still had some questions in the back of our minds—we knew they were a great team—but we wanted another chance at them.

The first day of practice that week, Coach K walked into the locker room and talked to us with his usual passion and energy. He said, "Don't believe anything you read this week. I'm going to be talking about how great they are, but I'm telling you now, you are going to beat them." It's hard to explain, but he had that ability to make you believe and to get it done.

My main job against Vegas was to take care of the basketball and maintain the pace of the game. We still wanted to run, but Coach K wanted me to be smart about it and pick our spots. He didn't want to get into a full-court, up-tempo game with them. The other key thing for me was to focus on getting back on defense and not letting them get the uncontested dunks and layups they got against us the first time.

The key plan for the team was to not play against center George Ackles. That allowed Christian to roam around on defense and to help out on Johnson. Ackles hurt us occasionally with offensive rebounds because there was nobody to check him, but it worked out.

I liked playing in the Hoosier Dome. People said they didn't shoot well in domes, but I liked the atmosphere. In the ACC, we played in places where the fans are right on top of you, but the setup in Indianapolis really helped my peace of mind. The crowd was still there, but it was like the court was on an island.

I remember reading a lot before the game and getting irritated, like a controlled fire was building in me. It's not that they weren't a great team, but nobody was giving us a chance. I was able to use that.

We knew we had to come out and get off to a good start. We scored off the opening tip and were up like 14-6 by the first TV time-out. That really gave us confidence. We needed that. They still had that mystique, but after the first few minutes, we knew we could play with them.

That first half I got the sense that I was playing in a great game. I knew they were very good and they were making a lot of plays, but so were we. We had a lot of confidence. Everybody on that team brought a lot to the table. I never had the sense that we were outmanned.

I think the important thing is that we were never intimidated. A lot of teams lost to that Vegas team before they ever took the court.

At the half, we were down 43-41, but at that point, we knew we were right in the game. We knew we were doing what we had to do. I don't remember anything dramatic in the locker room at halftime. Personally, I was just using the time to get whatever rest I could.

It was a physical game, but if I took a hit, I didn't care. I could have put a helmet on and played football. I had a hard foul on Anderson Hunt in the second half. It was my way of letting my teammates know they were not going to dunk on us. I thought after what happened the year before that was an important message to send.

It must have been frustrating for UNLV. We had seen their margins of victory. They had had their way with everybody they had played that season, but they couldn't break us. They'd hit us with a knockout punch, but we wouldn't go down.

Our goal was to get them in a close game and see how they'd react. They hadn't been in a close game and we had played a lot of them. It was a critical play for us when (UNLV point guard) Greg Anthony fouled out. He orchestrated everything for them.

I thought the key moment was when they went up five with just over two minutes left. I felt like they had all the momentum. I knew what they were thinking—get one stop, then start to work the clock and we'd have to foul them.

They were in the "Amoeba" (zone defense). They were very good in it. You could rarely find creases in it and they had a lot of long defenders who were quick to react. That made it very difficult to get a shot off.

I later heard that on TV, Billy Packer was saying we didn't need a three. It's funny, it seems to happen a lot—an announcer will be talking about how great some guy is at the free throw line and he'll miss. This was like that in reverse.

I wasn't hung up on taking a three. It was just an instinct. If I had a shot, I wanted to take it. It just happened to be a three, and when it went in, it was a one-possession game. I thought that was the turning point; the momentum was back on our side.

We forced them into a shot-clock violation. I don't remember much about the sequence, except that I was guarding Hunt (who had taken over at point guard) and I was trying to put more pressure on him than I did when I was guarding Anthony. I did not respect his ability to penetrate.

Everything seemed to fall into place down the stretch. Brian made a great slashing move to the basket for a three-point play that gave us the lead.

Larry Johnson tied it up after we gave him an extra free throw on a lane violation. He had a little hitch in his motion and we were warned about that all week. Thomas Hill fell for it, but it could have been any of us.

(With the score tied, Laettner rebounded Thomas Hill's miss and was fouled with 12.7 seconds left. UNLV called timeout).

I remember sitting there and Coach saying, "after Christian makes these two free throws . . ." I think Christian had the will to make them anyway, but that's an example of the way Coach K instilled confidence. Naturally, Christian made both shots.

Coach K wanted to extend pressure after the free throws to make them use the clock to push it up. Not having Anthony to orchestrate things really hurt them. I was on Hunt, and I didn't want him to get the ball because I knew he could beat us with a three. I wish my arms were two inches longer; I could have gotten a finger on the ball. He got off a long, off-balance shot that hit the back of the rim and rebounded long to me.

At that point, the game was over and everybody was jumping around and I was still dribbling. The game was so good, I didn't want it to end. I couldn't believe it was over. Grant finally had to grab me.

We had our celebration on the floor. We had invested so much in the game, we had to celebrate. But we also knew what we still had to do. We knew that to beat a team like Vegas and then lose to Kansas in the finals would be a complete screwup.

THE AFTERMATH

Duke didn't screw up. Less than 48 hours after edging UNLV 79-77 in the semifinals, the Blue Devils came back and beat Kansas 72-65 in the title game to give the school its first national championship.

"We wanted to win it for Coach K," Hurley said. "He deserved it after getting so close so many times before. Maybe we didn't have the same emotion [against Kansas as against UNLV], but we played with the same determination. The guys were a little worn down, but we did what we had to do."

Hurley was the only Duke player to go all 40 minutes in both games. He scored 12 points against UNLV (hitting 3-of-4 three-pointers), passed out seven assists and committed just three turnovers. He scored another 12 points against Kansas in the championship game, passing out nine assists and committing three turnovers.

"For Bobby to play the two games he played against the pressure he faced with no turnovers—or just a few—and with so many assists . . . I can't imagine how he did it," Krzyzewski said.

In hindsight, Hurley's three-pointer with 2:14 to play against UNLV rivals the buzzer-beater teammate Christian Laettner would hit a year later against Kentucky as the most important shot in Duke basketball history. Without that shot, it's unlikely that Duke would rally for the victory over the Runnin' Rebels and would not have won the 1991 national title.

And without that title, would Duke have been such a confident, dominant team in 1992?

"We were excited to be No. 1 [in preseason]," Hurley said of the 1992 season. "We got out of the gate fast when we took apart St. John's in the old ACC/Big East Challenge. We were cruising right along until I broke my foot in the first half at Carolina."

Indeed, Duke was 17-0 and ranked No. 1 when Hurley was hurt late in the first half of the game at UNC. He tried to play in the second half, going a gritty 37 minutes, but he was clearly hobbled, and the Blue Devils lost a 75-73 heartbreaker.

Hurley missed the next five games as his foot healed, including another close loss at Wake Forest. But he returned a week earlier than projected—just in time to power the team's postseason drive for a second straight national title.

"We knew all year that was what the season was about—the tournament," Hurley said.

The Blue Devils got off to a fast postseason start in 1992 by routing UNC in the ACC Tournament title game. Hurley had 11 points and 11 assists as Duke reversed the 1991 loss to the Tar Heels with a 94-74 victory. In a sense, it was very much like the 1991 UNLV win in that Duke got revenge for a rout the previous season.

"It had that same kind of emotion," Hurley said. "We were reminded of what had happened the year before. Winning like that gave us a lot of momentum since they were a Final Four-capable team."

Duke's own path to the 1992 Final Four was not easy. Hurley faced a particularly tough challenge against Seton Hall in the regional semifinals in the Meadowlands. Not only were the Pirates led by his former high school teammates Terry Dehere and Jerry Walker, but his younger brother Danny was the starting point guard.

"When Danny was guarding me, it was . . . different," the former Duke star said. "I like to attack my opponent, but that was hard to do against Danny."

Hurley played a sloppy game against Seton Hall. He shot poorly and scored just four points in Duke's 81-69 victory. However, he bounced back two days later to play a major role in one of the great games in college basketball history. Hurley went all 45 minutes of Duke's 103-102 overtime victory over Kentucky, scoring 22 points and passing out 10 assists for the Blue Devils.

"In a way, the game was very similar to our Vegas win," Hurley said. "I think the Kentucky game had more drama, but the Vegas game was played at a higher level. Kentucky's style was that they were willing to give up some things, believing that their pressure would create more things for them. They made a lot of big shots—the kind we usually make."

But Christian Laettner made the biggest shot, taking a 75-foot pass from Grant Hill and hitting the 15-footer than won it at the buzzer. Hurley was the second option on the play, running down the left sideline.

"I had virtually the same view of Christian's shot as I did of the one he hit to beat UConn in 1990," Hurley said.

The junior point guard was more than a spectator the next week in Minneapolis, where Duke participated in its fifth straight Final Four. He had to pick up the slack in the semifinals as Laettner struggled. Hurley poured in a career-high 26 points, including six three-pointers as Duke edged Indiana in the semifinals.

Krzyzewski credited Hurley for the victory.

"I don't think we win without Hurley," Krzyzewski said. "He had one of those magnificent games. He was playing at a much higher level than any of our other players."

Hurley suggested that it was his turn to take over.

"Indiana was focused a lot on Christian," Hurley said. "That and everything that Christian went through after Kentucky, I knew he might struggle. It was like he was emotionally drained. I didn't see the same fire from him. But that's what separated our team. We had a lot of different people who could step up."

Hurley stepped up again at halftime of the title game. Duke was trailing Michigan's Fab Five 31-30 at the break.

"Brian and Christian provided most of the vocal leadership for that team," Hurley explained. "But that night Brian was hurt and Christian was struggling. When we got to the locker room, I still didn't see that look in [Christian's] eyes, Thomas Hill and I stepped up and laid into everybody. It seemed to work. But that half really belonged to Grant. His athleticism was the biggest factor down the stretch."

Krzyzewski told reporters that Hurley's halftime speech turned the tide.

"Bobby does not speak out all that often," the Duke coach said. "It sends chills down my spine to see Bobby do something like that. He told them, 'I'm out there giving 110 percent. Why can't you give 110 percent?'"

Hill's 18 points helped Duke pull away for the surprisingly easy 71-51 victory that capped Duke's second straight national championship. But it was Hurley, with a modest nine points and seven assists in the title game who claimed the Final Four MVP Award.

Hurley returned for his senior year, hoping to become the first player in NCAA history to start in four straight national title games. For much of the season, that looked like a distinct possibility. Duke started strong, upsetting Michigan in Cameron and climbing to No. 1 in the national rankings.

The Blue Devils were 19-3 and ranked No. 3 nationally when disaster struck. Grant Hill, who was emerging as the superstar he would become, broke a bone in his ankle in a loss to Wake Forest and was sidelined for the next month.

"The margin of error for us that season wasn't very large," Hurley said. "Grant was a huge part of that team."

Duke still managed to eke out four more ACC wins in eight games before the gifted junior returned. It was during that stretch, Hurley became the NCAA's career assist leader, passing N.C. State's Chris Corchiani in his final home game against Maryland.

"That's what I was all about," Hurley said. "I was lucky enough to play with some great players. I loved running the break and giving it up to Grant Hill or Brian Davis or Thomas Hill and watching them finish with a dunk. That's just my nature. I'd get more of a kick from that than from scoring myself."

While Grant Hill returned in time for the NCAA Tournament, Duke suffered another blow when starting center Cherokee Parks badly sprained his ankle in the first half of a second-round loss to Cal. Hurley scored a career-high 32 points in the 82-77 loss, but with Duke up one, Jason Kidd came up with a loose ball in the lane and converted a three-point play that gave the Bears the lead.

"That was a lot of crazy stuff at the end," Hurley said. "I still remember the shot I took [after Kidd's basket]. I got a good look and the ball hit every part of the rim before bouncing off."

Coach K cried in the postgame press conference as he realized that Hurley's career was over. He understood just what the slender point guard had brought to his program. It was more than the 1,731 points and the NCAA-record 1,076 assists. More importantly, it was all the winning that Hurley had contributed to—the two national titles, consecutive seasons of 29-9, 32-7, 34-2, 24-8, and an 18-2 record in NCAA Tournament play.

"Bobby Hurley had a storied career," Krzyzewski said. "I'm just glad I was along for the story. The last four years how we've played has been measured by how Bobby did. He's one of the special players in the history of the Atlantic Coast Conference. He's hit more big shots and made more big defensive plays . . . and he did it for almost 40 minutes a game."

REFLECTIONS ON DUKE

Hurley's game was highly prized by NBA scouts, and the Sacramento Kings took him with the seventh pick in the first round. Tragically, Hurley would never get the chance to prove himself in the NBA. He got off to a promising start, averaging seven points and six assists in his first 19 games, but barely two months into his rookie season, he was involved in a near-fatal traffic accident as he was leaving the Arco Arena after a night game. His SUV was hit broadside by a drunk driver, driving without lights, who plowed through a red light.

Hurley was critically injured. He spent months in the hospital, then even more months trying to rehabilitate his body after the accident. Although he returned to play parts of four seasons for the Kings, he never regained the full athleticism that he had before the accident.

"It's disappointing because I loved playing and I really enjoyed the competition," Hurley said. "To have that taken away was tough. It's not as big an issue with me today as it was when I was 30. Now I'm older, I have kids, and I've moved on to other things."

One of those things is horse breeding. Hurley started by buying two inexperienced horses and has expanded his enterprise from there. One of his early purchases, a horse named Songandaprayer, was good enough to run in the Kentucky Derby.

"I did it initially because I thought it would be fun," he said. "I've always liked horses and racing. I've really enjoyed the experience."

And Hurley enjoyed his days at Duke, when he was college basketball's most successful point guard.

"It's nice to think of that stuff," he said. "Looking back and knowing I was a part of what I was a part of . . . that's very satisfying."

CHAPTER 19

CHRIS CARRAWELL

Chris Carrawell never set foot in a gym until he entered high school.

His basketball education came on the concrete outdoor courts in St. Louis, where as a 12- and 13-year-old, he routinely took on grown men in the city's ubiquitous pickup games.

"I got beat up a lot," Carrawell said. "I was tall for my age—maybe 6-1. I was hoping to grow to be 6-9 because my favorite player was Magic Johnson and I thought that if I could grow to be 6-9, I could be Magic Johnson."

Carrawell admired the versatility of Johnson's game. He was too young to see it in person, but he read about Johnson's performance as a rookie in the NBA playoffs. The former Michigan State star played point guard for the Lakers, but in Game 6 of the 1980 NBA Finals, L.A. big man Kareem Abdul-Jabbar was sick, and Johnson moved to center and led the Lakers to the championship.

"He was able to play every position," Carrawell said of his hero. "That's what I wanted to do. I was able to do a lot of different things at an early age."

Carrawell never did grow quite as tall as his hero, but even after he topped out at 6-foot-6, the St. Louis schoolboy was recognized very early as a budding star. The summer after his sophomore season at Cardinal Ritter High School, Carrawell took the Nike All-Star Camp by storm, excelling in a setting that included such future stars as Kevin Garnett, Vince Carter, Ron Mercer, and Trent Tucker. Later that summer, Carrawell attended the 5-Star Camp in Pennsylvania and beat out Carter, Tucker, and Stephon Marbury for the MVP honors in the all-star game.

Going into his junior season at Cardinal Ritter, Carrawell was rated one of the top five prospects in his class by respected prep analyst Bob Gibbons.

Then disaster struck.

"We were playing East St. Louis and it was a rough game," Carrawell said. "I remember that Gene Keady was there watching when I went up for dunk and one of their players undercut me. I landed on my left shoulder and I dislocated it."

Carrawell returned to action and led Cardinal Ritter to the state title, but the injury limited his game—especially his shooting. Worse, because he overcompensated and tried to do too much with his right side, his right shoulder began to pop out of the socket. The injured prospect should have undergone surgery after the season, but Carrawell didn't want to miss the summer AAU camps, so he played with a sling under his jersey.

"I slipped in the ratings," he said. "I never talked about [the injury]. I never made excuses. I just played. I started reading that I was overrated. A lot of schools fell off me."

But not Duke.

Blue Devil coach Mike Krzyzewski, anxious to rebuild his talent base after the disaster of 1995, continued to pursue the tough St. Louis playground product.

"Coach K was one of the few guys who saw what was happening," Carrawell said.

A few other coaches were willing to gamble on the injured prep star—Clem Haskins at Minnesota, John Calipari at UMass, Jim Boeheim at Syracuse, and Charlie Spoonhaur at St. Louis. Before he could make a choice, Carrawell had to get over his dislike of Duke.

"I was a big Vegas fan [in 1991]," he said. "I kind of liked Grant Hill, but I didn't like Christian Laettner or Bobby Hurley. I liked Larry Johnson and the [Michigan] Fab Five. I didn't like Duke, but I respected them. You've got to respect greatness."

Krzyzewski helped convince Carrawell that he'd fit in at Duke.

"When Coach K took me in a back room and told me I could be a star there—how could I turn him down?" Carrawell asked. "Then I visited the campus and thought, 'This is unreal!' It was so different

Chris Carrawell—trying his best to look like (and play like) Magic Johnson.

from my background. But I knew I would do well there. After my visit, I was sold on Duke."

THE SETTING

Carrawell knew he was entering a rebuilding situation. Duke was coming off consecutive seasons of 13-18 and 18-13 when he signed, along with Nate James and Mike Chappell.

"When my class came in, Coach was coming off a couple of sub-par years," he said. "The glory days, you thought, were behind. Well, we turned it around—and I think I had something to do with it."

Indeed, Carrawell, still hampered by two unstable shoulders, made his impact felt early in his freshman season. He didn't do much scoring, but he was willing to do other things to get in the lineup—play defense, rebound, set screens, and handle the ball.

"Magic Johnson could do anything," Carrawell said. "He had the mentality to play point guard, but he could also play 2, 3, 4, even center. That's what I wanted to be. If I could do it, I would."

Carrawell first cracked the starting lineup in January, replacing 6-feet-11 center Greg Newton as a starter in a homecourt victory over a North Carolina team that featured future pros Antawn Jamison and Vince Carter. But it was a week later that Carrawell came of age. Duke traveled to Winston-Salem to try to snap a nine-game losing streak to Wake Forest, the nation's No. 2-ranked team.

"They had Tim Duncan, the best player in the country, and a frontline with Ricky Peral and my old high school teammate, Loren Woods," he said. "We were playing three guards and two forwards and they had a frontline of 6-11, 6-10, and 7-1. But we hung with them.

"With about seven or eight minutes left, I was sitting next to Coach K when Duncan slammed one against Newton. Coach turned to me and said, 'You've got Duncan.' Well, you know how when you get nervous, you get this big lump in your stomach? That's how I felt. I was saying a big prayer as I went into the game."

The 6-foot-6 freshman took his place defending the 6-foot-11 National Player of the year.

"I fronted him, I face-guarded him, I pushed him outside—anything to keep him from getting the ball," Carrawell said. "He didn't get many touches."

With Duncan "out" of the game, Duke took a one-point lead with just over a minute left.

"There was a play where [Wake Forest guard] Tony Rutland got past [Duke's Steve Wojciechowski]," Carrawell said. "I was caught in between. Do I leave Duncan and rotate over to stop Rutland or do I stay with Duncan? I watched Rutland go up for the layup and I got there at the last minute. I was lucky enough to not only block the shot, but to trap it against the glass. I came down with it, but because I was a horrible free-throw shooter [thanks to the bad shoulders], I got rid of it right away. I got it to Trajan [Langdon] and he made two free throws and we had a cushion."

Duke held on for a 73-68 victory that proved pivotal in the ACC regular-season race. Carrawell had just seven points and seven rebounds in the victory, but his defense on Duncan down the stretch was decisive.

"That was the defining moment in my career," Carrawell said. "That's when I knew I could play in this league, and that's when everybody knew Duke was back."

The Blue Devils ended up edging the Deacons for the ACC regular-season title and finishing 24-9. A year later, Krzyzewski added one of his most celebrated recruiting classes—Elton Brand, Shane Battier, Chris Burgess, and Will Avery.

Suddenly Duke was one of the nation's most talented teams again.

The influx of talent relegated Carrawell to a supporting role for the next two seasons. He had off-season surgery after his freshman year to repair his shoulders, and it paid off with improved shooting. His scoring average jumped from 5.5 points a game as a freshman to 10.1 as a sophomore, and 9.9 as a junior.

But Krzyzewski didn't need a lot of scoring from Carrawell on teams that boasted the firepower of Brand, Langdon, and Avery.

"For two years, I played in the shadow of Elton Brand and Trajan Langdon," Carrawell said. "You can't have five guys trying to score all the time. I knew my role was to make those guys better."

So Carrawell did the dirty work. He was the team's premier lockdown defender and was an effective rebounder. He would hit an occasional three-pointer and he could spell Avery at the point when necessary.

That became necessary late in the 1999 season when foul trouble sidelined Duke's playmaker late in a titanic game between No. 1 Duke and No. 8 St. John's in Madison Square Garden.

"They were really loaded—Ron Artest, Erik Barkley, Bootsie Thornton—and we were the best team in the country," Carrawell said. "It was a Sunday game at noon on national TV with Spike Lee there at courtside. It was a real battle. Elton fouled out. Will Avery fouled out. Trajan had four fouls."

But Carrawell stepped up and helped Duke survive the 92-88 overtime thriller. He finished with 17 points, nine rebounds, and six assists in 40 minutes of action.

"That was almost a Magic Johnson game," he said.

Carrawell got to play on two great teams as a sophomore and a junior. The 1998 Blue Devils went 15-1 in the league, 32-4 overall, and finished No. 3 in the final AP poll. The 1999 team was even better: 16-0 in the ACC, 37-2 overall, No. 1 in the final AP poll, and NCAA runner-ups.

At first, Carrawell thought that Duke would be loaded again for his senior season. True, Langdon would be gone and Brand, the consensus national player of the year, was almost certain to become the first Duke undergraduate to jump to the NBA, but Carrawell remained optimistic at first.

"We thought we'd be right back there," Carrawell said. "But then Chris Burgess announced he was transferring, and when we heard that Will Avery and Maggette were leaving [for the NBA], it was like, 'Wow!'"

The early departures left Carrawell, Battier, and James as the only three players with any real experience returning in 1999-2000. Krzyzewski was bringing in another highly touted recruiting class, but Jason Williams, Carlos Boozer, and Mike Dunleavy would just be freshmen.

"Shane, Nate, and I looked at each other and said, 'Now, we're the guys,'" Carrawell said. "That spring, Coach was laid up after hip surgery and there was a lot of negative stuff being tossed around. We were in the office and I said, 'Let's go see Coach.' The three of us drove out to see him and talk to him about all the guys leaving. You could tell he was down. I told him, 'If you're willing to coach us, we'll be good.'

"He told us, 'I'm going to coach you guys,' and at that point, I knew I was going to have a great senior year. From that point, I dedicated myself to being the best player I could be. I knew I'd have to be more selfish as a shooter. I knew I'd have to be in great shape."

A change in the Duke coaching staff helped that happen. Former Blue Devil star Johnny Dawkins joined Coach K's staff and fashioned an unprecedented off-season conditioning program.

"It was like Marine boot camp," Carrawell said. "Before my junior year, we didn't condition at all. We just played pickup. Johnny and our new strength coach, Will Stevens, put together a conditioning program like no other."

But despite all the preparation, Carrawell's senior season did not get off to a promising start. The Blue Devils opened the year with a doubleheader in New York's Madison Square Garden, losing heartbreakers to Stanford and Connecticut.

"We didn't play well and we lost to two great teams," Carrawell said. "That's a tough way for the freshmen to start—against two tough teams in Madison Square Garden. Coming back, I stood up on the bus and said, 'We're going to get back, work hard, and we're going to win one game at a time."

And that's exactly what happened. Duke went home and beat a couple of patsies, then traveled to Anaheim and beat Southern Cal. On the way home, the Devils stopped in Chicago and edged Illinois in the United Center. The wins kept coming—a close call at home against DePaul and another thriller on the road at Michigan, followed by a trio of soft touches before the ACC opener at Virginia.

Carrawell scored 25 as Duke knocked off the Cavs to stretch its winning streak to 10 straight. He had 20 points in a win at Maryland. The winning streak stretched to 13 straight with victories over Georgia Tech and Florida State.

Next up was N.C. State, looking to crack the top 25 after starting 12-2. It was an interesting coincidence that Duke was looking for its 27th straight ACC regular-season victory—a streak that stretched back to a loss at North Carolina on February 2, 1998. A win over the Pack would match the ACC record, set by David Thompson's N.C. State champions of 1973-74.

The 2000 Wolfpack players were determined to prevent that from happening. Guard Anthony Grundy told reporters, "Duke is not a dominant team. They're beatable."

Even though nobody had beaten the Devils since Stanford and Connecticut back in early November, when N.C. State invaded Cameron Indoor Stadium on the night of January 19, 2000, Grundy's statement seemed reasonable. Carrawell and company were still working to establish themselves as a great team.

THE GAME OF MY LIFE
DUKE VS. N.C. STATE, JANUARY 19, 2000
BY CHRIS CARRAWELL

There was some bad blood between us and N.C. State. Kenny Inge didn't get along with Battier and they had knocked us out of the ACC Tournament my freshman year. But we respected them. They had some good players—[Damon] Thornton, [Damien] Wilkins, Inge, Justin Gainey. They were talented and Coach [Herb] Sendek had those guys playing tough defense.

We saw it as a must-win game. They were certainly playing well at the time. It was one of those nights when you walk into Cameron and you feel the excitement—the Crazies are going nuts, Dick Vitale's there—it's just wild.

In the first half, I was playing well. I attacked all night. They were very physical, so I was very aggressive and I got to the foul line a lot. We looked at the matchups to start the game and [Anthony] Grundy was guarding me. He was like 6-foot-2 and I was 6-foot-6. I had been playing with Battier and Nate so long, all it took was a little eye contact to call for the ball. Shane lobbed it down to me and I shot it right over Grundy. The second time down, the same thing.

We got off to an early lead, but they fought back. I remember it was really physical. N.C. State would really get up and guard you. Nothing was easy.

The game was close, back and forth all the way. The next thing I knew, we were down one with less than a minute to play. We called a play for me—it was a pick and roll out top. We used the high pick and roll a lot. Damien Wilkins was guarding me now. He had more size, but he was a freshman and I thought, "If I can get in the lane, I'll either get a shot off or get fouled."

But he played it well and stayed in front of me. He cut me off, so I used a spin move—it was one of my favorite moves—and got past him for a finger roll that put us up one.

At the other end, Shane and Jason [Williams] trapped Gainey. He ended up calling timeout, but they didn't have any more timeouts so it was a technical foul. We got to shoot free throws and got the ball, which led to more free throws. Suddenly, we were up five [with 12 seconds left] and we think the game's won.

But we let Gainey drive through us for a quick basket—too quick. I tried to make a quick inbounds pass to Jason, but I made a bad pass and he lost it out of bounds. So they had the ball down three with just a few seconds left. Coach told us to foul before they could try a three-point attempt.

Shane fouled Gainey. It was clearly a foul before the shot, but the ref called it differently. He gave Gainey three shots [with 0.8 seconds left]. He could tie the game at the line. He hit the first, but missed his second free throw.

Now, we knew that he was going to miss the next one on purpose. But with just 0.8 seconds left, all they could do was try to tap it in. There was no time to rebound, go down, and then go back up with a shot.

Justin missed perfectly. They crashed and the refs were not going to call a foul. You wouldn't believe all the stuff going on in the lane. There were muggings going on. Then some freshman I never heard of before or since [Marshall Williams] made a perfect tap, the ball went in and we headed to overtime.

I had played all 40 minutes and at this point I had five minutes to go. I was crushed. We were up five with 12 seconds to go; we were sure we were going to win. After that, there wasn't much left in the tank.

That's when our conditioning kicked in. I was able to catch my breath and in the huddle before the overtime, I said, "We're not losing this game." We went out and they scored the first basket in overtime, but then we took control.

The reason we were so tough is because we had so many leaders. I wouldn't be the only one in the huddle saying we were going to win. I'd say it, then Shane would say it, and then Nate would say it. That happened all the time that season.

The leaders on that team, we weren't stars at first. But we knew what it took to win.

AFTERMATH

"Guts—we really had to fight," Carrawell told reporters in the Duke locker room. "That was a playground kind of game, a bring-your-lunch-bucket kind of game. I've always wanted to be in this situation."

Duke's 92-88 victory over N.C. State matched the ACC record for consecutive conference regular-season wins. Three days later, the Blue Devils beat Wake Forest to break the record. The winning streak stretched to 31 straight before Maryland upset Duke in Cameron.

That would be the team's only loss en route to a 15-1 regular-season finish—and a fourth straight ACC regular-season title.

For Carrawell, the N.C. State win would be a watershed event in the way he was perceived around the league. Before the season, the ACC media voted on the projected ACC player of the year—Maryland's Terrence Morris led the voting, followed by Wake Forest's Robert O'Kelley, and Shane Battier.

Carrawell did not get a single vote.

But after the Duke senior scored 30 points against N.C. State—going all 45 minutes in the overtime win—writers began to suggest that he might be the league's most valuable player.

"I think that was the game that pushed me into the forefront," Carrawell said. "I had had good games at Virginia and at Maryland, but after I scored 30 points against State, it was different. People notice scoring. All the other stuff—the rebounding, the defense, everything else—I had been doing that for three years. But I didn't get noticed when Elton and Trajan were doing the scoring.

"If you score, you get more attention. All of a sudden, people noticed all the other things I did. I got attention for being an all-around player."

Carrawell was the definition of an all-around player. As a senior, he averaged 16.9 points, 6.1 rebounds, and 3.2 assists. He also averaged 35.6 minutes a game and had career highs in field-goal percentage, free-throw percentage, and three-point percentage. He was the best wing defender in the ACC.

Krzyzewski lavished praise on his senior captain.

"Carrawell, what a magnificent warrior," he told reporters after the N.C. State win. "I'm really honored to be his coach. He's the best."

The ACC media, who didn't give Carrawell a single preseason player of the year vote, gave him the postseason award by a wide margin over Battier. After winning third-team All-ACC honors as a junior, Carrawell was a unanimous first-team pick as a senior, as well as a consensus first-team All-American.

"Winning player of the year meant a lot to me," Carrawell said. "To have my name on the trophy with Michael Jordan, Tim Duncan, and Grant Hill was a great achievement."

Amazingly, despite losing five of the top seven players on the 1999 Final Four team, Duke finished 29-5 in 2000. When Cincinnati, who was ranked No. 1 for most of the season, lost in the Conference USA Tournament, the Blue Devils climbed to the top spot in the final AP poll.

"To start the season and 0-2 and finish No. 1 a year after losing so many players, I don't think that's talked about enough," Carrawell said. "Maybe that's because we didn't win [the NCAA championship]. We didn't have enough players. We only had six players all season, and after Mike Dunleavy got sick, we were down to five at the end of the year.

"Duke did win it the next year and I think we laid the groundwork for that."

REFLECTIONS ON DUKE

Carrawell was bitterly disappointed when he was not taken in the first round of the NBA draft. Picked 41st overall by San Antonio, the Duke star was released by the Spurs before he could play a game in the league.

"How can I be the top player in the ACC and a first-team All-American and not get drafted until the second round?" Carrawell asks today. "What more could I have done? When I left Duke, I was the winningest player in ACC history. I thought basketball was about winning."

Indeed, Carrawell's winning percentage is unmatched. Duke was 124-20 with him in the lineup, winning four ACC regular-season and two tournament titles in his four years. His last two Duke teams finished No. 1 in the final AP poll. His Blue Devil teams were 58-6 in ACC regular-season play, 8-2 in the ACC Tournament and 11-4 in NCAA Tournament play.

Despite his failure to crack the NBA, Carrawell has pursued his pro basketball career in places such as Lithuania and the Netherlands. He was the MVP of the American Basketball Association in 2006.

"I'm in a great situation," Carrawell said. "I'm married. I have my degree. I still love to play this game."

He has given up any hope of playing in the NBA.

"I'll be 30 this year—for me, it's past," he said. "I'll play as long as I can, maybe until I'm 36 or 37, then I'll get into coaching. Maybe I'll end up back on the Duke bench."

If Carrawell can bring the same toughness and will to win he brought as a player, he'd be a welcome addition to any staff.

CHAPTER 20

JASON WILLIAMS

Jason Williams was a late bloomer on the basketball court.

Unlike so many of today's prospects, he did not grow up on the AAU circuit—identified early and heralded as the next superstar. Even though Williams grew up in the basketball hotbed of New Jersey and made the varsity squad as a freshman at St. Joseph's High School, he resisted the lure of the hardwood game. The young man known to his friends as "Jay Dub," didn't follow the sport on television and he put much of his early efforts toward soccer and making the chess club.

All that changed as Williams entered his junior season at St. Joseph's. The future Duke star saw a list of the top basketball prospects in New Jersey—and his name was not on it.

"I was not even ranked in state!" Williams said, the outrage still evident in his voice a decade later. "My whole life, I've been the guy people counted out. My idea is that I would outwork everybody. I've always had a strong work ethic."

As Williams focused his work ethic on basketball in his junior season, he led St. Joseph's to the finals of the New Jersey state championships and emerged as one of the top prospects—not just in Jersey, but also in the nation. That spring, he visited the University of North Carolina for a prep all-star tournament and was dazzled by the jerseys hanging from the rafters of the Smith Center.

"I was really intrigued by Carolina," Williams said. "Growing up, I didn't follow basketball that much, so I wasn't aware of who the top teams were. I had already fallen in love with Rutgers—a lot of my friends and classmates were going there. I knew Duke and Carolina always battled it out, so I gave them a look."

Williams was regarded at the time as a slightly undersized scoring guard. He essentially played small forward at St. Joseph's.

"I went to Nike camp that summer and focused on showing people that I could pass," he said. "I averaged 17 assists per game and was rated the top point guard in the class."

But North Carolina coach Bill Guthridge didn't see it that way.

"I went to Carolina for an unofficial visit, and he told me they saw me more as a scoring guard," Williams said. "They already had Ron Curry and Ed Cota [at the point] and he didn't have room for me."

Duke's Mike Krzyzewski took a different approach.

"Coach K recruited me as a point guard," Williams said. "He and [assistant coach] David Henderson watched every one of my games at Nike."

Krzyzewski persisted in his pursuit even after Mark Taylor, Williams' coach at St. Joseph, told the Duke coach that his star was better suited to play as a wing guard or small forward.

"During one visit, Coach K told me that he thought I could be the best point guard in the country," Williams said. "He asked my high school coach and he said, 'I don't see him as a point guard.'"

Williams played his senior year at St. Joseph's on the wing, leading the team back to the state finals and averaging 24.0 points a game. He finished as the school's all-time leading scorer and earned the Morgan Wooten Award as the nation's best prep player.

That spring, Williams got a chance to play point guard in the McDonald's All-America game, where he had 20 points and six assists. He added 29 points and 11 assists in the Capital Classic, and then led a team of American prep stars to victory in the Nike Hoop Summit, with 18 points and 11 assists.

It was beginning to look like Krzyzewski's minority opinion about Williams' point guard potential would prevail. And Williams never had any doubt about his decision to sign with Duke.

"That was the best decision I ever made," he said.

THE SETTING

When Jason Williams signed with Duke in the fall of 1998, he never expected to come in and start right away. The 1998-99 Blue

Jason Williams shows his strength as he drives into traffic.

Devils boasted a superb young point guard in sophomore Will Avery.

Avery was so good that Krzyzewski (and Williams) expected him to turn pro a year early. That would give Williams a year to learn the position as a backup, and then step in as a starter in 2000-01. But Avery had his own schedule. He surprised the Duke coach in the spring of 1999 by declaring for the NBA draft. That created a void that thrust Williams into the starting point guard role before he was ready.

"We had no one else who could play it," Williams said. "I came in thinking I would be a backup, then I have to start. I had to fight it."

Early on it was a struggle. Williams made his debut against Stanford in Madison Square Garden and missed 12 of 15 shots in a one-point loss. One night later, he was 5 of 17 in a close loss to defending national champion UConn.

Duke was 0-2 for the first time since 1959. Krzyzewski would have liked to pull Williams out of the starting lineup to take some of the pressure off his overmatched freshman. Unfortunately, he had no other options. Duke was so thin at the point that Krzyzewski had given a scholarship to Andre Buckner, the younger brother of Clemson standout Greg Buckner, who had been planning to walk on at Tennessee. Krzyzewski signed Buckner as a practice player—so Williams would have somebody to work against in scrimmages. But he was never an option to start.

Instead, Williams stayed in the lineup, learning the position under fire.

"I made a lot of blunders," he said. "I didn't have the position mastered and I was out of shape. Not out of basketball shape, but out of Duke basketball shape."

After that nightmarish weekend in New York, Williams—and Duke—began to play better. The freshman point guard was solid as the Blue Devils beat Southern Cal in Los Angeles and edged Illinois in Chicago. Then, Williams tallied 15 points, 10 assists, and six steals as Duke beat DePaul in overtime.

But the real sign of Williams' growing maturity came in the ACC opener at Virginia. The Blue Devil freshman endured a rough shooting night—a five-of-18 performance that evoked memories of the opening weekend in New York. But the outcome was different because the young point guard played a superb floor game (seven assists and just two turnovers) and with the game on the line, stepped up and hit the game-clinching shot.

That would prove to be Williams' signature moment—no one else in Duke history ever displayed such an ability to overcome a bad game so often by stepping up and making a winning play.

"That's the mentality that made me what I am," Williams said.

It's the mentality that would turn his 2001 visit to Maryland into one of the classic games in Duke history.

Williams, who arrived at Duke knowing little more about the ACC other than North Carolina was supposed to be the Blue Devils' big rival, was soon educated about the growing antipathy between Duke and Maryland.

Gary Williams had inherited a probation-plagued program in 1989, but turned Maryland into a national power by the time Jason Williams arrived at Duke. But the high-strung Terrapin coach had endured a singular lack of success against Krzyzewski and the Blue Devils. His frustration was shared by Maryland's fandom.

Jason Williams got a taste of the growing bitterness when Duke played at College Park in early January of his freshman season. The Blue Devils smashed Maryland with relative ease, as they had done so often in that era. That only spurred the fans at Cole Field House into an even greater level of hysteria. The Duke players and their families behind the team bench were showered with debris.

"Carlos Boozer's mother was hit by a glass water bottle," Williams said. "I was hit in the head by a penny."

What hurt even more was that Duke's freshman point guard was outplayed by Maryland's freshman point guard. Steve Blake had 12 points and eight assists in a losing cause, while Williams only managed six points, five assists and eight turnovers.

Still, the victory over Maryland was Duke's 11th in a row following the team's two opening losses in New York. The winning streak stretched to 18 straight before it was snapped—by Maryland in Cameron.

The defeat was marked by another sub-par performance by Williams in his matchup with Blake. The Duke point guard managed just nine points against his new rival. He did have 10 assists, but he also had seven turnovers as the Terps snapped Duke's 46-game home-court winning streak.

That proved to be the only loss Duke suffered in the ACC that season. The Blue Devils won both the regular-season and tournament titles, and when Cincinnati, the season-long No. 1 team, was upset in the Conference USA Tournament, 27-4 Duke took over the No. 1 spot in the final AP poll.

On paper, it was not a bad season for Duke's freshman point guard. He averaged 14.5 points and 6.5 assists. More importantly, he quarterbacked the nation's No. 1 team to a 29-5 final record (after an NCAA Sweet 16 loss to Florida) and also earned the Everett Case Award as the most valuable player in the ACC Tournament.

A great freshman season, right?

"Wrong," Williams said. "I didn't think I had a good freshman season at all. Chris Carrawell and Shane Battier were the reason we finished No. 1. It was a very difficult year for me."

Williams responded to his personal frustration by doing what he always did—he worked harder. First, he reshaped his body.

"My freshman year I was too heavy," he said. "I stayed at Duke that summer and worked out with [assistant coach Johnny Dawkins]. I got down to 187 pounds and found that I was so much quicker and faster. Later that summer, I played in the World Games. It was a great experience. I found my shot again, like in high school. It was a real confidence boost."

Williams led a team of U.S. all-stars in scoring, assists, and shooting percentage. He joined teammate Shane Battier on a select group of college players that helped prepare the NBA stars on Team USA for the 2000 Olympic Games. Williams was clearly the one collegian who proved he could play with the pros.

The "new" Jason Williams was on display as Duke opened the 2000-01 season with 18 wins in 19 games. He returned to Madison Square Garden and helped Duke win the preseason NIT with victories over Texas and Temple. His 23 points and seven assists were too much for Illinois in Greensboro. He poured in 30 points, hitting eight of 10 three-pointers, as Duke knocked off Temple in Philadelphia for a second victory over the Owls (an Elite Eight team that season) in less than a month. He embarrassed future ACC member Boston College with 34 points and nine assists and he had 26 points and five assists in the team's one loss, at Stanford.

By the time Duke readied for its trip to Cole Field House in late January, Williams had raised his scoring average to well over 20 points a game. More significantly, his shooting percentage had jumped from 41.7 as a freshman to over 47 percent as a sophomore. His three-point percentage was up from 35 percent to over 42 percent.

But Williams still had something to prove going into the game with No. 8 Maryland. He still had to overcome his personal nemesis, Steve Blake.

JASON WILLIAMS

THE GAME OF MY LIFE

DUKE VS. MARYLAND, JANUARY 27, 2001

BY JASON WILLIAMS

Steve Blake was a good defender, but the thing I always tell people is that it wasn't just Steve stopping me. Juan Dixon was a good help defender and they had big guys like Chris Wilcox to defend the lane. So it wasn't Steve locking me up. It was their team defense.

I was looking forward to the game at College Park. I had family in the Maryland area, so I always had a lot of people I knew there. It was a tough atmosphere. When you go to Duke, you know you'll be hated by a lot of people and loved by a lot of people. We are resented because of all the attention we get. But we didn't ask for the media hype. We never asked Dick Vitale to sing our praises all the time.

The atmosphere at Cole Field House was so ugly. I wanted to silence those people who said, "Maryland has your number."

We were really ready to play, but then everything went wrong. Coach K later had a great analogy for it. He said it's like being in a rush looking for your keys. You search high and low, but can't find them anywhere. You're late and you get more and more frantic until you finally give up and lay down on the couch and there your keys are, right underneath you.

That was us. That was me. I was trying to play so hard and trying to beat them so badly that I was putting too much pressure on myself.

I remember when it turned. It was during that timeout (with 1:01 left and Maryland leading 90-80). I remember it like it was yesterday. The Maryland fans were chanting, "Overrated, overrated." There was kind of an eerie silence in the huddle, and then Shane said, "Let's fight this thing to the end."

I hit a driving lay-up, then freshman Chris Duhon and I singled out Drew Nicholas. Steve had fouled out and Drew was playing for him. He was a good player, but he didn't have as much experience. Chris was our energy man. It was like he had drunk a million Red Bulls.

Chris was covering Drew. I told him, 'You and I are going to trap him. Let him catch it in the corner, then we'll trap him."

That's what we did. I stole the ball and hit a three.

We fouled Drew right away after that. They had been doing a lot of trash talking during the game and we couldn't talk back because we were losing. When we fouled Drew and were walking to the other end of the floor before he took his shots, we were pouring it in his ear.

He missed both shots, we came down and I got another quick three.

I'll never forget the look in their eyes. Their fans were quiet. They were flabbergasted. We knew the basketball gods were on our side.

When we got it into overtime, I knew we were going to win. I remember when Shane got that game-clinching block on Juan Dixon, the feeling that we had pulled it off.

That game says a lot about our team's mindset. It was our mindset for the rest of the year. A month later, we lost Carlos Boozer, but we believed and we kept fighting.

THE AFTERMATH

Williams finished with 25 points and five assists, but those numbers don't tell the real story of his contribution to Duke's 98-96 victory. What really mattered was his eight points in 13 seconds that turned a hopeless 90-80 deficit into a 90-88 thriller. It was Nate James who forced the overtime with two free throws with 21.9 seconds left, but it was Williams' burst—his eight points and his steal—in that 13-second stretch that gave Duke life.

In the overtime, Williams hit two free throws to give Duke its first lead of the game, then set up the game-winning three-pointer from Battier with a classic drive and kick out. It was a pretty good point guard move for a guy once thought to be more of a wing guard.

The victory in College Park proved to be the first of four classic games between the Blue Devils and Terps that season. Duke was winning the rematch in Durham when, early in the second half, Boozer went down with a broken foot. The injury to the team's only big man not only led to a loss to Maryland, it also seemed to doom Duke's chances in the postseason.

But as Williams said, the Devils "kept believing and kept fighting." Krzyzewski revamped his lineup, inserting energy man Duhon as a backcourt mate to Williams. He unveiled his new lineup in the regular-season finale at North Carolina. The Blue Devils blitzed the Tar Heels on their own home court to win a share of the ACC regular-season title.

A week later in Atlanta, Duke and Maryland dueled again in front of more than 30,000 fans in the ACC Tournament semifinals at the Georgia Dome. Williams poured in 19 points against his nemesis and a last-second tap-in by Nate James secured the 84-82 victory. That win put Duke in the ACC title game against North Carolina. It was supposed to be a thriller between the league's two regular-season co-champs. Instead, the Blue Devils simply blew the Tar Heels out of the Georgia Dome, running away with a 79-53 victory.

But the victory was somewhat soured as Duke's Williams went down late with a sprained ankle. With Boozer still sidelined and now the team's All-America point guard hobbled, how could the Devils survive in postseason?

"I couldn't believe it," Williams said. "I was feeling so good. I was starting to come into my prime. Then, oh man, to blow out my ankle against Carolina?"

Williams was not expected to play in Duke's NCAA opener against Monmouth. But his father reminded him of something from his high school days.

"I rolled an ankle in high school, then came back and in the next four games, I averaged over 38 points a game," Williams said. "That made me think, 'Maybe this happened for a reason.'"

Williams started and scored 22 points in 20 minutes against Monmouth. Two days later, he scored 31 points and passed out nine assists in a second-round victory over Missouri. He was even better in Philadelphia for the Sweet 16. The sophomore point guard scored 17 straight points during a second-half run and finished with 34 as Duke held off UCLA. And in the regional finals, Williams added 28 more in a victory over Southern Cal.

"Then I get to the Final Four and I'm so cold—I can't make a shot," Williams laughed.

That's a slight exaggeration. Williams did drop off his torrid pace, but he still contributed 23 points as Duke erased a 22-point first-half deficit against Maryland in the semifinals. The last of their four classic duels in 2001 followed much the same script as the first—Maryland building a huge lead, but Duke rallying for the victory.

Williams had another off-form shooting performance in the title game, but strong performances from Battier and Mike Dunleavy put Duke in position to win. The key shot turned out to be a classic play by Jason Williams—after missing nine of his first 10 three-point attempts, in the closing seconds he calmly stepped behind a Battier screen and knocked down the three-pointer that clinched Duke's third national title.

Williams, who averaged 21.6 points and 6.1 assists per game, won the NABC National Player of the Year Award, although, teammate Shane Battier swept the other player of the year awards. Duke's sophomore point guard was a consensus All-American and was projected as the top pick in the NBA draft, despite his public pronouncement that he'd been returning to Duke for his junior year.

"I thought all along that I'd handle the decision at the end of the season," he said. "I just wanted the media to leave me alone. I remember, I got a call from Michael Jordan [then the general manager of the Washington Wizards, which owned the No. 1 pick]. He told me that he wanted to play with me in D.C.

"I sat down with Coach and with my mother and father and we talked about it. The thing I appreciate is they never pressured me to do anything. They left it to me. But Coach did say something that made an impression. He said, 'Jason, don't be the norm. Be special.' That made me think of a poem by Robert Frost: 'I took the path less traveled and that has made all the difference.'"

So Williams passed up the chance to be the No. 1 pick in the 2001 NBA Draft. He returned to Duke in 2001-02 and anchored another great Duke team. This time, he swept the national player of the year awards as he averaged 21.3 points and 5.3 assists for a 31-4 team. The Devils lost the ACC regular-season race to Maryland, but won a fourth straight ACC championship by beating N.C. State in the tournament finals. Duke finished No. 1 in the final AP poll for the third time in Williams' three years at Duke.

The season—and his career—came to a frustrating end as Indiana upset Duke in the Sweet 16 in Lexington. Williams almost pulled the game out with a remarkable play in the final seconds. Down four with just seconds remaining, he converted a three-pointer as he was fouled. Unfortunately, he missed the game-tying free throw, and Boozer's attempt to follow the miss was thwarted by Indiana's Jared Jeffries at the buzzer.

Williams finished his college career with 2,079 points—the greatest three-year total in Duke history—and 644 assists. He quarterbacked teams that won 95 games (against 13 losses) and won a national title, three ACC championships, and three times finished No. 1 in the final AP poll. He also earned his degree in just three years.

"I wouldn't take anything about my career back," Williams said. "Not even the Indiana game we lost. I had the ball in my hand with a chance to make a play at the end of the game. That's all I ever wanted."

REFLECTIONS ON DUKE

Williams' decision to return for his junior year didn't prove costly, although the presence of China's giant prospect, Yao Ming, in the draft dropped the Duke star from the probable No. 1 spot in 2001 to the No. 2 position in 2002.

Williams still earned a lucrative contract from the Chicago Bulls. He was cast as the centerpiece of that team's efforts to rebuild after the departures of Michael Jordan and Scottie Pippen from the championship teams of the 1990s. As a rookie point guard, Jason Williams averaged 9.7 points and 4.7 assists as a part-time starter, and though he wasn't good enough to turn things around right away, he showed enough promise to convince the Bulls he was their playmaker of the future.

The biggest problem Williams endured that season was his name. Not only was there another NBA point guard named Jason Williams (a Florida product playing at the time for the Memphis Grizzlies), but former NBA forward Jayson Williams was in the news when he was accused of killing a limousine driver. It was suggested that Duke's Jason Williams might want to change his first name to "Jay" in order to avoid confusion and protect his marketing potential.

"My manager and I were having that discussion before I was to do an interview for NBA TV," Williams said. "I told him I'd think about it. But a reporter for the *New York Times* overheard what we were talking about and printed a story: 'Jason Williams to change name.' After that, everybody called me Jay. But I never changed it . . . I'm still Jason Williams."

The identity problems became moot on June 19, 2003, when Williams was seriously injured in a motorcycle accident. He severed a vital nerve in his left leg, fractured his pelvis and tore three ligaments in his left knee. He required extensive physical therapy to even walk again. Doctors gave him little or no chance to ever play basketball again.

"I remember being in a wheelchair three months after the accident," Williams said. "I was talking to my father about whether I could come back and play in the NBA. He told me, 'It's not whether you can . . . it's whether you want to.'

"I battled all the way back and when I put on a Nets jersey in preseason [before the 2006-07 season] I was almost there. But I realized that I didn't have the same love for the game. It wasn't fun for me any more. I didn't want to play for just a paycheck."

Williams still plays in a rec league in New York and every summer he returns to Duke and plays with his former teammates and other former Blue Devil standouts. He's done television commentary for ESPN, and he's putting his Duke degree to work as an executive for 24 Hour Fitness, the nation's largest privately owned fitness chain.

"I don't want people to think, 'He didn't make it all the way back,'" Williams said. "I went to school because I wanted to get into business. To my way of thinking, I've won in so many aspects of life."